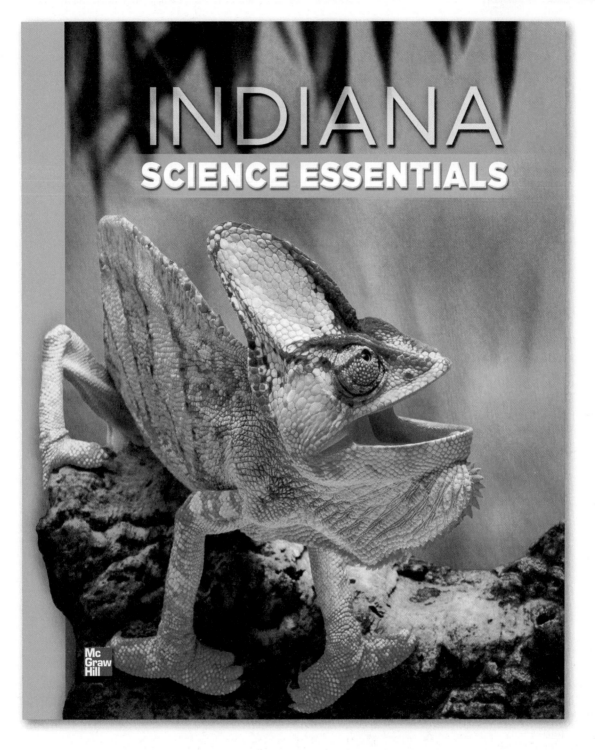

INDIANA
SCIENCE ESSENTIALS

Mc Graw Hill

Bothell, WA • Chicago, IL • Columbus, OH • New York, NY

Program Authors

Dr. Jay K. Hackett
Professor Emeritus of Earth Sciences
University of Northern Colorado
Greeley, CO

Dr. Richard H. Moyer
Professor of Science Education and Natural Sciences
University of Michigan-Dearborn
Dearborn, MI

Dr. JoAnne Vasquez
Elementary Science Education Consultant
NSTA Past President
Member, National Science Board and NASA Education Board

Mulugheta Teferi, M.A.
Principal, Gateway Middle School
Center of Math, Science, and Technology
St. Louis Public Schools
St. Louis, MO

Dinah Zike, M.Ed.
Dinah Might Adventures LP
San Antonio, TX

Kathryn LeRoy, M.S.
Chief Officer
Curriculum Services
Duval County Schools, FL

Dr. Dorothy J. T. Terman
Science Curriculum Development Consultant
Former K-12 Science and Mathematics Coordinator
Irvine Unified School District, CA
Irvine, CA

Dr. Gerald F. Wheeler
Executive Director
National Science Teachers Association

Bank Street College of Education
New York, NY

Contributing Authors

Dr. Sally Ride
Sally Ride Science
San Diego, CA

Lucille Villegas Barrera, M.Ed.
Elementary Science Supervisor
Houston Independent School District
Houston, TX

American Museum of Natural History
New York, NY

Contributing Writer

Ellen C. Grace, M.S.
Consultant
Albuquerque, NM

RFB&D learning through listening Students with print disabilities may be eligible to obtain an accessible, audio version of the pupil edition of this textbook. Please call Recording for the Blind & Dyslexic at 1-800-221-4792 for complete information.

The McGraw-Hill Companies

Mc Graw Hill **Macmillan/McGraw-Hill**

Send all inquiries to:
Macmillan/McGraw-Hill
8787 Orion Place
Columbus, OH 43240-4027

ISBN: 978-0-02-114382-5
MHID: 0-02-114382-X

Printed in the United States of America.

2 3 4 5 6 7 8 9 10 QDB 15 14 13 12 11

Content Consultants

Paul R. Haberstroh, Ph.D.
Mohave Community College
Lake Havasu City, AZ

Timothy Long
School of Earth and Atmospheric Sciences
Georgia Institute of Technology
Atlanta, GA

Rick MacPherson, Ph.D.
Program Director
The Coral Reef Alliance
San Francisco, CA

Hector Córdova Mireles, Ph.D.
Physics Department
California State Polytechnic University
Pomona, CA

Charlotte A. Otto, Ph.D.
Department of Natural Sciences
University of Michigan-Dearborn
Dearborn, MI

Paul Zitzewitz, Ph.D.
Department of Natural Sciences
University of Michigan-Dearborn
Dearborn, MI

Editorial Advisory Board

Deborah T. Boros, M.A.
President, Society of Elementary Presidential Awardees
Second-Grade Teacher
Mississippi Elementary
Coon Rapids, MN

Lorraine Conrad
K–12 Coordinator of Science
Richland County School District #2
Columbia, SC

Kitty Farnell
Science/Health/PE Coordinator
School District 5 of Lexington and Richland Counties
Ballentine, SC

Kathy Grimes, Ph.D.
Science Specialist
Las Vegas, NV

Richard Hogen
Fourth-Grade Teacher
Rudy Bologna Elementary School
Chandler, AZ

Kathy Horstmeyer
Educational Consultant
Past President, Society of Presidential Awardees
Past Preschool/Elementary NSTA Director
Carefree, AZ and Chester, CT

Jean Kugler
Gaywood Elementary School
Prince George's County Public Schools
Lanham, MD

Bill Metz, Ph.D.
Science Education Consultant
Fort Washington, PA

Karen Stratton
Science Coordinator K–12
Lexington District One
Lexington, SC

Emma Walton, Ph.D.
Science Education Consultant
NSTA Past President
Anchorage, AK

Debbie Wickerham
Teacher
Findlay City Schools
Findlay, OH

The American Museum of Natural History in New York City is one of the world's preeminent scientific, educational, and cultural institutions, with a global mission to explore and interpret human cultures and the natural world through scientific research, education, and exhibitions. Each year the Museum welcomes around 4 million visitors, including 500,000 schoolchildren in organized field trips. It provides professional development activities for thousands of teachers; hundreds of public programs that serve audiences ranging from preschoolers to seniors; and an array of learning and teaching resources for use in homes, schools, and community-based settings. Visit www.amnh.org for online resources.

Indiana Science Standards

The Nature of Science

Students gain scientific knowledge by observing the natural and constructed world, performing and evaluating investigations and communicating their findings. These principles should guide student work and be integrated into the curriculum along with the content standards on a daily basis.

Standards	Page Numbers
• Make predictions and formulate testable questions. • Design a fair test. • Plan and carry out investigations as a class, in small groups or independently, often over a period of several class lessons. • Perform investigations using appropriate tools and technology that will extend the senses. • Use measurement skills and apply appropriate units when collecting data. • Test predictions with multiple trials. • Keep accurate records in a notebook during investigations and communicate findings to others using graphs, charts, maps and models through oral and written reports. • Identify simple patterns in data and propose explanations to account for the patterns. • Compare the results of an investigation with the prediction.	Explore, pp. 20–21, 36–37, 62–63, 80–81, 104–105, 118–119, 142–143, 156–157, 174–175, 196–197, 212–213 Be a Scientist, pp. 1–11, 46–49 Focus on Skills, pp. 168–171, 206–209

The Design Process

As citizens of the constructed world, students will participate in the design process. Students will learn to use materials and tools safely and employ the basic principles of the engineering design process in order to find solutions to problems.

Standards	Page Numbers
• Identify a need or problem to be solved. • Brainstorm potential solutions. • Document the design throughout the entire design process. • Select a solution to the need or problem. • Select the most appropriate materials to develop a solution that will meet the need. • Create the solution through a prototype. • Test and evaluate how well the solution meets the goal. • Evaluate and test the design using measurement. • Present evidence using mathematical representations (graphs, data tables). • Communicate the solution including evidence using mathematical representations (graphs, data tables), drawings or prototypes. • Communicate how to improve the solution.	Explore, pp. 212–213, 232–233 Focus on Skills, pp. 242–245 Math in Science, pp. 228–229

Standard 1: Physical Science

Core Standard:
Provide evidence that heat and electricity are forms of energy.

Core Standard:
Design and assemble electric circuits that provide a means of transferring energy from one form or place to another.

Standards	Page Numbers
4.1.1 Describe and investigate the different ways in which heat can be generated.	Unit 1 Lesson 1, pp. 18–29
4.1.2 Investigate the variety of ways that heat can be generated and move from one place to another and explain the direction in which the heat moves.	Unit 1 Lesson 1, pp. 18–29
4.1.3 Construct a complete circuit through which an electrical current can pass as evidenced by the lighting of a bulb or ringing of a bell.	Explore, pp. 36–37
4.1.4 Experiment with materials to identify conductors and insulators of heat and electricity.	Focus on Skills, pp. 30–33 Be a Scientist, pp. 46–49
4.1.5 Demonstrate that electrical energy can be transformed into heat, light, and sound.	Unit 1 Lesson 2, pp. 34–45

Indiana Science Standards

Standard 2: Earth Science

Core Standard:
Observe, investigate and give examples of ways that the shape of the land changes over time.

Core Standard:
Describe how the supply of natural resources is limited and investigate ways that humans protect and harm the environment.

Standards	Page Numbers
4.2.1 Demonstrate and describe how smaller rocks come from the breakage and weathering of larger rocks in a process that occurs over a long period of time.	Unit 2 Lesson 1, pp. 60–73 Math in Science, pp. 76–77 Writing in Science, pp. 74–75
4.2.2 Demonstrate and describe how wind, water and glacial ice shape and reshape earth's land surface by eroding rock and soil in some areas and depositing them in other areas in a process that occurs over a long period of time.	Unit 2 Lesson 1, pp. 60–73
4.2.3 Demonstrate and describe how earthquakes, volcanoes, and landslides suddenly change the shape of the land.	Unit 2 Lesson 2, pp. 78–89 Reading in Science, pp. 90–91
4.2.4 Investigate earth materials that serve as natural resources and gather data to determine which are in limited supply.	Unit 3 Lesson 1, pp. 102–113 Reading in Science, pp. 114–115
4.2.5 Describe methods that humans currently use to extend the use of natural resources.	Unit 3 Lesson 2, pp. 116–127 Writing in Science, pp. 128–129
4.2.6 Describe ways in which humans have changed the natural environment that have been detrimental or beneficial.	Unit 3 Lesson 2, pp. 116–127

Standard 3: Life Science

Core Standard:
Observe, describe, and ask questions about structures of organisms and how they affect their growth and survival.

Standards	Page Numbers
4.3.1 Observe and describe how offspring are very much, but not exactly, like their parents or one another. Describe how these differences in physical characteristics among individuals in a population may be advantageous for survival and reproduction.	Unit 4 Lesson 1, pp. 140–151 Unit 4 Lesson 3, pp. 172–181
4.3.2 Observe, compare, and record the physical characteristics of living plants or animals from widely different environments, and describe how each is adapted to its environment.	Unit 4 Lesson 2, pp. 154–167 Reading in Science, pp. 152–153, 182–183
4.3.3 Design an investigation to explore how organisms meet some of their needs by responding to stimuli from their environment.	Unit 4 Lesson 2, 154–167
4.3.4 Describe a way that a given plant or animal might adapt to changes arising from human or non-human impact on the environment.	Unit 4 Lesson 3, pp. 172–181

Standard 4: Science, Engineering and Technology

Core Standard:
Design a moving system and measure its motion.

Standards	Page Numbers
4.4.1 Investigate transportation systems and devices that operate on or in land, water, air and space and recognize the forces (lift, drag, friction, thrust and gravity) that affect their motion.	Unit 5 Lesson 2, pp. 210–225 Writing in Science, pp. 226–227
4.4.2 Make appropriate measurements to compare the speeds of objects in terms of distance traveled in a given amount of time or time required to travel a given distance.	Unit 5 Lesson 1, pp. 194–205 Focus on Skills, pp. 206–209
4.4.3 Investigate how changes in speed or direction are caused by forces; the greater the force exerted on an object, the greater the change.	Unit 5 Lesson 1, pp. 194–205
4.4.4 Define a problem in the context of motion and transportation and propose a solution to this problem by evaluating, reevaluating and testing the design, gathering evidence about how well the design meets the needs of the problem, and documenting the design so that it can be easily replicated.	Unit 5 Lesson 3, pp. 230–241

Be a Scientist

◀ Making a model can help you understand how something works.

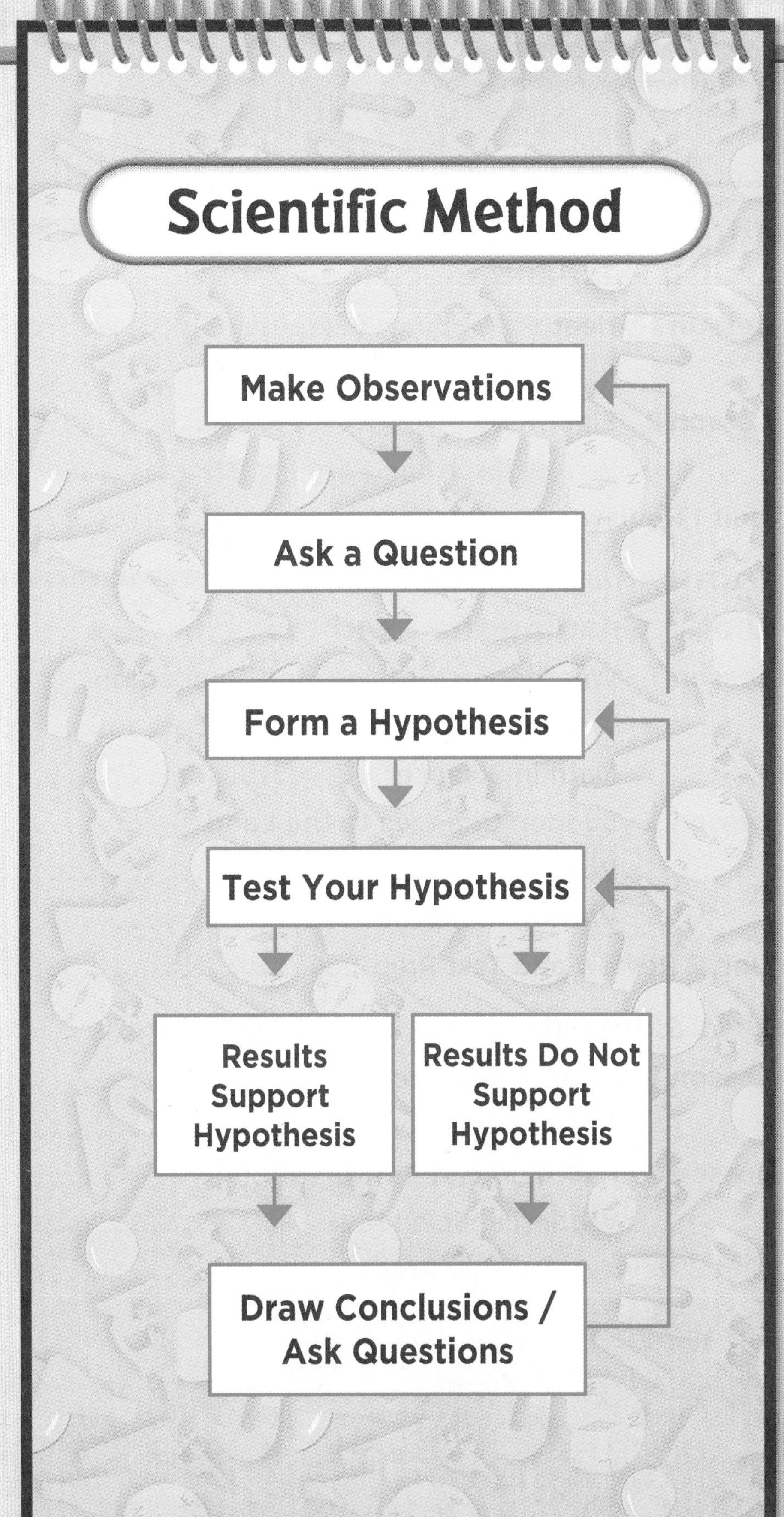
Scientific Method
Make Observations
Ask a Question
Form a Hypothesis
Test Your Hypothesis
Results Support Hypothesis
Results Do Not Support Hypothesis
Draw Conclusions / Ask Questions

Indiana Science

LIFE SCIENCE

SCIENCE, ENGINEERING AND TECHNOLOGY

Online Resources

Animations

Science in Motion Animations online at www.macmillanmh.com

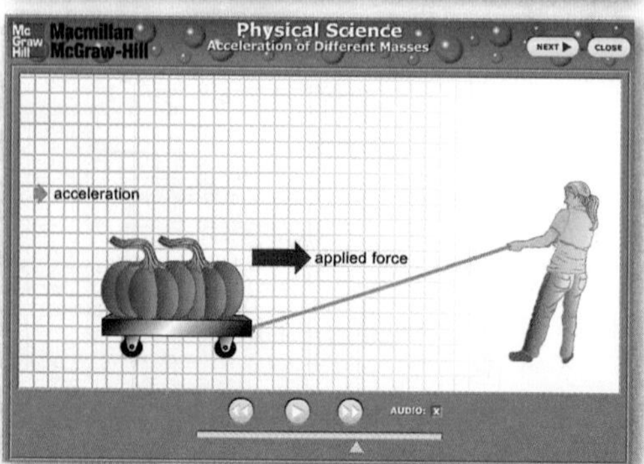

Additional Student Resources

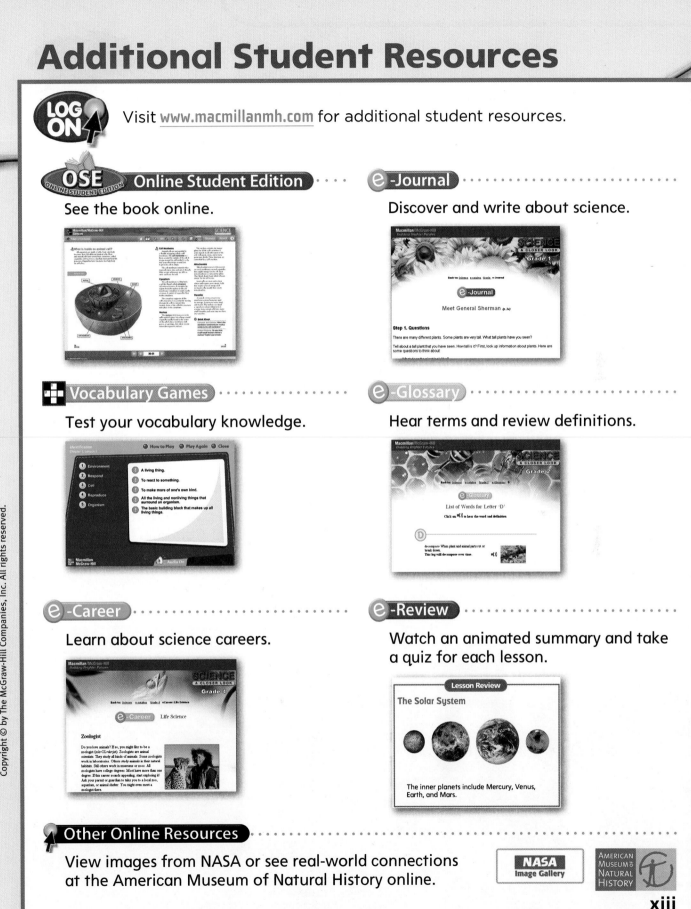

Visit www.macmillanmh.com for additional student resources.

Online Student Edition

See the book online.

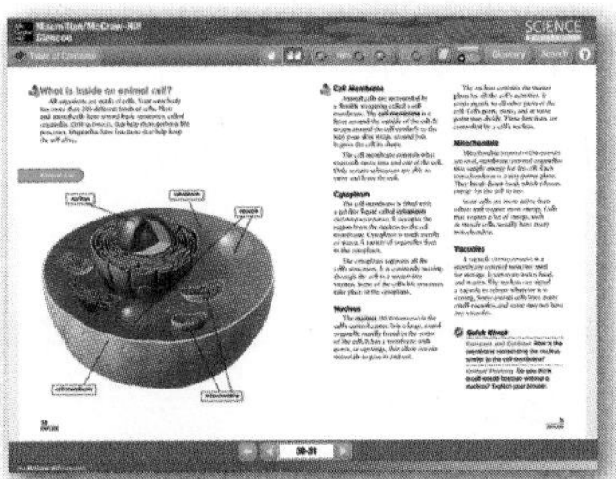

e-Journal

Discover and write about science.

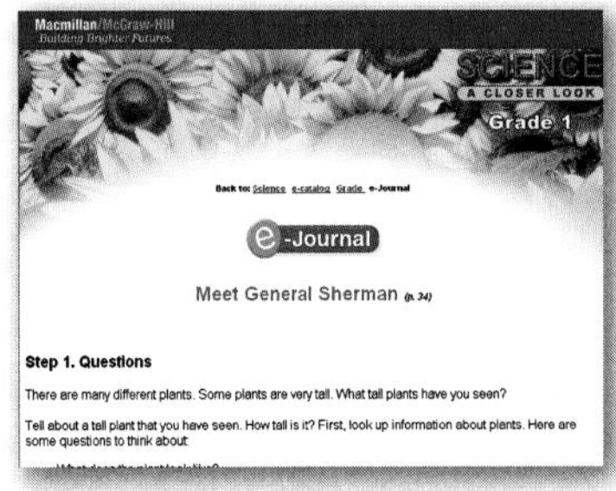

Vocabulary Games

Test your vocabulary knowledge.

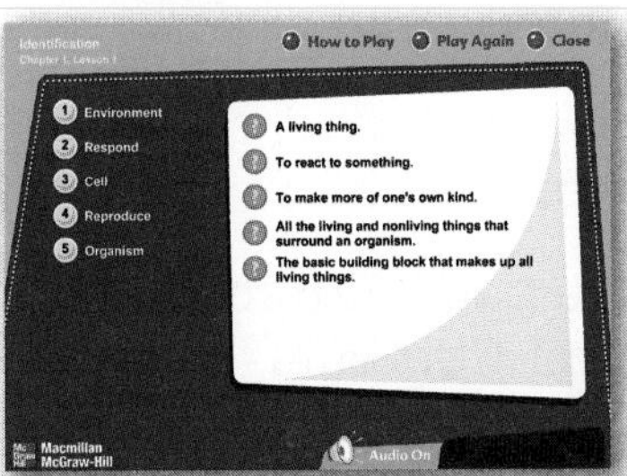

e-Glossary

Hear terms and review definitions.

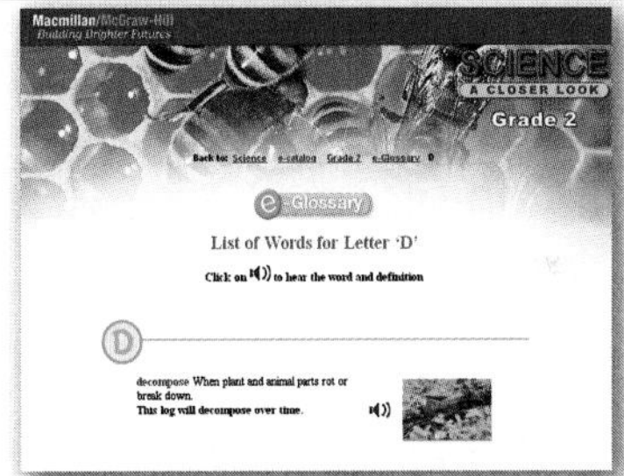

e-Career

Learn about science careers.

e-Review

Watch an animated summary and take a quiz for each lesson.

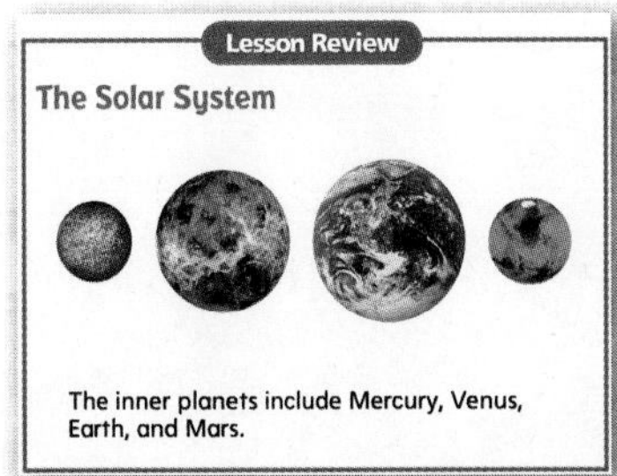

Other Online Resources

View images from NASA or see real-world connections at the American Museum of Natural History online.

Activities and Investigations

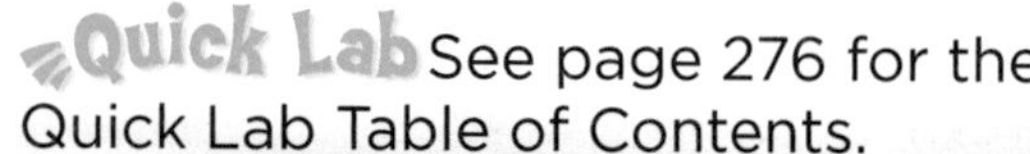

See page 276 for the Quick Lab Table of Contents.

INDIANA

Be a Scientist

Mount Etna is the largest active volcano in Europe.

Mount Etna, Italy

Be a Scientist

The Scientific Method

The Nature of Science Students gain scientific knowledge by observing the natural and constructed world, performing and evaluating investigations and communicating their findings. These principles should guide student work and be integrated into the curriculum along with the content standards on a daily basis.

Francesca studies volcanoes in their natural settings.

Jim studies volcanoes in the laboratory.

Look and Wonder

Jim Webster and Francesca Sintoni are geologists (jee•OL•uh•jists). They work at the American Museum of Natural History in New York City. Geologists are scientists who study what goes on inside and outside Earth. Jim and Francesca are curious about volcanoes like the ones pictured here on the islands of Indonesia. They want to understand more about why volcanoes erupt. What do you think happens inside Earth that sends these clouds of ash and gas into the sky?

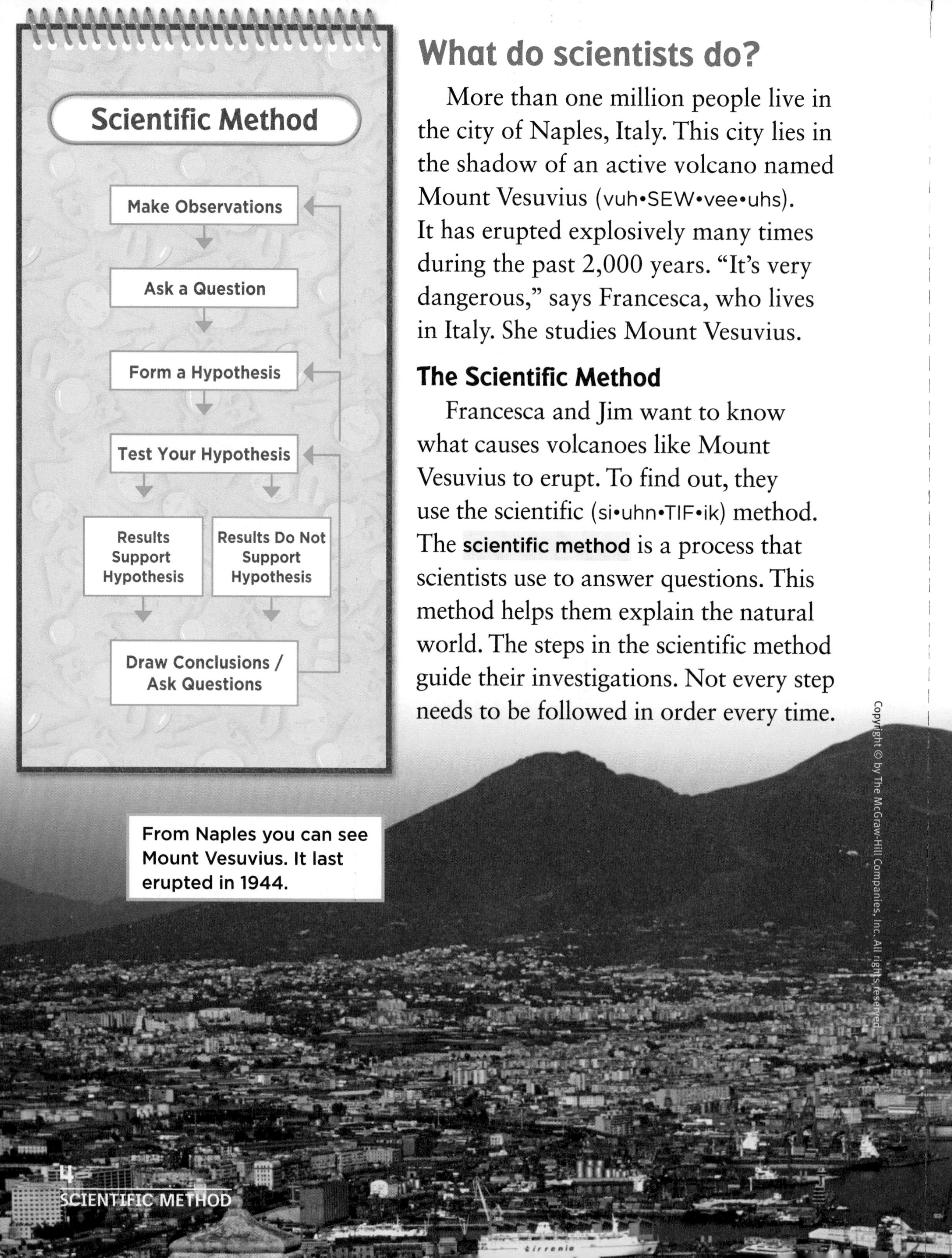

What do scientists do?

More than one million people live in the city of Naples, Italy. This city lies in the shadow of an active volcano named Mount Vesuvius (vuh•SEW•vee•uhs). It has erupted explosively many times during the past 2,000 years. "It's very dangerous," says Francesca, who lives in Italy. She studies Mount Vesuvius.

The Scientific Method

Francesca and Jim want to know what causes volcanoes like Mount Vesuvius to erupt. To find out, they use the scientific (si•uhn•TIF•ik) method. The **scientific method** is a process that scientists use to answer questions. This method helps them explain the natural world. The steps in the scientific method guide their investigations. Not every step needs to be followed in order every time.

From Naples you can see Mount Vesuvius. It last erupted in 1944.

Asking Questions

Volcanoes are filled with melted rock called *magma*. Magma is found deep inside Earth. Sometimes a gas is present in the magma. The gas may have water vapor, chlorine, or other substances in it.

When magma erupts from a volcano, lavas (LAH•vuhz) form. Many lavas are filled with small holes. These holes were once bubbles of gas in the hot magma.

Jim and Francesca ask why some volcanic eruptions are more explosive than others. They already know that water vapor affects how volcanoes erupt. Based on what they know, Jim and Francesca make a prediction. They predict that other substances will also affect volcanic eruptions. One variable (VAYR•ee•uh•buhl) they want to test is a substance called chlorine. A **variable** is something that changes, or varies.

Forming a Hypothesis

Jim and Francesca form a hypothesis (hi•PAH•thuh•sis). A **hypothesis** is a statement that can be tested to answer a question. Their hypothesis states that if magma has chlorine, then a volcano will have a larger explosion.

Quick Check

1. What is the "why" question that Jim and Francesca want to answer?

____

____

____

Francesca and Jim want to know why volcanoes erupt the way they do.

How do scientists test their hypotheses?

Can Jim and Francesca do research in an active volcano? No! Instead they use a laboratory, or lab for short. An instrument in Jim's lab models the heat and pressure deep inside a volcano. "We're trying to imitate the temperature and pressure inside Earth's crust," Jim explains.

Selecting a Strategy

To test their hypothesis, Jim and Francesca need to collect evidence. They decide to perform a set of experiments. An **experiment** is a scientific test that can be used to support or disprove a hypothesis. The pair design a set of experiments to test the effects of chlorine.

Planning a Procedure

Jim and Francesca write the steps of their procedure clearly. That way, they and others can repeat their experiments. Why? Good experiments are done again and again. If the results are similar, the evidence is stronger.

The plan is to add known amounts of chlorine to volcanic rock samples. Chlorine is the only variable they will change. The variable that changes in an experiment is the *independent variable*. Most experiments test only one independent variable at a time.

A good experiment also has *controlled variables* that are kept the same. Here, the scientists plan to control the mass, pressure, and temperature of each sample. How will they know if chlorine has any effect? They will count the number of holes in each rock. These holes are their dependent variable.

Quick Check

2. Why are Jim and Francesca unable to collect data directly from an active volcano?

____

____

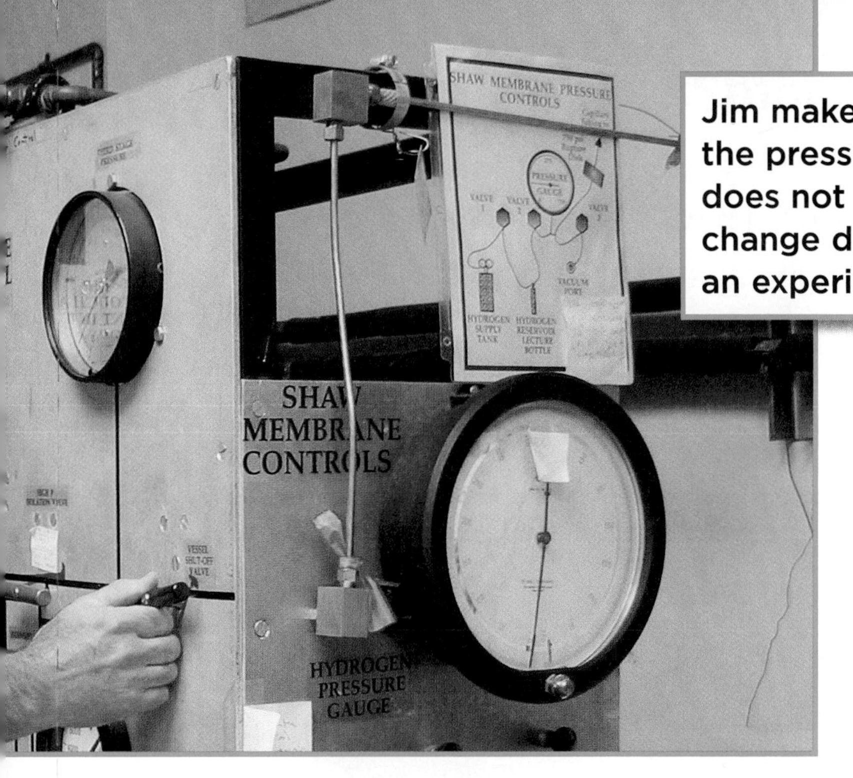

Jim makes sure the pressure does not change during an experiment.

Underline the sentence on this page that describes how Jim and Francesca test their independent variable.

Collecting Data

Jim and Francesca follow their plan. They pour crushed rock and water into tiny metal capsules. They add different amounts of chlorine. One capsule has no chlorine.

Francesca puts the sealed capsules inside a strong steel cylinder. Then Jim increases the pressure inside the cylinder. He also increases the temperature to about ten times hotter than a pizza oven!

After one week, it is time to cool the cylinder and open it. Jim and Francesca open the capsules. They observe the cooled rocks under a microscope. They count and record the number of holes. Later, they repeat the experiment exactly. They make sure the data are dependable.

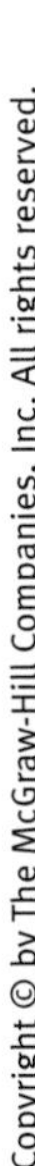

Quick Check

3. What are the controlled variables in their experiment?

___

___

___

The holes in volcanic rock were once gas bubbles that formed inside magma.

How do scientists analyze data?

When Jim and Francesca collect data, they keep careful records of their observations. They record how much chlorine went into each capsule. They carefully describe each tiny piece of cooled rock. They record the number of holes. Then they organize all this data in a way that makes sense.

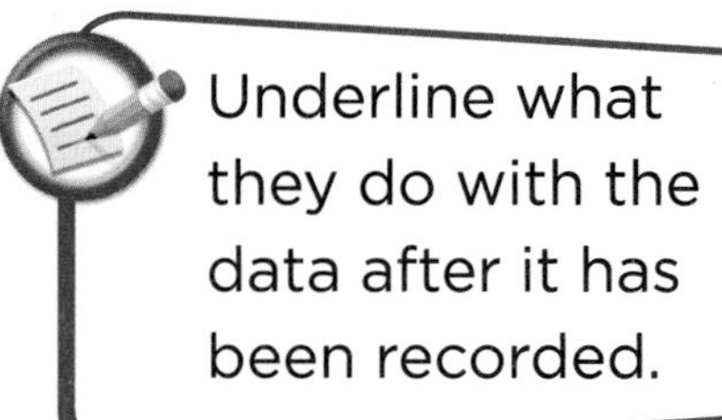

Underline what they do with the data after it has been recorded.

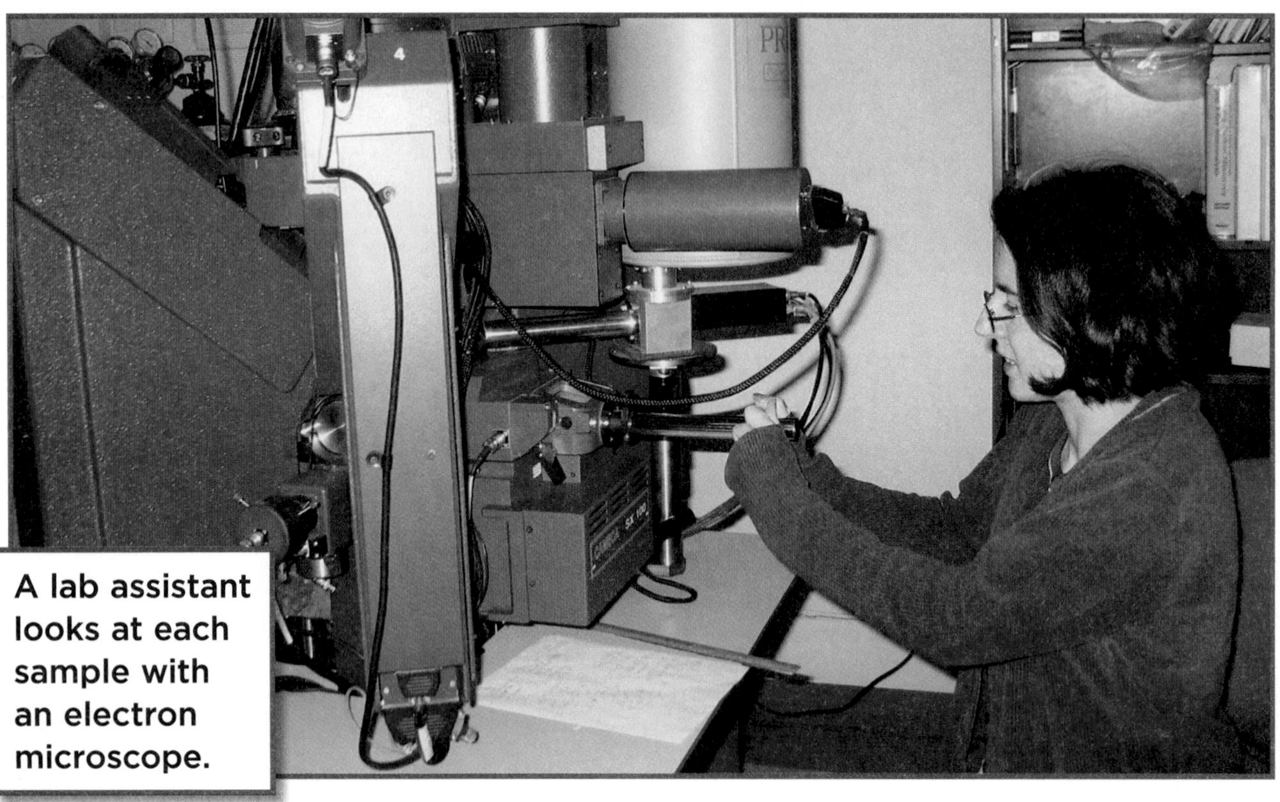

A lab assistant looks at each sample with an electron microscope.

Comparing Samples

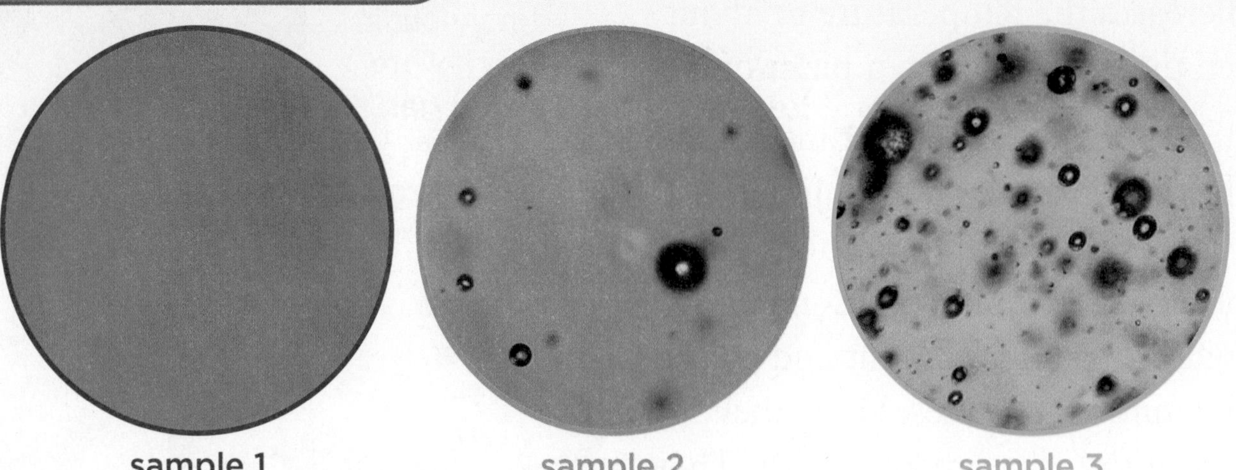

sample 1 | sample 2 | sample 3

Data Chart				
Run	Temperature	Pressure	Chlorine	Bubble
1	920°C	**200 MPa**	0%	none
2	920°C	**200 MPa**	0.8%	some
3	920°C	**200 MPa**	0.9%	many

Looking for Patterns

The table above has some of the results from Jim and Francesca's study. In total, they ran about 50 experiments. Each one took about one week to complete. That means it took almost a year to collect their data!

After Jim and Francesca organize all their data, they look for patterns. What do their data show? When a sample has more chlorine, the cooled rock has more holes. The control sample, without chlorine, has no holes at all.

Checking for Errors

As they go along, Jim and Francesca review their procedures. They check that the experiments were run correctly. If they find any errors, they cannot use the data. Errors mean they must try again.

✓ Quick Check

4. Why do scientists organize the data they collect?

____

____

____

____

5. What will Jim and Francesca do if they find an error in their experiment?

____

____

How do scientists draw conclusions?

Now Jim and Francesca must decide whether their data support their hypothesis. They compare their results with lavas from Mount Vesuvius and other explosive volcanoes. This comparison allows them to draw their conclusion.

Does more chlorine in the magma cause a bigger explosion? "Yes, it does!" Francesca exclaims.

The results of an experiment do not always support the tested hypothesis. This can be a useful outcome. When a hypothesis is not supported, scientists ask why. They may decide to test the hypothesis with new experiments using different methods.

Sometimes scientists conclude that a hypothesis is incorrect. When this happens, they often form a new hypothesis. Then they follow the steps of the scientific method once again.

Quick Check

6. If the data collected does not support the hypothesis, is the study a failure?

____

____

Mount Saint Augustine volcano, Alaska

Communicating

Jim and Francesca report their conclusions. This way, other scientists can do the same experiment and compare their results. Many scientists share their results so people can learn from their work.

Asking New Questions

A scientist's results may lead to new questions. Jim wants to know if chlorine affects eruptions at other volcanoes too. What other gases affect the size of eruptions? What else happens when a volcano erupts?

Today Jim studies Mount Saint Augustine volcano in Alaska. Like Mount Vesuvius, Mount Saint Augustine is an active volcano. It makes up its own island in Alaska's Cook Inlet.

Jim visits Mount Saint Augustine with other scientists. Together, they make new observations.

Quick Check

8. Why is the scientific method useful to scientists?

9. What other questions about volcanoes can you think of? Choose one. Form a hypothesis that could be tested.

10. What could scientists do if their data disproved their hypothesis?

Focus on Skills

▲ **Scientists first**

____________ an object or event to learn more about it.

Scientists use many skills as they apply the scientific method. Inquiry (IN•kwuh•ree) skills help you gather information and answer questions about the world around you. Here are some important inquiry skills that all scientists use:

Observe Use your senses to learn about an object or event.

Form a Hypothesis Make a statement that can be tested to answer a question.

Communicate Share information with others.

Classify Place things with similar properties into groups.

Use Numbers Order, count, add, subtract, multiply, or divide.

Make a Model Assemble something that represents an object, a system, or a process.

Fill in each blank on these two pages with one of the inquiry skills listed.

Before starting an experiment, scientists form a(n) ____________.

Scientists may use a chart like this to gather information. This chart may help a scientist ____________. ▶

Carton A	
Prediction	
Day	Observations
1	
2	
7	
10	

Use Variables Identify things that can control or change the outcome of an experiment.

Interpret Data Use information that has been gathered to answer questions, solve problems, or compare results.

Measure Find the size, distance, time, volume, area, mass, weight, or temperature of something.

Predict State a likely result of an event or experiment based on facts or observations.

Infer Form an idea or opinion from facts or observations.

Experiment Perform a test to support or disprove a hypothesis.

In the photograph, the girl is using a graduated cylinder to ____________ water. ▶

Inquiry Skill Builder

Throughout this book, you will find Inquiry Skill Builder activities. These activities will help you practice the skills that scientists use every day.

Safety Tips

In the Classroom

- Read all of the directions. Make sure you understand them. When you see "△ **Be Careful,**" follow the safety rules.
- Listen to your teacher for special safety directions. If you do not understand something, ask for help.
- Wash your hands with soap and water before an activity.
- Be careful around a hot plate. Know when it is on and when it is off. Remember that the plate stays hot for a few minutes after it is turned off.
- Wear a safety apron if you work with anything messy or anything that might spill.
- Clean up a spill right away, or ask your teacher for help.
- Dispose of things the way your teacher tells you to.
- Tell your teacher if something breaks. If glass breaks, do not clean it up yourself.
- Wear safety goggles when your teacher tells you to wear them. Wear them when working with anything that can fly into your eyes or when working with liquids.
- Keep your hair and clothes away from open flames. Tie back long hair, and roll up long sleeves.
- Keep your hands dry around electrical equipment.
- Do not eat or drink anything during an experiment.
- Put equipment back the way your teacher tells you to.
- Clean up your work area after an activity, and wash your hands with soap and water.

In the Field

- Go with a trusted adult—such as your teacher and a parent or a guardian.
- Do not touch animals or plants without an adult's approval. The animal might bite. The plant might be poison ivy or another dangerous plant.

Responsibility

Treat living things, the environment, and one another with respect.

INDIANA

Physical Science

Academic Standards for Science

Core Standard Provide evidence that heat and electricity are forms of energy.

Core Standard Design and assemble electric circuits that provide a means of transferring energy from one form or place to another.

A bolt of lightning is hotter than the surface of the Sun.

lightning over Indianapolis, Indiana

UNIT 1

Heat and Electricity

What do heat and electricity have in common?

____

____

____

____

____

____

Vocabulary

heat the movement of energy between materials because they are different temperatures

insulator a material that heat or electricity does not move through easily

conductor a material that heat or electricity moves through easily

electrical current a flow of charged particles

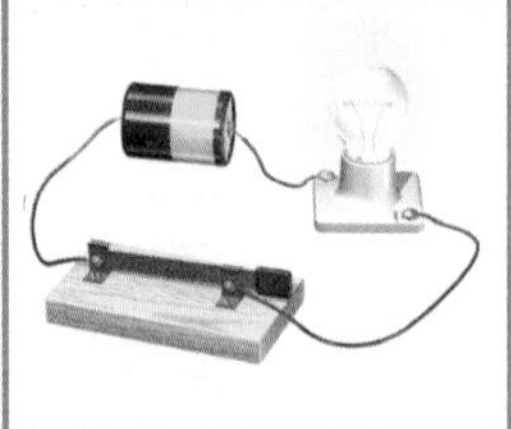

circuit a path with parts that work together to allow electrical current to flow

fuse a device that stops the flow of electrical current when it heats up

As you read the unit, complete the concept map about heat and electricity.

Energy Comparison	Heat	Electricity
Sources	The main source of Earth's heat is _______________.	A buildup of electrical charges is called _______________.
Movement	Heat moves from a(n) _______________ object to a(n) _______________ one.	Electrical current will only pass through a(n) _______________ circuit.
Changes	Sand heats up _______________ than water. An ice cube begins to _______________ when placed in warm water.	Electricity can be changed into motion, _______________, _______________, and _______________.
Uses	How I use heat: _______________ _______________ _______________	How I use electricity: _______________ _______________ _______________

Lesson 1

Heat

4.1.1 Describe and investigate the different ways in which heat can be generated.
4.1.2 Investigate the variety of ways that heat can be generated and move from one place to another and explain the direction in which the heat moves.

Look and Wonder

This grinding wheel wears away metal. What happens when the wheel spins against the metal?

Essential Question How can you describe heat?

Explore

What are some ways that heat is produced?

Purpose

Investigate situations that produce heat.

Materials

- rubber eraser

- thick rubber band

Procedure

1. **Observe** Place a rubber eraser against the back of your hand. Do the same with a thick rubber band. Does the rubber feel warm, hot, or cool?

   ____

2. **Observe** Stretch and release the thick rubber band 30 times. Test how it feels against the back of your hand. Is it warm, hot, or cool? Rub the eraser on a rough surface for 30 seconds. Test how it feels. Is it warm, hot, or cool?

   ____

   ____

   ____

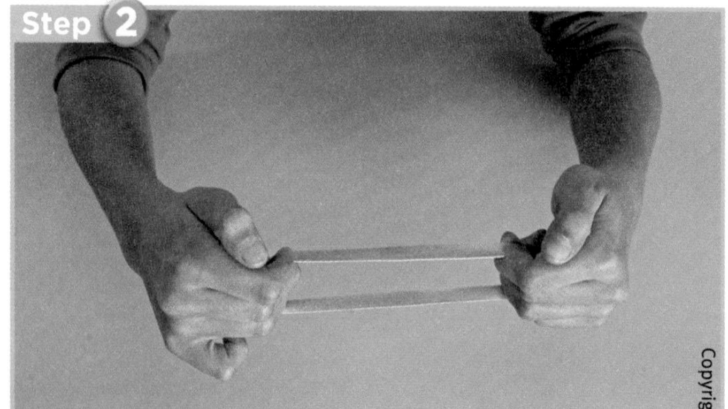

3. **Communicate** Describe how the rubber band and the rubber eraser changed.

   ____

4. **Experiment** How will rubbing your hands together affect their temperature? Touch the palms of your hand to your forehead. Observe how warm they are. Rub your hands together for 30 seconds. Then test them again to see how they feel after rubbing. Record your results.

   ____

The Nature of Science Make predictions and formulate testable questions.

Draw Conclusions

5 **Infer** What could you put on your hands to keep them from warming up when rubbed?

____

Explore More

Experiment What are some other ways that you can produce heat? Make a plan to find out. When your teacher has approved your plan, conduct your investigation and record your results.

____

____

Open Inquiry

How does the number of times you rub your hands or pull the rubber band affect how warm it gets? Think of your own question. Make a plan and carry out an experiment to answer your question.

My question is: ______________________

____

____

How I can test it: ______________________

____

____

My results are: ______________________

____

____

Read and Respond

What is heat?

Have you ever put your hands on a bowl of hot soup? What happened? Your hands got warm. Heat moved from the hot bowl to your hands. **Heat** is the movement of energy between materials because they are different temperatures. Heat can move through solids, liquids, and gases. It can even move through space. Heat always moves from a warmer material to a cooler one.

Through what can heat move? Underline the correct words in the first paragraph.

Heating Materials

Some objects heat up faster than others. For example, at the beach you will find sand and water. Both are warmed by the Sun. The sand gets very hot, but the water stays much cooler.

Quick Check

1. **What happens when an ice cube is placed in a warm glass of water?**

____

____

____

Glue your Notebook FOLDABLES® here. Use Foldable I on page 290.

Heat All Around

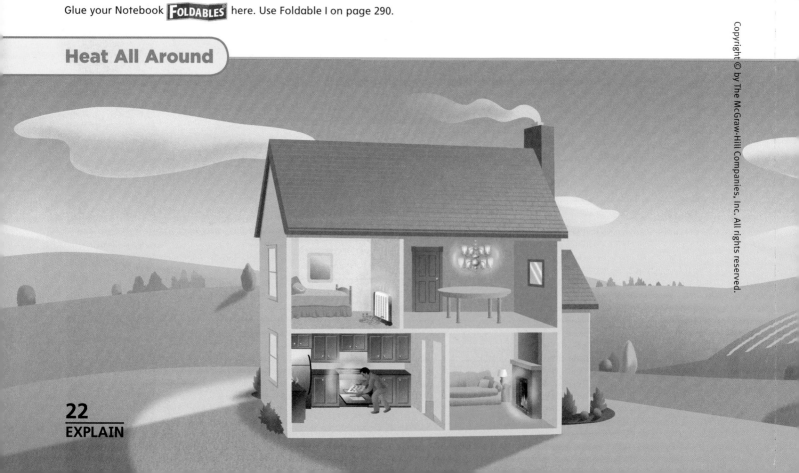

Sources of Heat

The Sun is Earth's main source of heat. A source is where something comes from. The Sun's heat warms the air, land, and water. Without the Sun's heat, it would be too cold on Earth for most living things to survive.

Fires, light bulbs, and stoves are some other sources of heat. Fires produce heat as materials burn. Light bulbs and some stoves use electricity to produce heat. Rubbing two objects together can also produce heat. This is why your hands get warm when you rub them together.

Quick Check

2. How could you find out if an object is getting hotter?

____

____

____

____

Quick Lab

To learn more about how heat affects materials, do the Quick Lab on page 277.

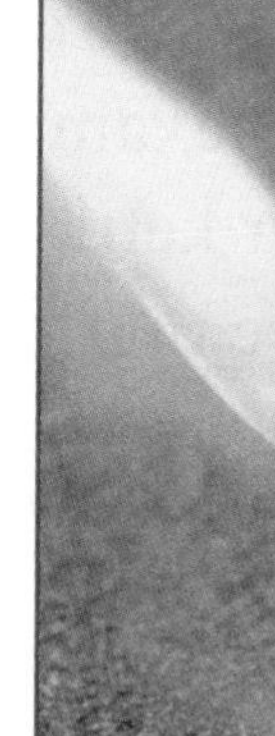

▲ A lit match is a source of heat.

Read a Diagram

Name the sources of heat you can find in this picture.

____

____

See page 255 for more practice reading diagrams.

What are conductors and insulators?

Heat does not move well through all materials. To stay warm, we trap heat around our bodies. Jackets, mittens, and blankets are examples of insulators (IN•suh•lay•tuhrz). An **insulator** is a material that heat does not move through easily. Wool, cotton, and fur are materials that make good insulators.

Heat moves easily through other materials, such as metals. For example, heat moves easily through the copper kettle shown below. Heat moves from a stove to the kettle. The kettle gets warm. The water inside the kettle also gets warm.

Materials such as metals are good conductors (kuhn•DUK•tuhrz). A **conductor** is a material that heat moves through easily. Conduction (kuhn•DUK•shun) is the process of passing heat from one material to another.

Underline the names of materials that make good insulators in the first paragraph on this page. Circle the names of materials that make good conductors in the second paragraph.

Mittens are good insulators for your hands.

A kettle is a good conductor for heating liquids.

Conductors feel cold to the touch. Look at the picture below. The carpet and tile floors are both the same temperature. However the tile floor feels cold because it conducts heat away from the boy's skin. The carpet feels warm because it insulates the boy's skin.

There are many natural insulators. Your skin is an example. Some animals, such as seals and walruses, have a layer of fat called blubber. Birds have feathers. Other animals, such as dogs and cats, have fur.

Quick Lab

To learn more about heat and temperature, do the Quick Lab on page 278.

Quick Check

Circle the correct answer.

3. Which of these is an insulator?

   oven mitt

   meat thermometer

   cooking pot

4. Which of these is a conductor?

   skillet

   sweater

   hat

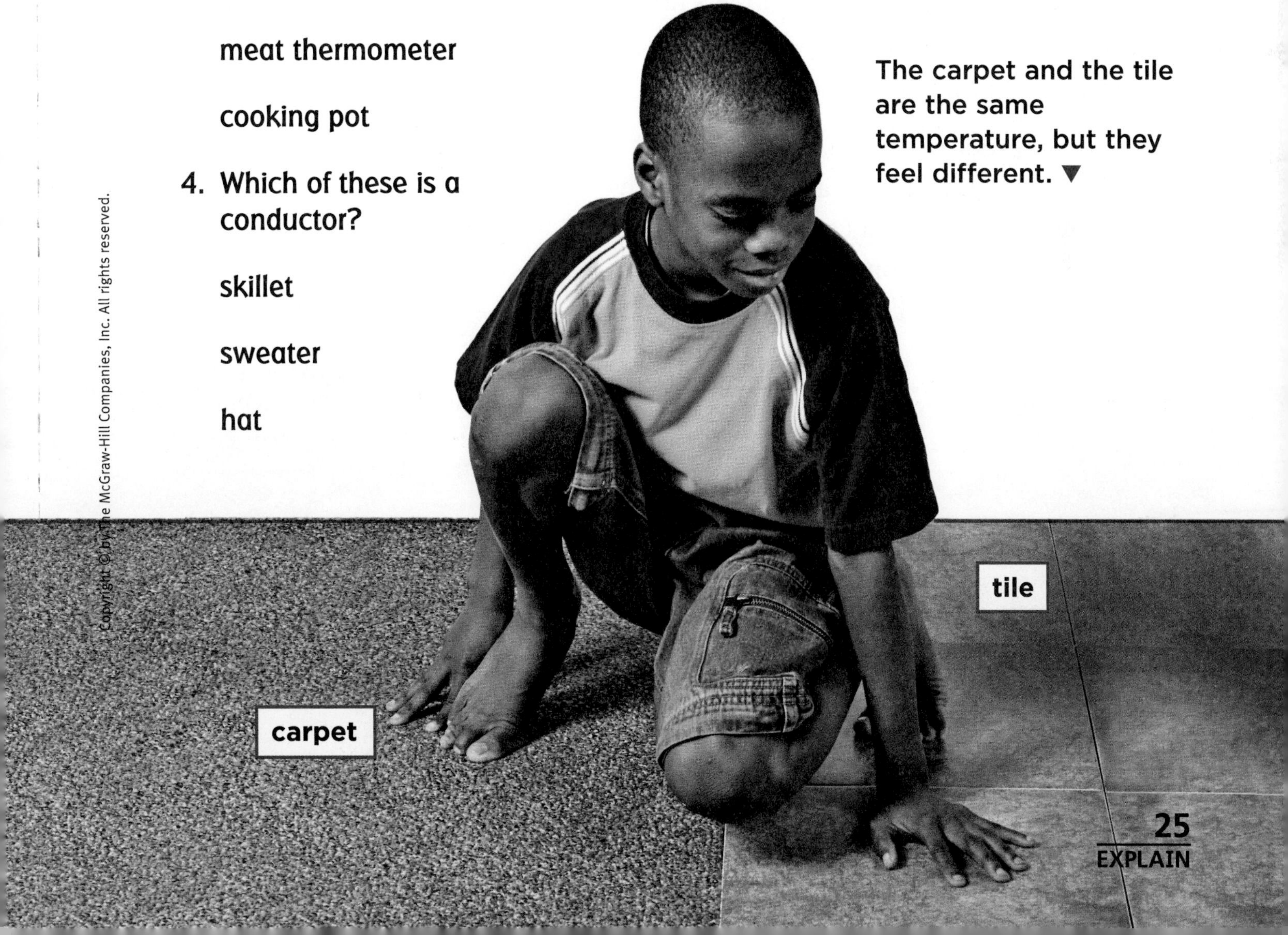

The carpet and the tile are the same temperature, but they feel different. ▼

How does heat move?

You have learned that heat can move easily through conductors. What are all the ways that heat can move?

In the last paragraph on this page, circle one example of radiation.

Conduction

Solids are heated mainly by conduction. Conduction often occurs between two objects that are touching. Conduction can also occur within an object. The handle of a metal pan heats by conduction.

What happens when you heat a pan on a stove? The fast-moving particles of the burner or flame hit the cooler particles of the pan. The cooler particles get energy. This makes the cooler particles start to move faster. Soon, the entire pan feels hot.

Radiation

Another way that heat moves is by radiation (ray•dee•AY•shun). **Radiation** is the movement of heat by wave energy, such as light waves. Radiation can move through space. Without radiation, energy from the Sun would not reach Earth.

Quick Check

5. How is radiation different from conduction?

____

____

____

____

East Pier Lighthouse, Michigan City, Indiana

The Sun's energy is transferred through space by radiation.

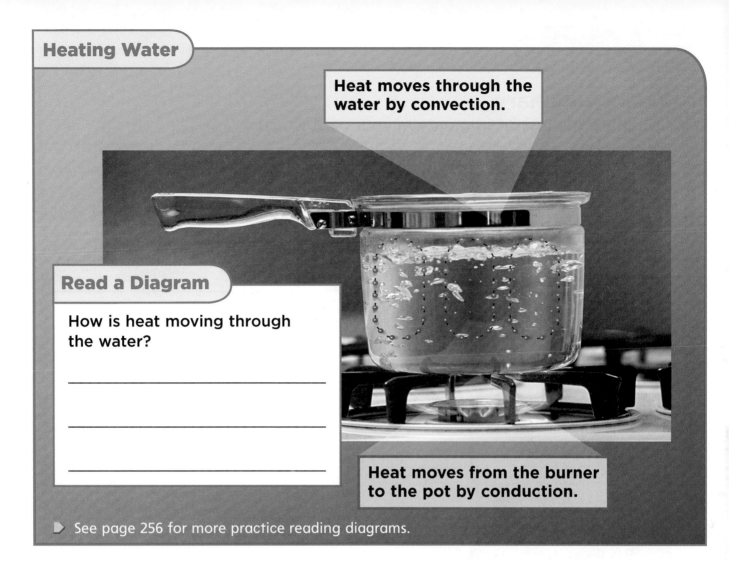

Heating Water

Heat moves through the water by convection.

Read a Diagram

How is heat moving through the water?

____

____

____

Heat moves from the burner to the pot by conduction.

See page 256 for more practice reading diagrams.

Convection

The third way heat moves is by convection (kun•VEK•shun). **Convection** is the movement of heat through liquids or gases.

If you want to boil water, you can heat it in a pot. As energy flows to the pot, the water heats. The water particles at the bottom of the pot heat first. The particles move faster and farther apart. The hot water rises. The cooler water at the top of the pot sinks, replacing the hot water. When all particles of water move at the same speed, the water boils. Bubbles form.

In the water shown above, draw arrows to show the direction that water particles are moving.

Quick Check

6. **Will hot air rise or fall? Explain.**

____

____

Visual Summary

Complete the lesson summary in your own words.

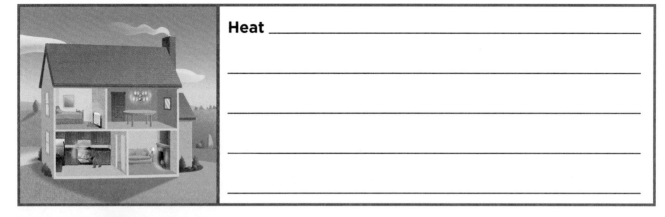

Heat ______________________________

____

____

____

____

Conductors and Insulators ______________________________

____

____

____

____

Radiation and Convection ______________________________

____

____

____

____

Make a FOLDABLES® Study Guide

Make a three-tab book. Use it to summarize what you learned about heat.

Think, Talk, and Write

1. **Vocabulary** The flow of energy between materials because they are different temperatures is called ________.

2. **Classify** Give three examples of heat flow. Classify each example as conduction, convection, or radiation.

Example	Type of Flow

3. **Critical Thinking** Explain why you are cooler under the shade of a tree than in the sunshine.

4. **Test Prep** **Many pots and pans are made of metal because metal is a good**

   A conductor.
   B insulator.
   C heat source.
   D radiator.

Essential Question How can you describe heat?

Focus on Skills

Inquiry Skill: Infer

You just read that insulators do not transfer heat very well. One way to keep ice cubes from melting is to insulate them. Scientists experiment to find out which materials prevent the most heat transfer. After the experiment, they can **infer** which material will make the best insulator.

▶ Learn It

When you **infer**, you form an idea from facts or observations. It's easier to form an idea about a result when the information is organized. You can use charts, tables, or graphs to organize your data. That way you can quickly see any differences and begin to interpret the results.

4.1.4 Experiment with materials to identify conductors and insulators of heat and electricity.

▶ Try It

Use different materials to insulate ice cubes. Infer which material is best for slowing the ice cubes' melting.

Materials **scissors, paper, aluminum foil, plastic wrap, 4 ice cubes, tape, shallow dish**

1. Cut a piece of paper just large enough to cover one ice cube. Do the same with the aluminum foil and plastic wrap.
2. Wrap one of the ice cubes in the paper. Seal the paper well with tape. Place the sealed ice cube in the dish. Record the time in your chart.

	Paper	Foil	Plastic	Unwrapped
Start Time				
Melted				
Time to Melt				

3. Repeat step 2 with the aluminum foil.
4. Repeat step 2 with the plastic wrap. Leave a fourth ice cube unwrapped. In the chart, record the time you place each ice cube in the dish.
5. Observe the ice cubes in the dishes. Record the time when each ice cube melts completely.
6. Calculate the time it took for each ice cube to melt. Enter the times in your chart.

Focus on Skills

▶ Apply It

Interpret your data to infer which wrapper best insulated the ice cube.

1. Compare your result for the unwrapped ice cube to each of your other results. Which material was the best insulator? What was the time difference between that one and the unwrapped cube?

2. Which material was the poorest insulator? Why do you think so?

3. Why was it a good idea to keep one ice cube unwrapped?

4 What type of heat transfer did you investigate? Explain your thinking.

____

____

____

____

5 Based on your test results, you inferred which material insulated best. What changes could you make to improve the test?

____

____

____

____

Lesson 2

Electricity

4.1.5 Demonstrate that electrical energy can be transformed into heat, light, and sound.

Look and Wonder

Light bulbs have different parts inside them. It takes electricity to make these parts give off light. What is electricity? When can we see electricity in action?

Essential Question How do we use electricity?

Explore

What makes a bulb light?

Make a Prediction

How can you connect a battery, a wire, and a light bulb to make the bulb light up?

Test Your Prediction

1. **Experiment** Try to light the bulb using setups that include a light bulb, wire, and battery.
2. **Communicate** Draw each setup. Record whether or not the setup made the bulb light up.
3. **Communicate** When your light bulb is lit, compare setups with your classmates. Is there more than one setup that lights the bulb? Explain.

Glue your Notebook FOLDABLES here. Use Foldable 3 on page 292.

Materials

- D-cell battery

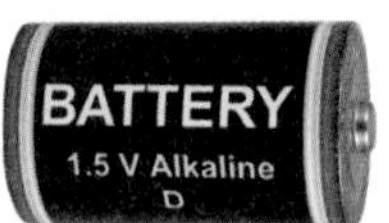

- one 20-cm piece of insulated wire

- light bulb

Step 1

Step 2

4.1.3 Construct a complete circuit through which an electrical current can pass as evidenced by the lighting of a bulb or ringing of a bell. The Nature of Science Keep accurate records in a notebook during investigations and communicate findings to others using graphs, charts, maps and models through oral and written reports.

Draw Conclusions

4. How many setups could you find that made the bulb light?

____

5. **Infer** Look at the setups that lit the bulb. What do you think is necessary to make the bulb light up?

____

____

____

Explore More

Experiment How could you turn a buzzer on and off using a battery, switch, and wires? Try it.

____

____

____

Open Inquiry

Can you make a setup with more than one light bulb? What will happen if one of the light bulbs is removed? Think of your own question about batteries, wires, and bulbs. Make a plan and carry out an experiment to answer your question.

My question is: ____

____

How I can test it: ____

____

My results are: ____

____

Read and Respond

What are electrical charges?

Have you ever had a shock from touching a doorknob? Why does this happen? The same thing that causes light bulbs to glow and lightning to strike causes this shock. All these things happen because of electricity.

Circle the two types of electrical charges named on this page.

All electricity is the result of the movement of electrical charges. You cannot see electrical charges. However, you can observe how objects with different charges interact.

There are two types of electrical charges. One is called positive. The other is called negative. A positive and a negative charge attract, or pull, each other. Similar charges, such as two positive charges, have the opposite effect. Similar charges repel, or push, each other.

Electrical charges can create a shock when you touch a doorknob.

Quick Check

1. **How will two negative charges affect each other? Explain.**

____

____

Static Electricity

Most objects have the same number of positive charges as negative charges. The charges are balanced, or equal. However when two objects touch, negative charges can move from one object to the other. Negative charges can build up on one object. That gives the object an overall negative charge. The buildup of electrical charges is called **static electricity.**

Rub a balloon on a sweater and hold it near a wall. The balloon sticks to the wall! When you rub the balloon, negative charges move from the sweater to the balloon. The balloon gets an overall negative charge. It repels the negative charges in the wall and attracts the positive charges. This causes the balloon to stick to the wall.

Static electricity is what sometimes causes you to get a shock when you touch a doorknob. When you walk across a carpeted floor, negative charges move from the floor to your body. You get a negative charge. When you touch a doorknob, the negative charges move from you to the metal knob. You feel this as a shock. A shock is also called a discharge. A discharge occurs when static electricity moves from one object to another. Lightning is also a discharge of static electricity.

Glue your Notebook FOLDABLES here. Use Foldable I on page 290.

Quick Lab

Experiment with static electricity. Do the Quick Lab on page 279.

▲ **The balloon has a negative charge. It attracts the positive (+) charges in the wall and repels the negative (–) charges. The balloon sticks to the wall.**

Quick Check

2. Which kind of electrical charge moves more easily?

___

What is electrical current?

You have read that charges can build up on objects. They can also be made to flow. A flow of electrical charges is called **electrical current** (KUR•unt). You use electrical current every day. Electrical current provides the energy for lights, radios, computers, hair dryers, and many other products. We use energy from electrical current to produce heat, light, sound, and motion.

 ***Quick Check***

Fill in the blanks.

3. An example of a machine that changes electrical current into motion is a(n) ________________.
4. A fluorescent bulb turns electrical current into ________________.

▲ Electrical current is changed into heat, light, and motion inside this toaster.

These headphones change electrical current into sound. ▼

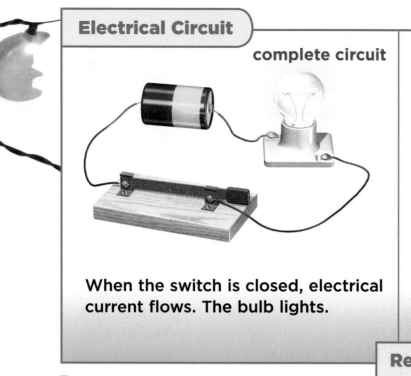

Electrical Circuit

complete circuit

When the switch is closed, electrical current flows. The bulb lights.

open circuit

When the switch is open, electrical current does not flow. The bulb does not light.

Read a Diagram

How could you light the second bulb?

___

See page 257 for more practice reading diagrams.

Circuits

Electrical current can move through a circuit (SUR•kut). A **circuit** is a path that allows current to flow. The diagram on this page shows a circuit. Wires connect the bulb to a battery. The battery is the circuit's power source.

To keep electrical current moving, a circuit cannot have any breaks, or openings. An unbroken circuit is called a *complete circuit*. A circuit with breaks is called an *open circuit*. Current does not flow through an open circuit.

Switches

You can use a switch (SWICH) to open or complete a circuit. A **switch** allows you to control the flow of electrical current. You use switches when you turn on a flashlight or ring a doorbell.

When a switch is in the "on" position, there is no gap in the path. The circuit is complete, and current can flow. Turn the switch off, and there is a gap in the path. The circuit is open, and current does not flow.

 **Quick Check**

5. When do you have a complete circuit in your home?

___

How do we use different materials in electrical circuits?

You know that heat flows well through some materials and poorly through others. The same is true of electrical current. Materials that allow current to flow through them are called **conductors**. Materials that do not allow current to flow through them are called **insulators**. How do we use these properties?

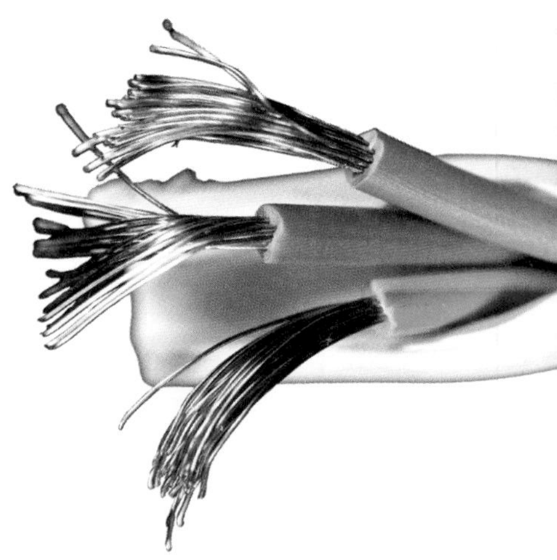

▲ Copper wires are conductors. The plastic around each wire is an insulator.

The electrical current in your home flows through wires. These wires are usually made of copper. Copper is a metal. It is a good conductor of electrical current. Most metals are good conductors.

Plastic is wrapped around the wires in your home because plastic is an insulator. The plastic coating protects you from getting a shock when you touch the wire. Glass, plastic, and rubber are insulators.

Electrical power line towers are made of metal, a conductor. Insulators are placed between the towers and the power lines. This prevents the towers from getting an electrical charge.

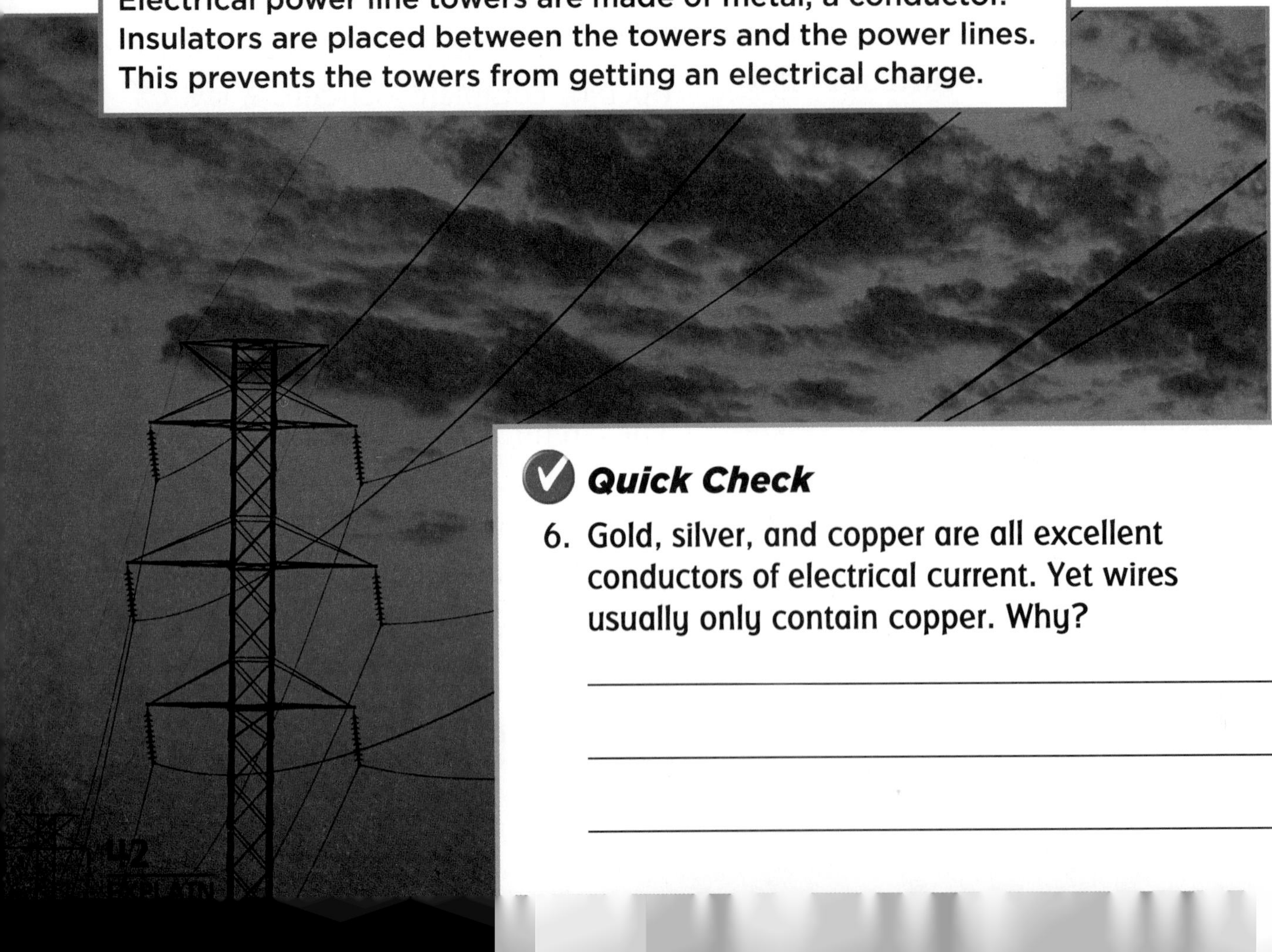

Quick Check

6. Gold, silver, and copper are all excellent conductors of electrical current. Yet wires usually only contain copper. Why?

____

____

____

Short Circuits

Resistance is the ability to oppose, or slow, current. Sometimes a circuit can accidentally have too little resistance. This is called a short circuit. A short circuit can occur where wires are torn or frayed.

A short circuit can be dangerous. The wires in the circuit can heat up and cause a fire.

Fuses and Circuit Breakers

A **fuse** is a device that helps prevent short circuits. A fuse has a thin strip of metal in it. The strip has high resistance. If too much current flows through, the metal strip heats up and melts. The circuit opens. This causes the current to stop flowing.

Fuses can be used only once. This means they must constantly be replaced. However, circuit breakers can be reset. A circuit breaker is a switch that protects circuits. When a dangerously high current flows through the circuit breaker, the switch opens. This stops the current.

If a fuse breaks, it cannot be reused.

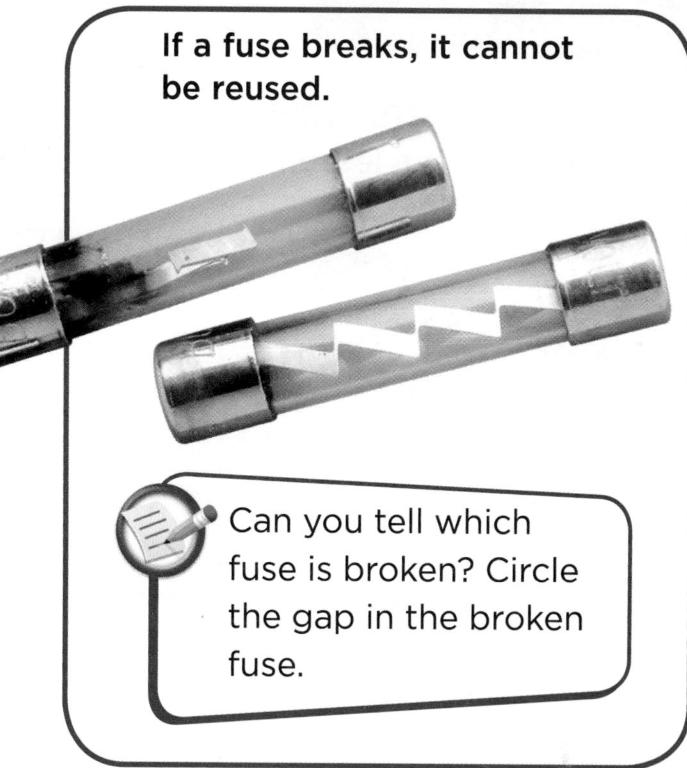

Can you tell which fuse is broken? Circle the gap in the broken fuse.

Most homes have circuit breakers. ▼

Quick Check

7. **Circuit breakers are used more often than fuses in new buildings. Why?**

____

____

Visual Summary

Complete the lesson summary in your own words.

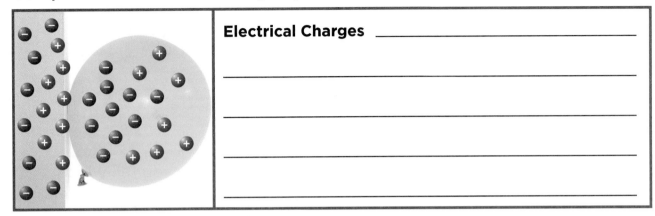

Electrical Charges ______________________________

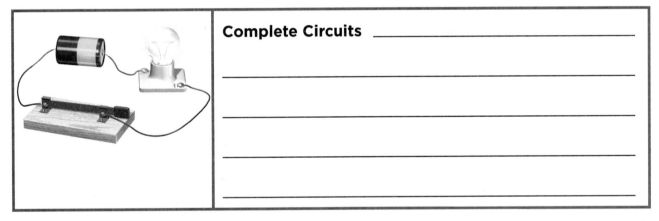

Complete Circuits ______________________________

Conductors and Insulators ______________________________

Make a FOLDABLES® Study Guide

Make a three-tab book. Use it to summarize what you learned about electricity.

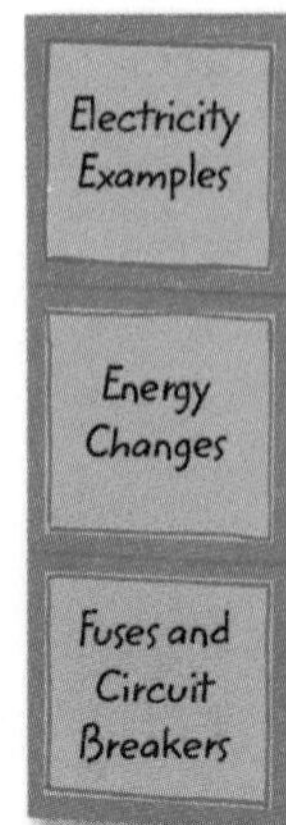

Think, Talk, and Write

1. **Vocabulary** A switch controls the flow of ________________.

2. **Main Idea and Details** What is electricity? Give details.

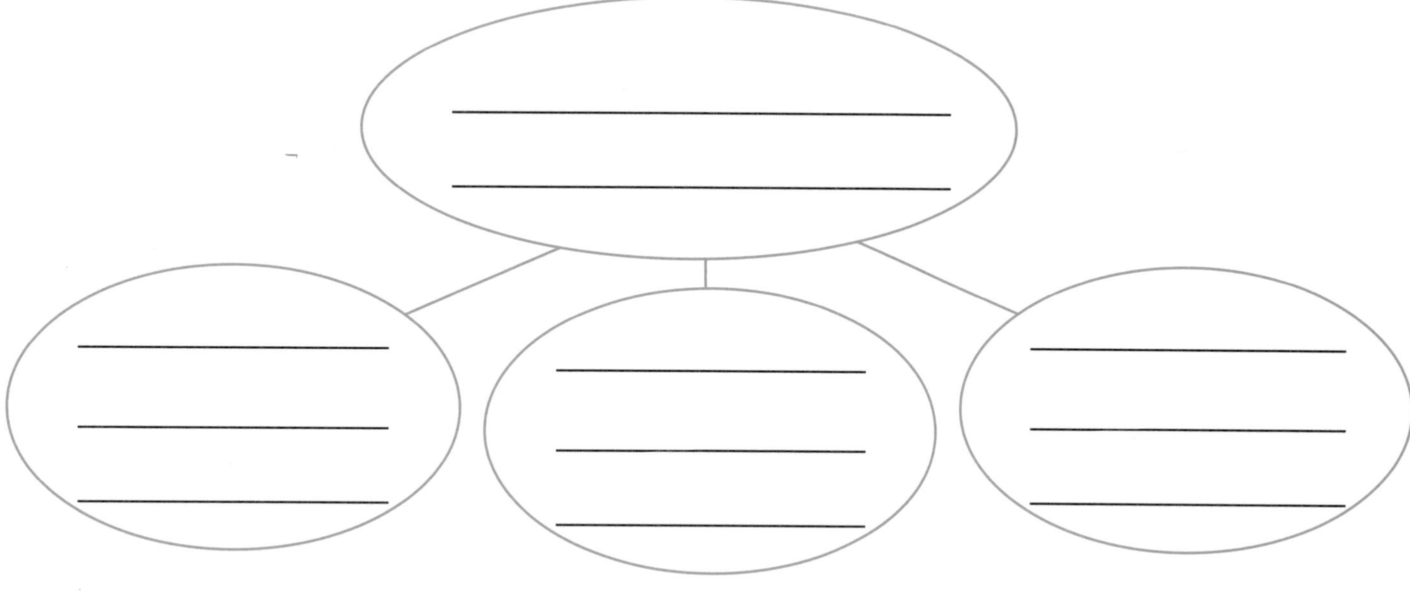

3. **Critical Thinking** You flip the switch on a flashlight. The light does not come on. List two things that might be wrong with the flashlight.

____

____

4. **Test Prep** **Which of these is the BEST electrical conductor?**

   A wood
   B plastic
   C rubber
   D copper

Essential Question How do we use electricity?

____

____

____

____

____

LOG ON e-Review Summaries and quizzes online at www.macmillanmh.com

Be a Scientist

Structured Inquiry

Which materials complete an electrical circuit?

Form a Hypothesis

Will a metal fork complete a circuit? Write your answer in the form "If I put a metal fork into a circuit, then the light bulb that is part of the circuit will . . . " What about an eraser and a lime? Will they complete a circuit? Write a hypothesis for the eraser and the lime too.

____

____

____

Test Your Hypothesis

1. You will make a circuit using a light bulb that will light when the circuit is completed. Gather the following materials: battery, battery holder, three pieces of wire, light bulb, bulb socket.

2. Put the battery in the battery holder. Screw the light bulb into the bulb socket. Connect a wire to each side of the battery holder.

3. Connect the free end of one of the wires to the bulb socket. Then connect a third wire to the bulb socket.

4.I.4 Experiment with materials to identify conductors and insulators of heat and electricity. **The Nature of Science** Keep accurate records in a notebook during investigations and communicate findings to others using graphs, charts, maps and models through oral and written reports.

4 **Experiment** Touch the free ends of the wires to the metal fork. Does the bulb light up? Record what happens in the chart below.

5 **Experiment** Repeat step 4 with a rubber eraser. Then, try the experiment with a lime that has been cut open. Record what happens in the chart.

Object Tested	Observations

Draw Conclusions

6 **Communicate** Describe what happens when the wires touch a conductor. Describe what happens when the wires touch an insulator.

____

____

____

____

7 **Infer** Which objects are conductors? Which are insulators?

____

____

Be a Scientist

Guided Inquiry

Which materials are the best conductors of electricity?

Form a Hypothesis

Think of other classroom objects you could test to find out if they conduct electricity. Write a hypothesis for each object.

____

____

____

Test Your Hypothesis

Test each object. Record your results and observations.

Draw Conclusions

Make a list of categories of materials (metals, liquids, solids, fruits, and so on). Which kinds of materials are the best conductors of electricity? Give evidence to support your conclusion.

____

____

____

____

____

Open Inquiry

Make your own conductivity tester. Test objects in your home to find out if they conduct electricity. Record your results. Share your results with your classmates.

My question is:

____

____

____

How I can test it:

____

____

____

My results are:

____

____

____

____

____

____

____

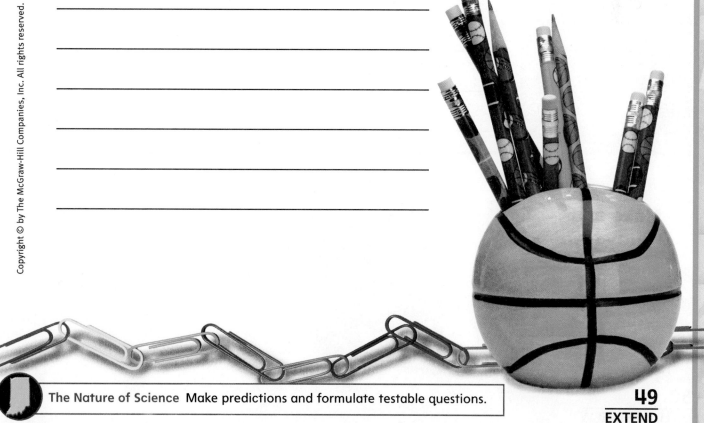

The Nature of Science Make predictions and formulate testable questions.

UNIT 1 Review

Visual Summary

Summarize each lesson in your own words.

Lesson 1 ______________________________

Lesson 2 ______________________________

Make a FOLDABLES® Study Guide

Glue your lesson study guides to a large sheet of paper as shown. Use them to review what you have learned in this unit.

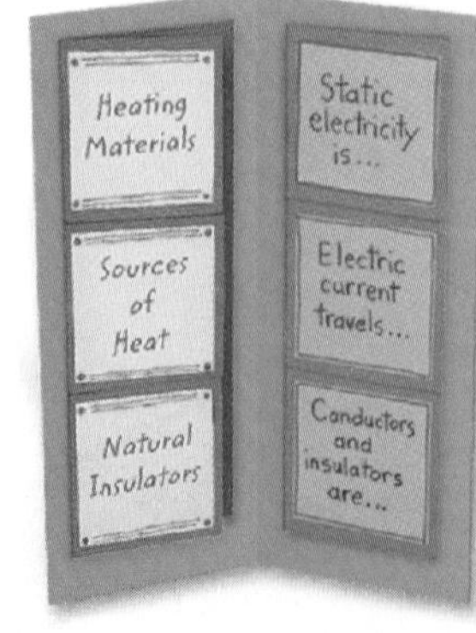

Vocabulary

DOK 1

Fill each blank with the best term from the list.

circuit, p. 41	**electrical current,** p. 40	**radiation,** p. 26
conductor, p. 24	**fuse,** p. 43	**resistance,** p. 43
convection, p. 27	**heat,** p. 22	
discharge, p. 39	**insulator,** p. 24	

1. A path that allows electrical current to flow is a(n) ________________.

2. The flow of energy from a warm object to a cold object is called ________________.

3. A material that heat or electricity does not move through easily is a(n) ________________.

4. A flow of charges is called ________________.

5. A material that heat or electricity flows through easily is called a(n) ________________.

6. The ability to slow electrical current is ________________.

7. The sudden movement of static electricity is a(n) ________________.

8. The process in which heat moves through liquids or gases is called ________________.

9. The Sun's energy is moved to Earth by ________________.

10. To prevent fires, some circuits have a(n) ________________.

e-Glossary Words and definitions online at www.macmillanmh.com

UNIT 1 Review

Skills and Concepts

DOK 2–3

Answer each of the following.

11. **Main Idea and Details** A boy touches a metal doorknob. He feels a shock. How can you explain this?

____

____

____

12. **Critical Thinking** You are given an unknown object that is long and thin. How could you test the object to see if it conducts or insulates heat?

____

____

____

13. **Summarize** What happens when an electrical switch is in the "off" position? What changes when the switch is turned on?

____

____

____

14. **Infer** Why are cooking pots made of metal?

____

____

15. **Summarize** Identify two electrical appliances that make light and heat.

____

Answer the following questions.

6. Name and describe the THREE WAYS that heat can move.
   4.1.2 (DOK 1)

7. Name THREE insulators of heat.
   4.1.4 (DOK 1)

8. Lisa designed a simple buzzer system for a school project. Her finished project is shown in the picture below.

   Name FOUR materials Lisa used to make her buzzer.
   4.1.3 (DOK 1)

   Describe how the buzzer system works. For example, describe what would trigger the buzzer?
   4.1.3 (DOK 3)

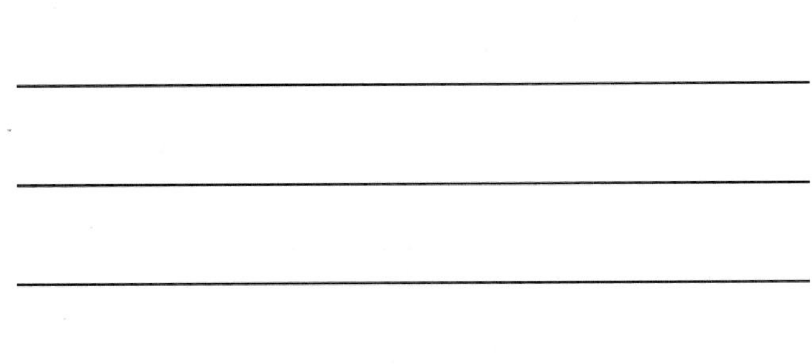

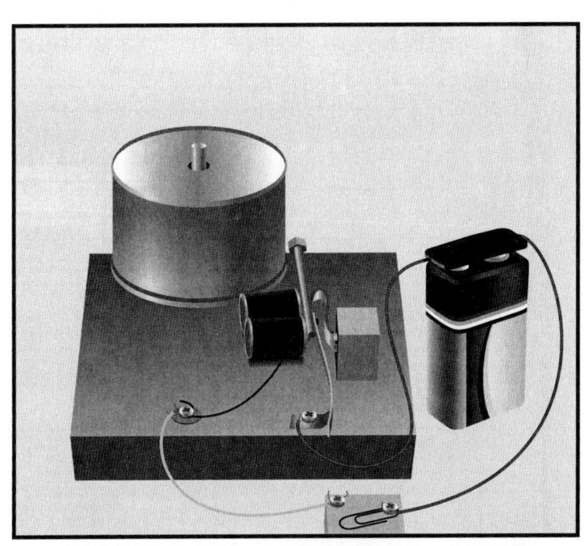

Electrician

▲ Electricians install wires, switches, and outlets.

Have you ever had a power failure in your home or school? Who do you call to fix it? You call an electrician! Electricians install alarms, repair switches, and replace wiring. They know how to handle anything that runs on electrical current.

Electricians know all about electricity. They are skilled in the use of tools. You can learn these skills in training programs in high school, college, and the military. You will need to be an apprentice, or helper, first. Then you can get your license.

Write About It

If you were an electrician, what kinds of problems would you solve? How would you solve them? Write a journal entry about a problem that an electrician might have to solve. Describe the steps that he or she would use to solve the problem.

____

____

____

____

____

____

LOG ON e-Careers at www.macmillanmh.com

Earth and Space Science

Academic Standards for Science

Core Standard Observe, investigate and give examples of ways that the shape of the land changes over time.

Core Standard Describe how the supply of natural resources is limited and investigate ways that humans protect and harm the environment.

Sand dunes are moving piles of sand.

Indiana Dunes National Lakeshore

UNIT 2

Shaping the Land

How does Earth's surface change?

____

____

____

____

____

____

____

Vocabulary

weathering the breaking down of rocks into smaller pieces

erosion the weathering and carrying away of rock, sand, and soil

deposition the dropping off of weathered rock, sand, and soil in a new place

earthquake a sudden shaking of the ground

volcano a mountain of hardened lava and ash

landslide the sudden movement of rocks and soil down a hill

As you read the unit, complete the chart about how different processes shape the land.

Processes That Shape the Land	Erosion	Deposition
Blowing Wind	▶ Wind picks up ______________ and ______________.	▶ Wind can blow sand into piles called ______________.
Moving Water	▶ Flowing water can create steep-sided valleys called ______________. ▶ Rainwater carries rock and soil particles into ______________ and ______________.	▶ Rivers flow into larger bodies of water such as lakes and ______________. ▶ Deposition by water builds up river banks, ______________, and ______________.
Flowing Glaciers	▶ Glaciers carve ______________ into rock. ▶ A glacier can erode hills and ______________.	▶ When they melted, glaciers deposited ______________ in northern Indiana. ▶ Glaciers deposited ______________ in the plains of central Indiana.

Lesson 1

Weathering, Erosion, and Deposition

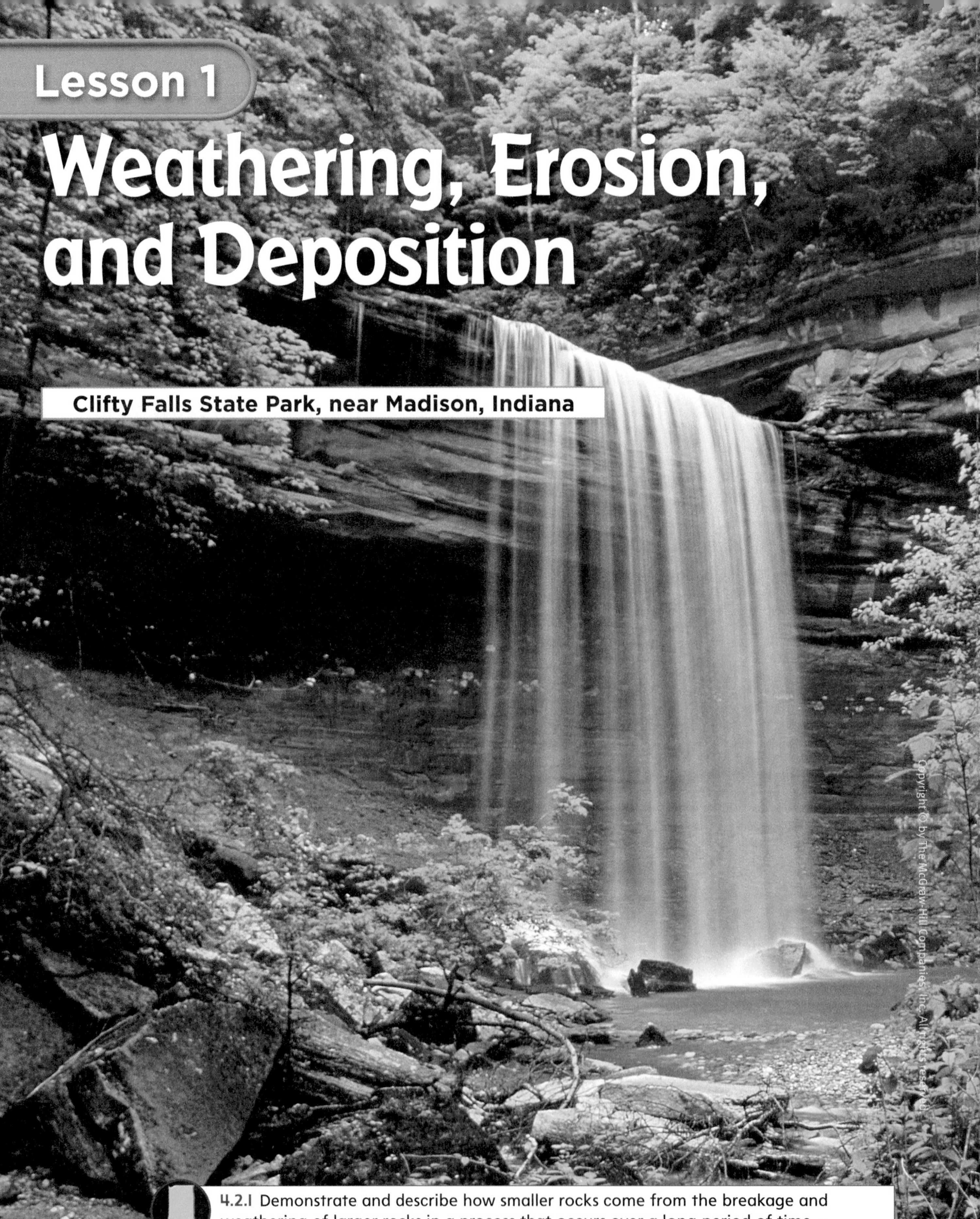

Clifty Falls State Park, near Madison, Indiana

4.2.1 Demonstrate and describe how smaller rocks come from the breakage and weathering of larger rocks in a process that occurs over a long period of time.
4.2.2 Demonstrate and describe how wind, water and glacial ice shape and reshape earth's land surface by eroding rock and soil in some areas and depositing them in other areas in a process that occurs over a long period of time.

Look and Wonder

Once this river flowed over rock. What happened to the rock? How did the waterfall form?

Essential Question How does the land change over a long period of time?

Explore

How can rocks change in moving water?

Materials

- sandstone rocks

- measuring cup

- 3 plastic jars with lids

- stopwatch

- hand lens

Form a Hypothesis

What happens to rocks when they move around in water? Write a hypothesis in the form, "If I shake rocks in water, then . . ."

____

____

Test Your Hypothesis

1. **Measure** Label the jars *A, B,* and *C*. Put the same number of similar-size sandstone rocks in each jar. Using the measuring cup, fill each jar with the same amount of water. Put a lid on each jar.

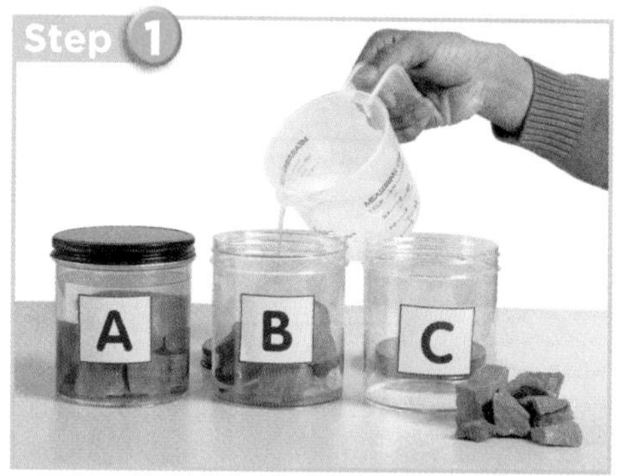

2. Let jar *A* sit. Do not shake it.
3. **Use Variables** Shake jar *B* hard for 2 minutes. Then let the jar sit.
4. **Use Variables** Shake jar *C* hard for 5 minutes. Then let the jar sit.
5. **Observe** Use a hand lens to observe the rocks in each jar. What happened? Did the results support your hypothesis?

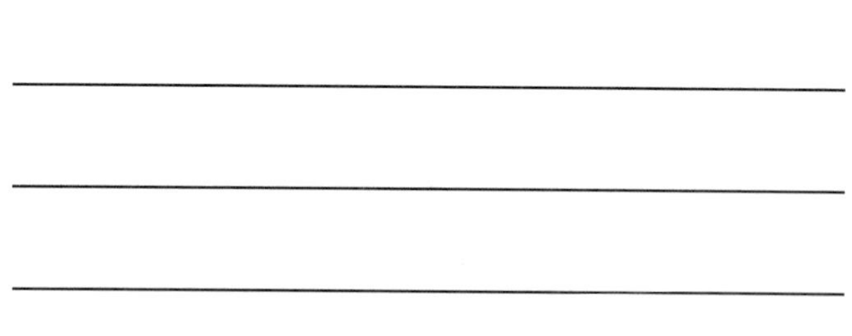

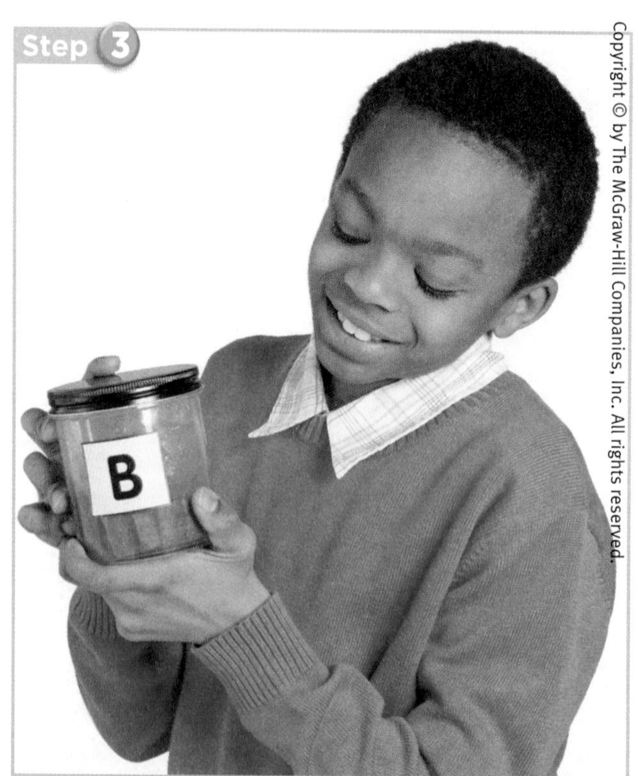

Draw Conclusions

6 **Infer** How can rocks change in moving water?

____

____

____

Explore More

Experiment Would the results be the same if a different kind of rock were used? Describe a fair test you could try.

____

____

____

Open Inquiry

In step 1, you used the same amount of water in each jar. This helped you perform a fair test. Now, think about whether rocks would break more easily without water in the jars. Formulate a question on this topic and then design and conduct a fair test to answer it.

My question is: _______________

____

How I can test it: _______________

____

My results are: _______________

____

____

The Nature of Science Design a fair test.

Read and Respond

What is weathering?

You might think that hard rocks cannot change or break, but they can. Large rocks break down into smaller rocks. Small rocks break down into sand. The breaking down of rocks into smaller pieces is called **weathering** (WETH•ur•ing). The weathering of rocks can take millions of years.

Underline four causes of weathering in the second paragraph on this page.

Causes of Weathering

Have you ever scraped yourself by bumping up against a rough surface? Scraping can cause weathering. Rock particles are picked up and carried by moving water and wind. The rock particles scrape against any rocks they bump into. Rain and ocean waves hit rocks and cause weathering. Even living things cause weathering. A plant's roots might grow in the cracks of a rock. The roots eventually split the rock apart.

In the distant future, the boulder shown below will probably look very different. Eventually, it may break down into small rocks and even sand. ▼

Quick Check

1. Where have you seen examples of weathered rocks?

____

____

____

Weathering can form caverns like this one in Marengo, Indiana.

Mirror Lake at Marengo Caverns

The combination of water and air can cause weathering. Have you ever seen an iron chain get rusty? Water and air changed the iron into rust. Rocks that have iron in them can rust too. This weakens the rock, making it easier to break down. Water and air also help break down limestone, a type of rock. This forms a special type of cave called a cavern. Southern Indiana has many caverns.

Freezing water can cause weathering. Water enters small cracks in rocks. When the water freezes, it expands, or takes up more space. This widens the cracks. Then the ice thaws and becomes liquid water again. Over time, repeated freezing and thawing breaks rocks apart.

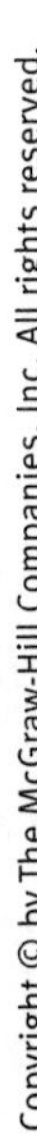

These hoodoos formed from water that froze and thawed inside cracks in the rocks.

Quick Check

2. How could you show that water expands when it freezes?

____

____

____

What is erosion?

Have you ever built a sand castle at the beach? Did waves wash it away? Waves crash against the shores of oceans and lakes, picking up beach sand and small rocks. Then the waves carry the pieces away. This is an example of erosion (i•ROH•zhun). **Erosion** is the weathering and carrying away of rock, sand, and soil. Erosion shapes and reshapes the land.

Causes of Erosion

Waves are not the only way that water causes erosion. Rainwater carries rock and soil particles into streams and rivers. The water flows downhill, carrying the particles along. In very cold places, glaciers (GLAY•shurz) cause erosion. A **glacier** is a thick sheet of ice that moves slowly across the land. The moving glacier scratches, breaks, and carries away everything in its path.

Wind also picks up weathered rock and soil particles. The wind carries them to new locations, where it drops them off. Gusts of wind can cause erosion quickly. Constant blowing of the wind can erode large amounts of sand.

Examples of erosion are all around you. You can find grooves carved into rock by glaciers. You can compare mountains of different ages. Young mountains have sharp, rocky peaks. Old mountains have smooth, round shapes. Over a long period of time, mountains become smoother and rounder.

Quick Check

3. Describe an example of erosion that you can see in Indiana.

____

____

____

Mount Horden, Frames Mountains, Antarctica

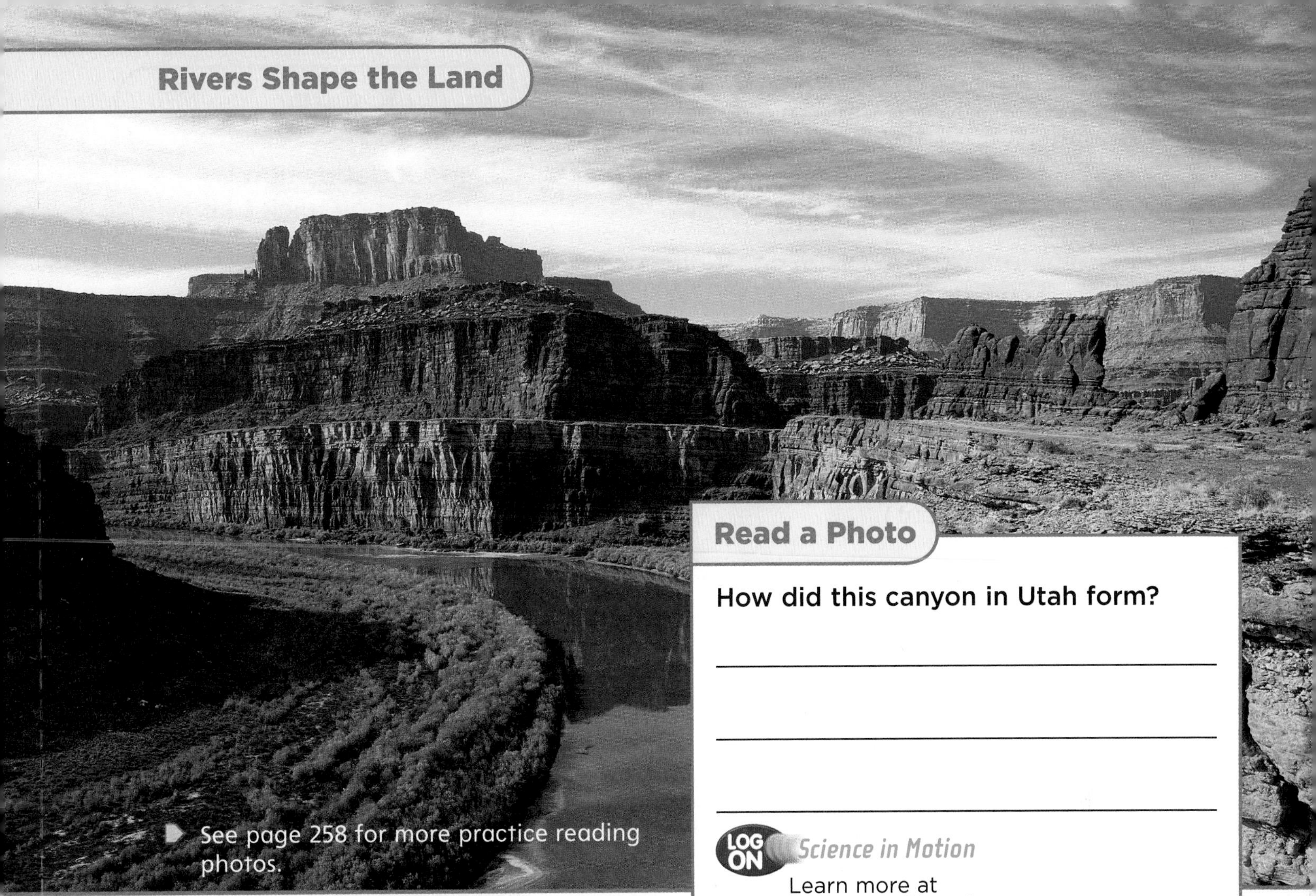

Read a Photo

How did this canyon in Utah form?

See page 258 for more practice reading photos.

LOG ON *Science in Motion* Learn more at www.macmillanmh.com

Rivers Erode the Land

The particles carried by a flowing river act like tiny drills. The particles slam into rocks and chip away at the rocks. This causes erosion along the sides and bottom of the river. This scratching and scraping is called abrasion (uh•BRAY•zhun). Abrasion is greater in a fast-moving river than in a slow-moving one.

The flow of water can create deep valleys. The Grand Canyon in Arizona shows how powerful a river can be. A canyon is a steep-sided valley. The Grand Canyon is 446 km (277 mi) long. It has an average depth of 1.6 km (1 mi). This canyon was carved over millions of years by erosion from the Colorado River.

Quick Check

Circle the correct answer.

4. What is another word for scratching and scraping?

erosion abrasion glacier

What is deposition?

Model deposition by doing the Quick Lab on page 280.

Eventually, a river flows into a larger body of water, such as a lake or an ocean. As the river enters the body of water, its speed slows suddenly. The river drops off the particles of rock, sand, and soil that it has been carrying. **Deposition** (deh•puh•ZIH•shun) is the dropping off of weathered rock, sand, and soil in a new place. The particles that are dropped off by the river are called sediment (SED•uh•ment).

Trace the outline of the delta in the picture on this page.

Sediment blocks the path of the river where it is deposited. The river shifts its course to pass on either side of the blockage. Over time, the deposits may take on the shape of a triangle or a fan. The formation is called a delta.

This delta formed where the Copper River meets Prince William Sound in Alaska.

Quick Check

5. Why do many deltas have the shape of a triangle?

____

____

Indiana Dunes

Over 20,000 years ago, a large, northern glacier moved south toward what is now Indiana. The glacier picked up sediment particles of all sizes. As the glacier melted, it deposited the sediment. The sand you see at Indiana Dunes National Lakeshore is part of that sediment. Most of the sediment was deposited as a mixture of small rocks, sand, and soil. This mixture is called **till**. Glaciers also deposited long mounds of sediment. These mounds are called **moraines** (muh•RAYNZ).

Today you can see a huge dune, or pile, of sand at Mount Baldy. Erosion and deposition from wind constantly shape and reshape sand dunes. In fact, the wind moves Mount Baldy over 1 meter (3 feet) every year. Waves from Lake Michigan replace some of the beach sand lost from wind erosion.

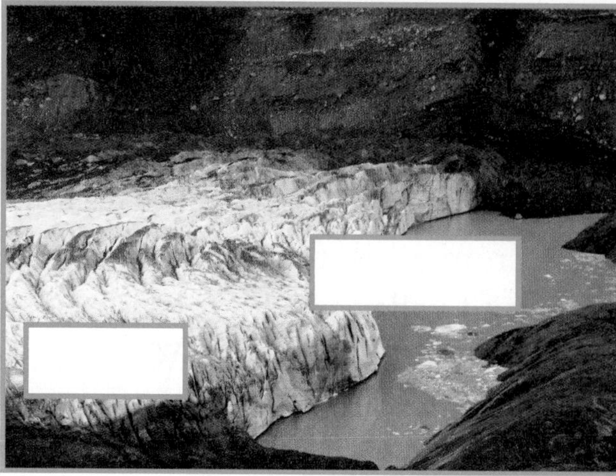

A glacier deposits mounds of sediment called moraines.

Draw arrows pointing to the glacier and the moraines in the picture above. Label the two features.

Quick Check

6. What would happen to a beach if erosion happened faster than deposition?

____

Mount Baldy at Indiana Dunes National Lakeshore

A glacier deposited the sand that formed Mount Baldy. Wind constantly changes the shape of the dune.

What are some features of Indiana's land?

About 2 million years ago, the first of several glaciers entered what is now Indiana. Moving from north to south, the glaciers eroded hills and valleys. In northern Indiana, the glaciers deposited moraines. Water from melting glaciers formed lakes. In central Indiana, glaciers spread till, leaving a nearly flat surface. This flat surface is called a till plain.

The pictures on the next page show some features of Indiana's land. Picture 1 shows a beach along the shore of Lake Michigan. Picture 2 shows a lake in Chain O'Lakes State Park. Both of these features were formed by the movement and melting of glaciers.

The glaciers never made it past central Indiana. This is why southern Indiana has hills and valleys. This region has many woodland areas and forests. Picture 3 shows a river valley in western, central Indiana. The picture was taken in Turkey Run State Park.

Southern Indiana contains two areas with plateaus (pla•TOHZ). Plateaus are high, flat areas. Most of Indiana's caverns are found in plateaus. Picture 4 was taken at Bluespring Caverns. These caverns are in Bedford, Indiana.

This salamander lives in Squire Boon Cavern. The cavern is located on a plateau in Corydon, Indiana.

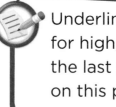

Underline the term for high, flat areas in the last paragraph on this page.

 ***Quick Check***

7. In which part of Indiana will you find the most farms? Explain.

____

____

____

Glue your Notebook FOLDABLES here. Use Foldable 8 on page 297.

Shapes of the Land in Indiana

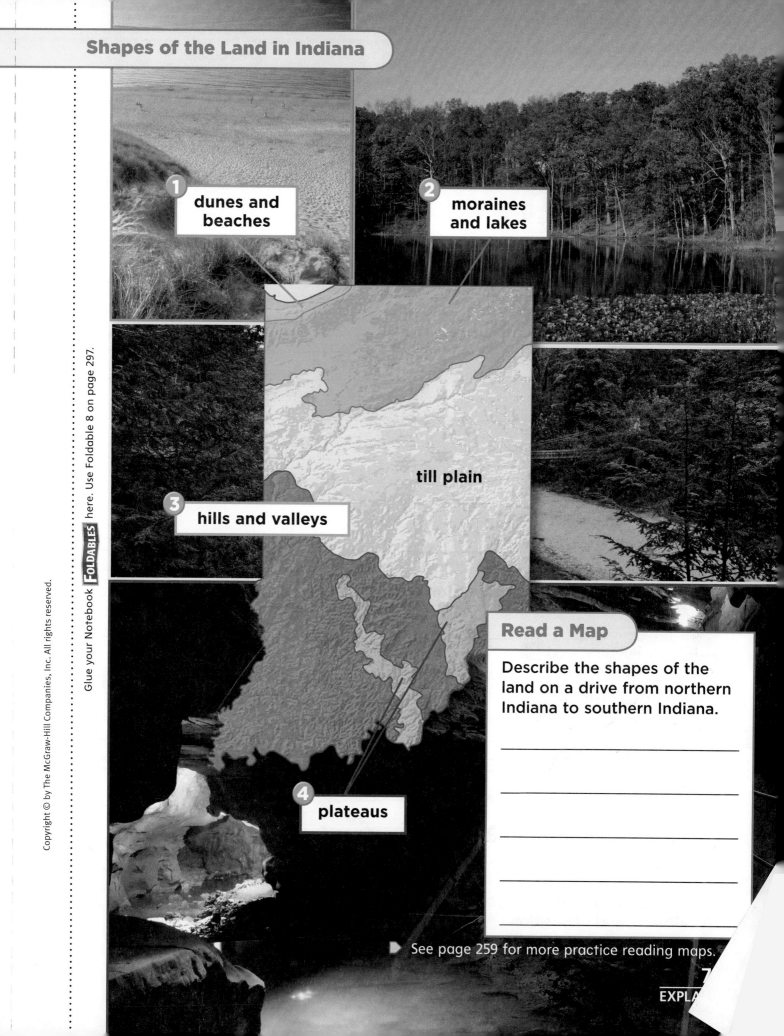

Read a Map

Describe the shapes of the land on a drive from northern Indiana to southern Indiana.

___

___

___

___

___

See page 259 for more practice reading maps.

Visual Summary

Summarize the lesson in your own words.

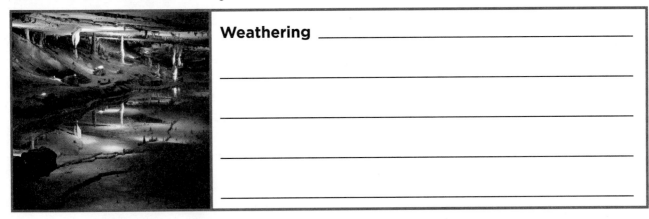

Weathering ______________________________

Erosion ______________________________

Deposition ______________________________

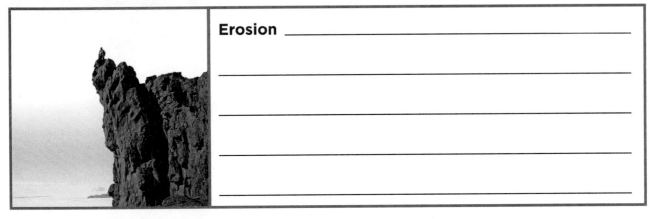

Make a FOLDABLES® Study Guide

Make a trifold book. Use it to summarize what you learned about weathering, erosion, and deposition.

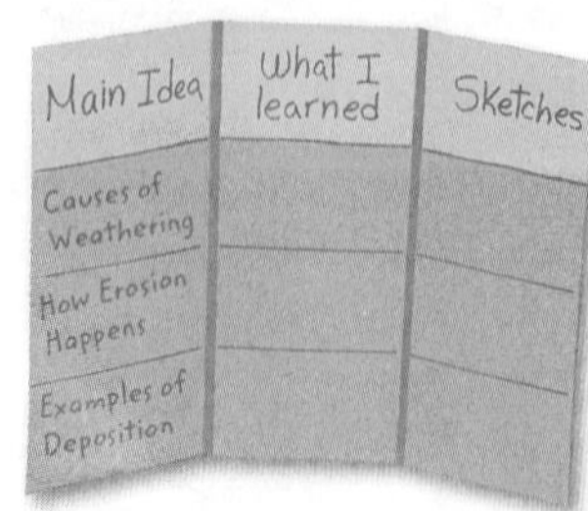

Think, Talk, and Write

1 **Vocabulary** A mixture of small rocks, sand, and soil deposited by a glacier is called ______________.

2 **Summarize** What causes the shape of the land to change?

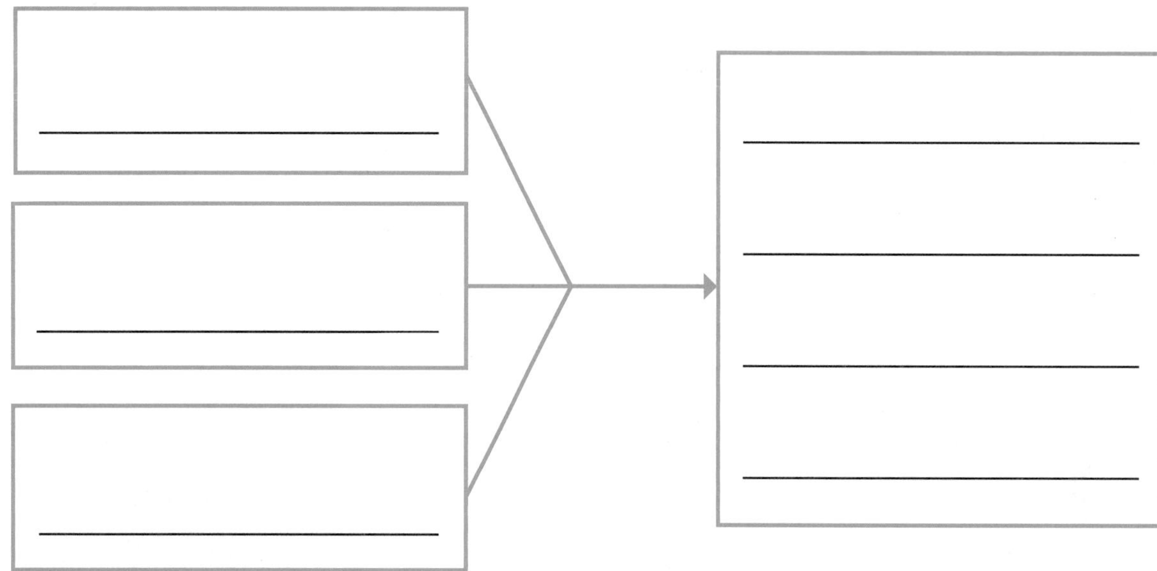

3 **Critical Thinking** A sidewalk crack became wider after a cold winter. Why?

____

____

4 **Test Prep** **Which of these is made of deposited materials?**

A moraine
B valley
C river
D glacier

How does the land change over a long period of time?

____

____

____

____

Land over Time

Mountains may seem like mighty giants. But are they? Weathering can break down even the tallest mountains. How does this happen?

Wind carries the seeds of plants from place to place. A seed can land on a patch of soil on rock. There the seed sprouts. The roots find small cracks in the rock.

As the roots grow, rainwater fills the cracks in the rock. If it gets cold enough, the water freezes into ice. The ice expands. The cracks widen. All this time, the roots grow bigger.

At some point, the cracks widen so much that pieces of rock break off. In time, these pieces get smaller. Over millions of years, weathering can break down an entire mountain!

Expository Writing

Good expository writing

- presents the main idea in a topic sentence;
- supports the main idea with facts and details.

Getting Ideas

Think about what you read in "Land Over Time." Then fill in the summary chart.

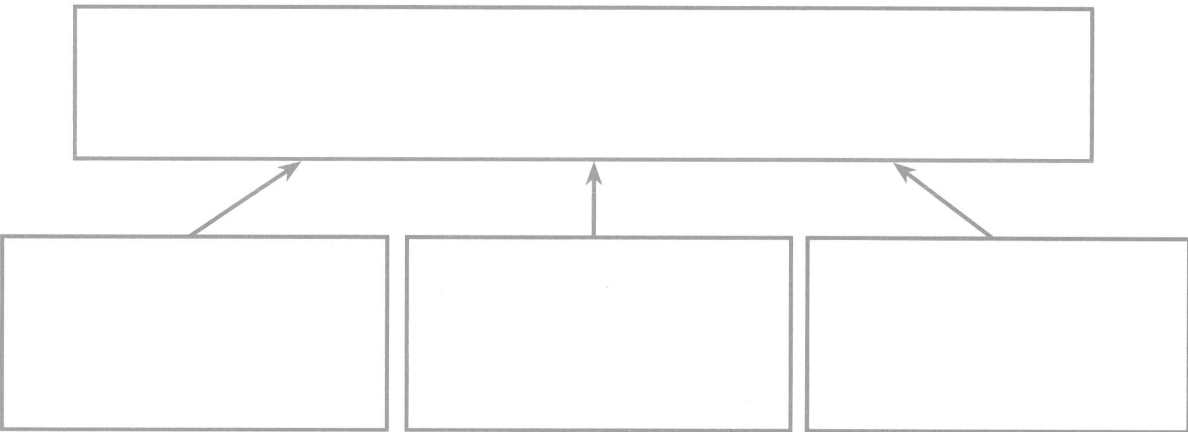

Write About It

Expository Writing Write a paragraph that summarizes "Land Over Time." Include the main idea and the most important details.

Glue your Notebook FOLDABLES® here. Use Foldable I on page 290.

Drafting

Begin drafting your summary.

Use a separate piece of paper. Include only important facts and details from "Land Over Time." Put them in your own words.

Now revise and proofread your writing. Ask yourself:

- Did I tell only the most important information?
- Did I provide details to support the main idea?

4.2.1 Demonstrate and describe how smaller rocks came from the breakage and weathering of larger rocks in a process that occurs over a long period of time.

DISAPPEARING MOUNTAINS

Mount McKinley

Mount Whitney

Mount Shasta

Wheeler Peak

This table shows the heights of some mountain peaks in the United States.

Heights of Mountain Peaks			
Mountain	**State**	**Height in Meters**	**Height in Feet**
Mount McKinley	Alaska	6,194	20,320
Mount Whitney	California	4,417	14,491
Mount Shasta	California	4,317	14,162
Wheeler Peak	Nevada	3,982	13,065

Mountains erode by small amounts. Suppose Mount McKinley erodes 2 m each year. How many years would it take for the mountain to be 6,174 m tall?

Problem Solving

- **To find the number of years, you can count backward by 2 from 6,194 m to 6,174 m.**

  6,192 6,190
  6,188 6,186
  6,184 6,182
  6,180 6,178
  6,176 6,174

  It would take 10 years.

- **Another way is to find the number of meters lost. Then you can divide the difference of meters by 2. 6,194 m − 6,174 m = 20 m**
  20 ÷ 2 = 10
  It would take 10 years.

Solve It

If the erosion rate is 1 m each year, what will be the height of:

1. Mount Shasta in 20 years? ____________

2. Mount Whitney in 15 years? ____________

3. Wheeler Peak in 80 years? ____________

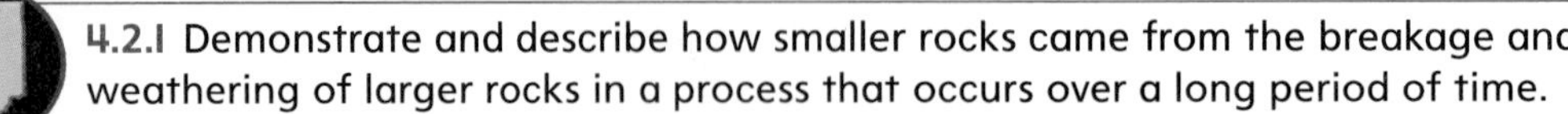
4.2.1 Demonstrate and describe how smaller rocks came from the breakage and weathering of larger rocks in a process that occurs over a long period of time.

Try It Again

The table below shows the heights of some mountain peaks around the world.

Heights of Mountain Peaks			
Mountain	**Country**	**Height (Meters)**	**Height (Feet)**
Everest	Nepal/Tibet	8,850	29,035
Annapurna	Nepal	8,090	26,545
Kungur	China	7,720	25,325
Aconcagua	Argentina	6,960	22,835
Huascarán	Peru	6,770	22,205

Solve these erosion problems. Show your work.

1. If Mount Everest is eroding by 5 m per century, how many centuries will it take for its height to be 8,800 m?

____

2. If Aconcagua is eroding at a rate of 6 ft per year, what will be its height in 50 years?

____

3. Suppose Kungur is eroding at the rate of 3 ft per year. How many years will it take for the mountain to be 25,265 ft tall?

____

Aconcagua

Mount Everest

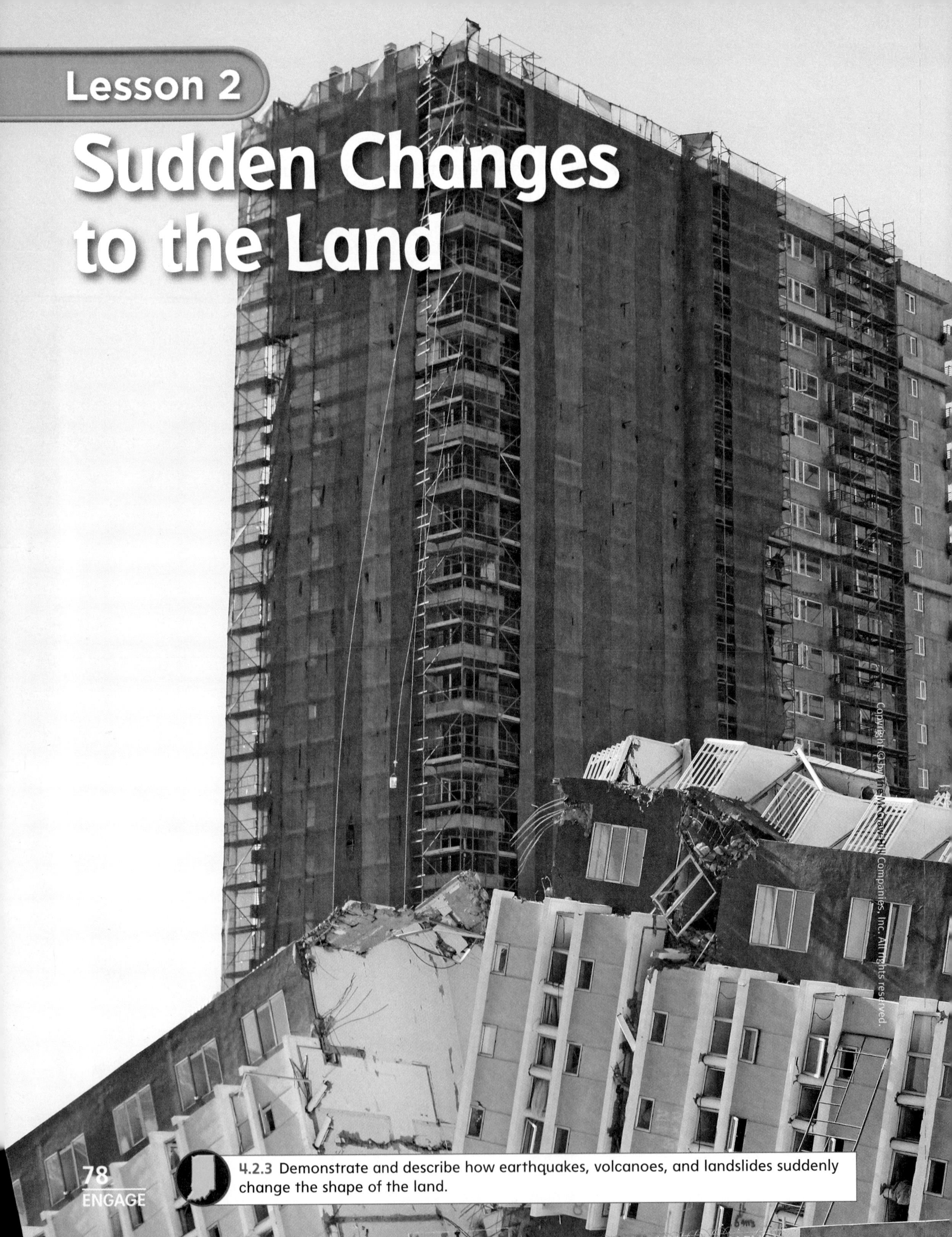

Lesson 2

Sudden Changes to the Land

4.2.3 Demonstrate and describe how earthquakes, volcanoes, and landslides suddenly change the shape of the land.

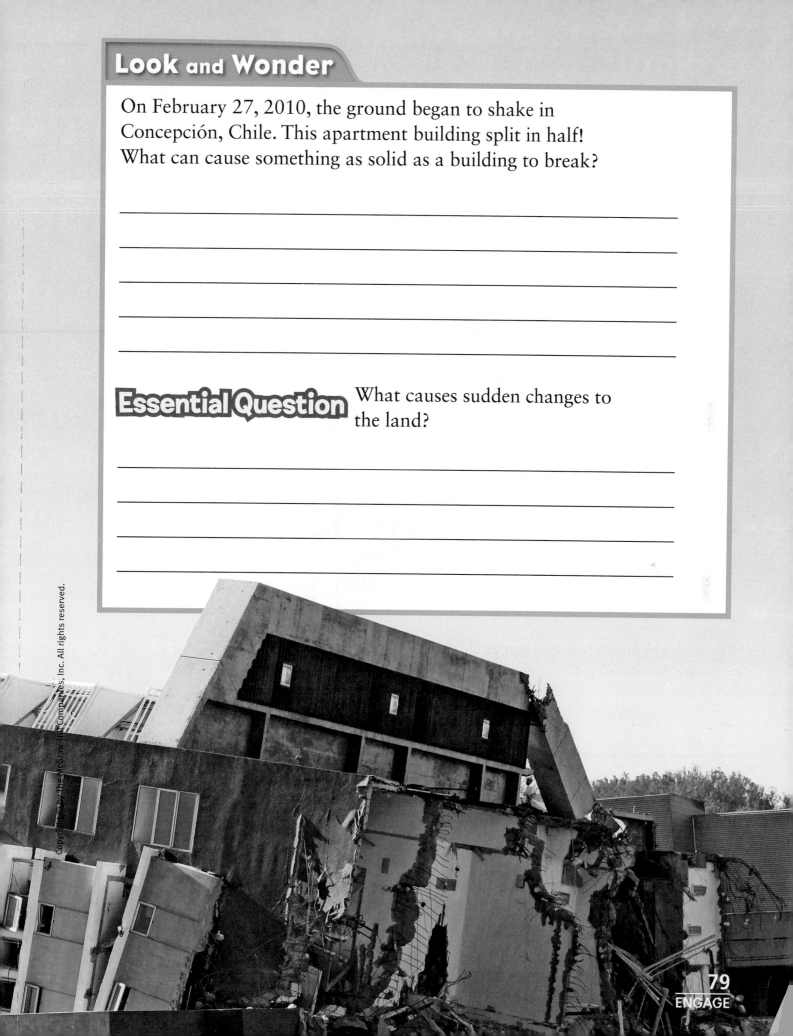

Look and Wonder

On February 27, 2010, the ground began to shake in Concepción, Chile. This apartment building split in half! What can cause something as solid as a building to break?

Essential Question What causes sudden changes to the land?

Explore

How does sudden movement change the land?

Purpose

Model what happens when the land suddenly moves.

Procedure

1. **Make a Model** Fill a pan halfway with sand. Form a mountain in the sand. This models a land surface.

2. Place blocks in the sand to model buildings. Add twigs to model trees.

Glue your Notebook FOLDABLES here. Use Foldable 3 on page 292.

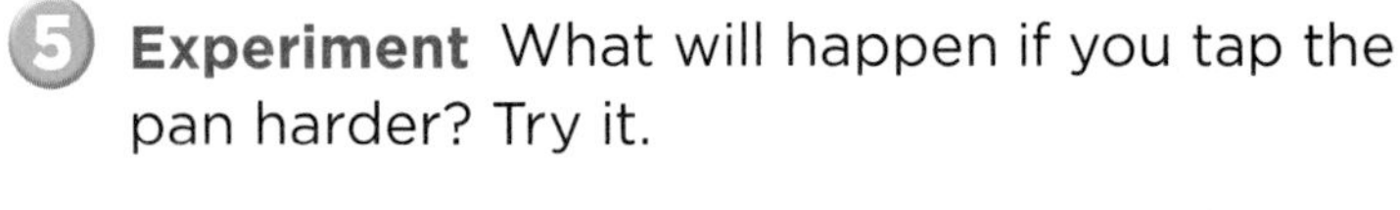

3. **Communicate** Draw your land surface.

4. **Experiment** What will happen if you tap the pan gently? Try it.

____

____

5. **Experiment** What will happen if you tap the pan harder? Try it.

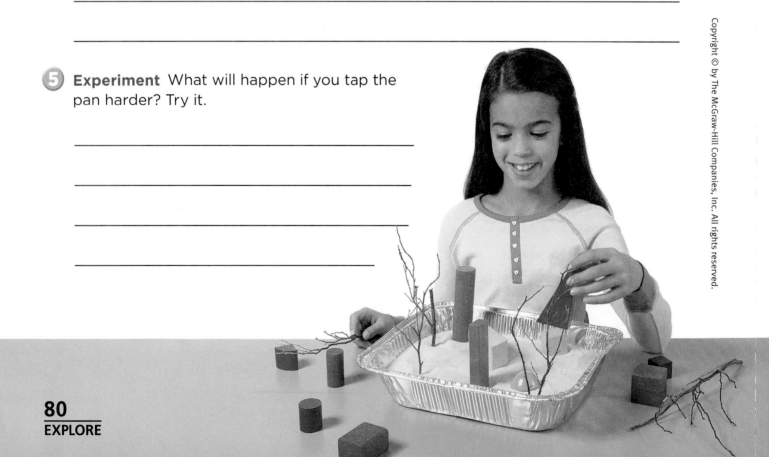

____

____

____

____

Draw Conclusions

6 **Infer** How can sudden movement change Earth's land?

____

____

7 Draw your land surface again, in order to show how it changed.

Explore More

Experiment Different rocks and soils make up the land. Does sudden movement change all land the same way? Make a plan to find out. Then try it. Describe your plan below.

____

____

Open Inquiry

Think about whether a liquid material will be affected differently by sudden movements of the land. Form a hypothesis and design a fair test to investigate it.

My question is: ______________________________

____

How I can test it: ______________________________

____

____

My results are: ______________________________

____

____

The Nature of Science Identify simple patterns in data and propose explanations to account for the patterns.

An earthquake broke apart Haiti's land in January, 2010.

Read and Respond

What are earthquakes?

You learned that weathering, erosion, and deposition slowly change the shape of the land. There are some events that can change Earth's surface in less than a minute. One example is an earthquake (URTH•kwayk). An **earthquake** is a sudden shaking of the ground. What causes an earthquake? How does it change the land? The answers are found under the ground.

Earth's Moving Crust

Earth's outside layer, the crust, is made up of huge slabs of rock. You might think that slabs of rock cannot move. They do move, however. Rocks deep below the ground can slowly slide past each other. They can also press against each other. This causes pressure to build up slowly over time. Think of a bent stick. When it is released suddenly, the energy from the bending snaps it back into shape. When rocks release their pressure, they also snap back. This causes an earthquake.

 ***Quick Check***

1. Name the outside layer of Earth's surface.

____

Earthquakes create vibration waves. The vibrations travel out from the earthquake's center, moving through the land. Some earthquakes are weak. They are not even noticed. Some feel like a truck rumbling by. Others are strong. Strong earthquakes can crack roads. Strong earthquakes can cause buildings and bridges to fall. They can even cause parts of mountains to collapse.

Tsunamis

Sometimes an earthquake occurs below the ocean. If the earthquake is strong enough, it can cause a tsunami (TSEW•NAH•mee). A **tsunami** is a giant wave of water. Tsunamis cause great damage along shorelines. They can change a shoreline in an instant. They can wash away beaches and destroy buildings, roads, and trees.

 ***Quick Check***

2. What are tsunamis? How do tsunamis suddenly change the shape of the land?

____

____

Where Earthquakes Start

For practice reading diagrams, see page 260.

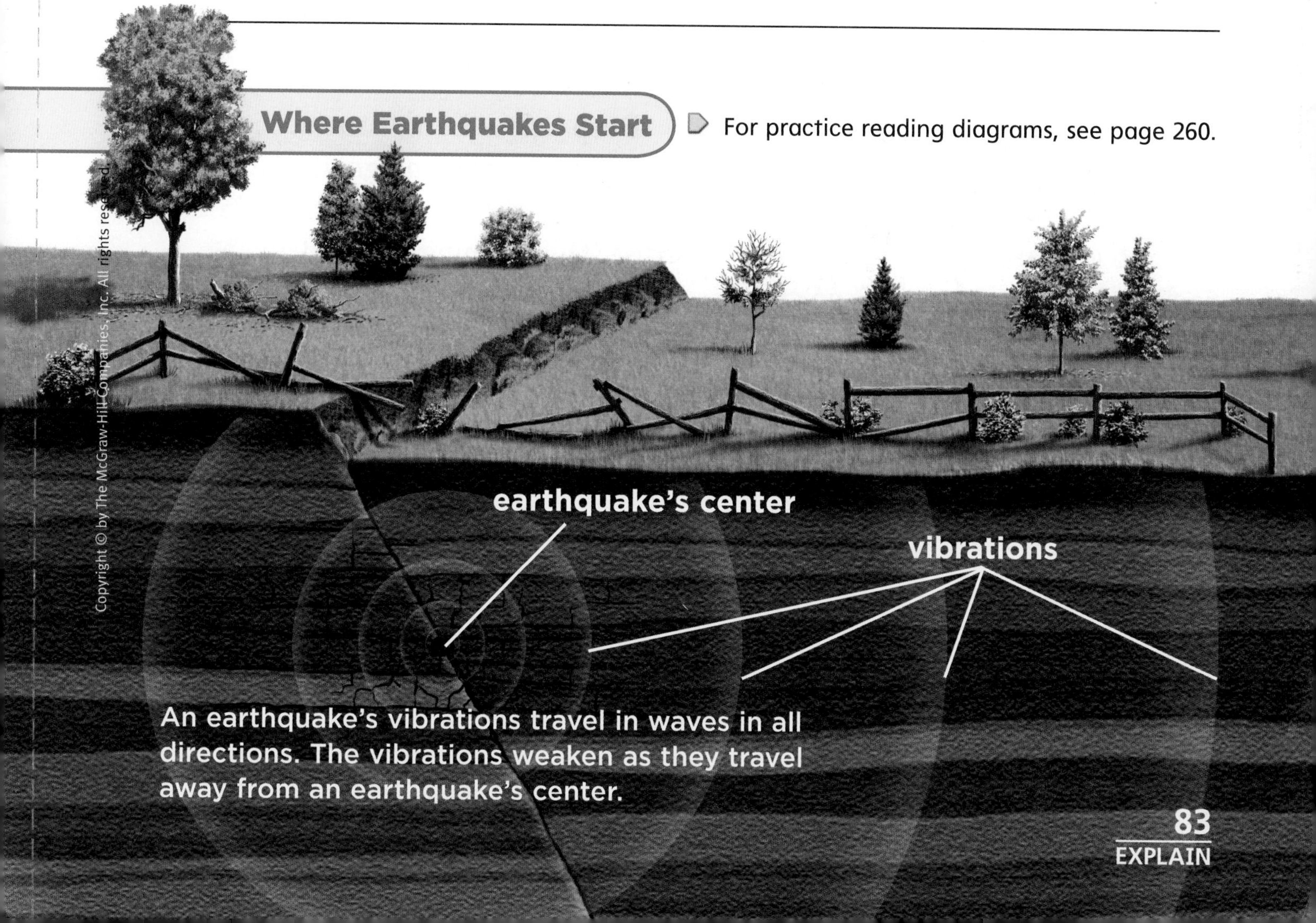

earthquake's center

vibrations

An earthquake's vibrations travel in waves in all directions. The vibrations weaken as they travel away from an earthquake's center.

Glue your Notebook FOLDABLES here. Use Foldable I on page 290.

How a Volcano Forms

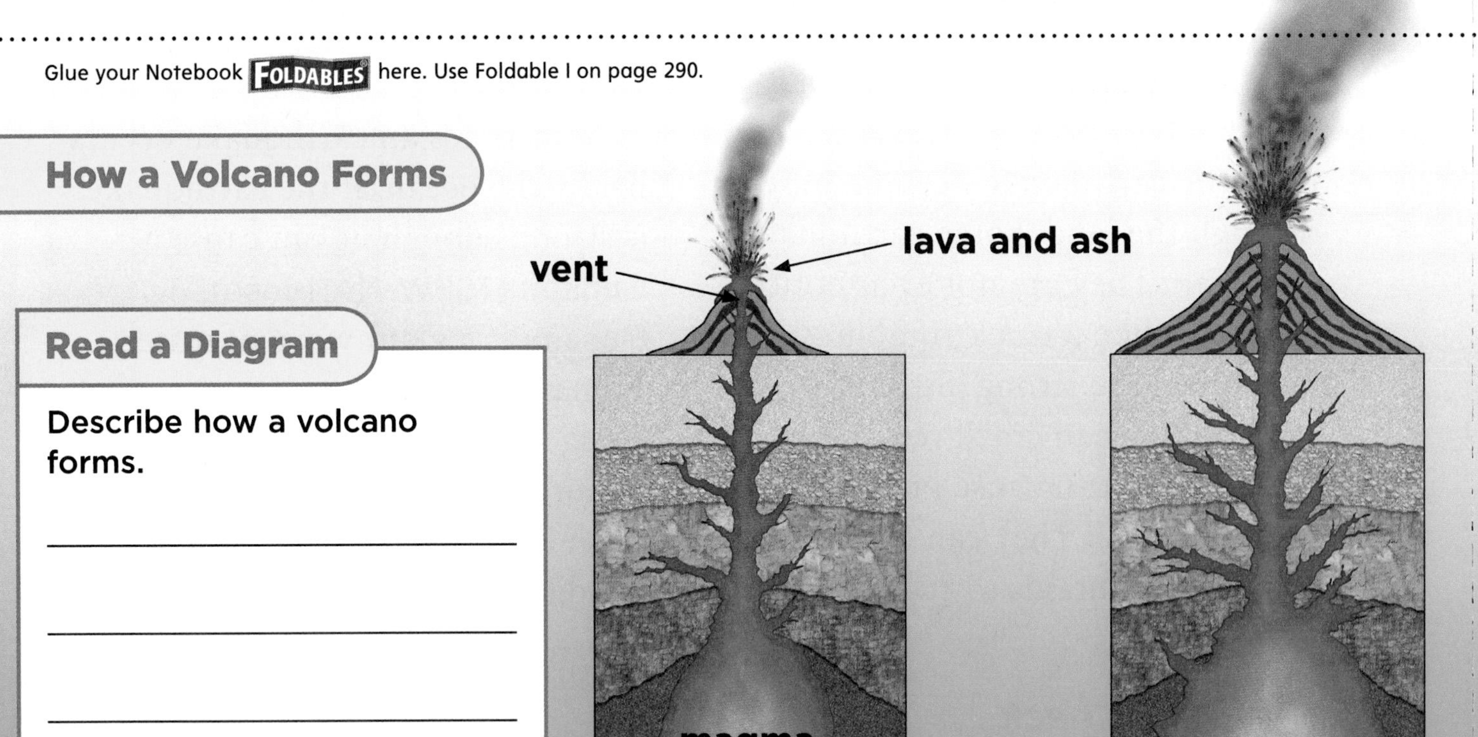

Read a Diagram

Describe how a volcano forms.

____

____

____

LOG ON *Science in Motion*
Learn more at www.macmillanmh.com

For more practice reading diagrams, see page 261.

What is a volcano?

Did you ever shake a can of soda and then open it? The gases inside the can probably caused the soda to spray out. This is similar to how a volcano (vahl•KAY•noh) sprays hot rock and ash into the air. A **volcano** is a mountain that builds up around an opening in Earth's crust. When the volcano sprays rock, ash, and gases into the air it is called an eruption (ee•RUP•shun).

Volcano Formation

Deep below Earth's surface is melted rock called magma. Magma can rise up through an opening in the crust. This opening is called a vent. Once magma reaches Earth's surface it is called lava. When lava flows over Earth's surface, it cools and hardens. Over time, a mountain forms from hardened lava and ash.

Quick Check

3. What is melted rock called when it is deep below Earth's surface?

____

4. What is melted rock called when it flows over Earth's surface?

____

Effects of Volcanoes

Lava can ooze from a volcano slowly. In other cases, lava can explode with great force. When a volcano explodes, a large part of the mountain can be blown away.

Volcanic eruptions can change the land around the volcano. Forests can be burned by hot lava flows. The local area can be buried in ash deposits. Some volcanoes have glaciers on top of them. When these volcanoes erupt, rivers of mud and rock can flow from the volcano. This causes rapid erosion.

To learn more about volcanoes, do the Quick Lab on page 281.

Active Volcanoes

The picture on this page shows Kilauea (kee•lou•WAY•uh) in Hawaii. Kilauea is an active volcano. Active volcanoes are those that scientists expect to erupt again. The United States has a lot of active volcanoes. Many of them are in Hawaii. Where are some of the others? Can you name any of them?

Kilauea is an active volcano on the island of Hawaii.

5. **Describe three ways that a volcano can change the land.**

____

____

____

What is a landslide?

Have you ever seen a pile of rocks at the bottom of a mountain? How did the rocks get there? Part of the answer is gravity. *Gravity* is a pulling effect that acts on all objects.

In the last paragraph on this page, circle four things that can lead to landslides.

Gravity can cause a landslide. A **landslide** is the sudden movement of rocks and soil down a hill. A landslide can cause a hill or mountain to change shape quickly.

Sometimes a landslide is caused by an earthquake. Volcanic eruptions and storms can also cause landslides. Human activity, such as clearing the land of trees in hilly areas, can make landslides more likely to occur.

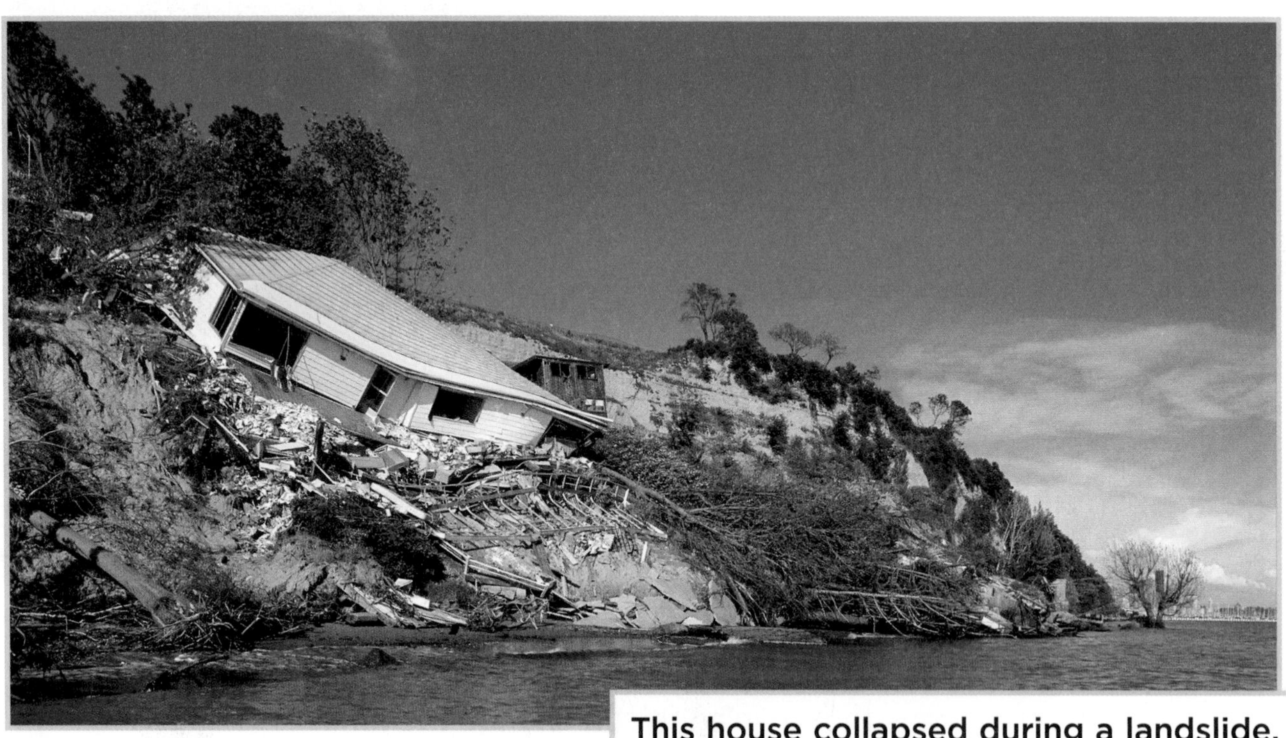

This house collapsed during a landslide.

Quick Check

Circle the answer that best completes the sentence.

6. Gravity ______________ objects.

pushes   pulls   holds

Mudslides

When it rains, some water soaks into the ground. At some point the ground can no longer absorb water. Then the remaining water mixes with the soil and forms mud. Eventually, the mud contains so much water that it cannot stay on the slope. If a lot of mud flows down the slope, it can knock down trees. It can destroy whatever is in its path. The movement of wet soil and rocks down a slope is called a mudslide. A mudslide can cause rapid erosion of rocks and soil.

Lahars

A lahar (luh•HAHR) is similar to a mudslide. In a lahar, a mix of mud, ash, and rock rush down a volcano. Lahars are triggered by volcanic eruptions. They change the landscape around a volcano.

▲ A mudslide is a type of landslide. It can quickly erode a hillside.

Quick Check

7. Compare and contrast mudslides and lahars. Use the graphic organizer below.

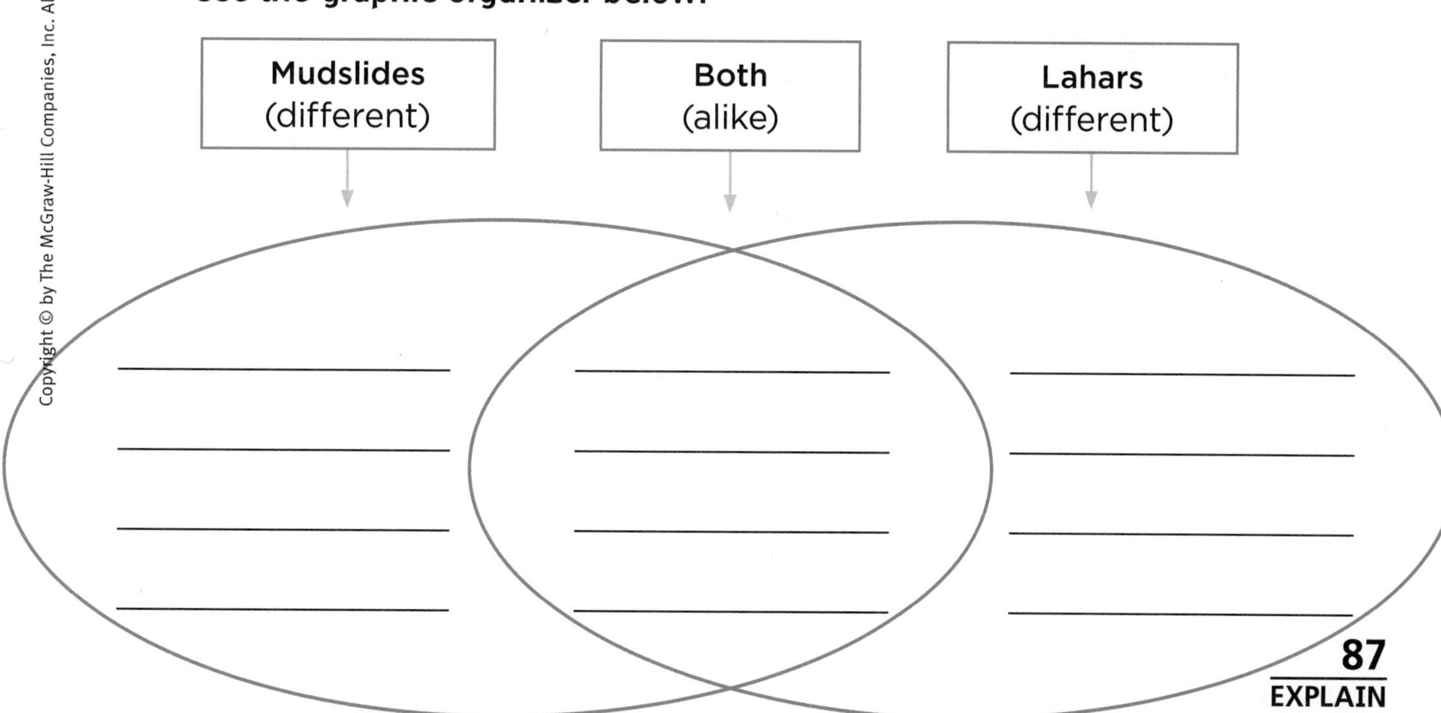

Visual Summary

Complete the lesson summary in your own words.

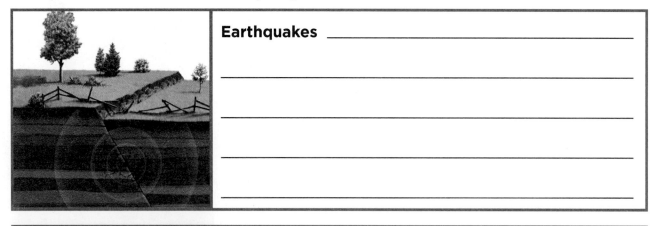

Earthquakes ______________________________

____

____

____

____

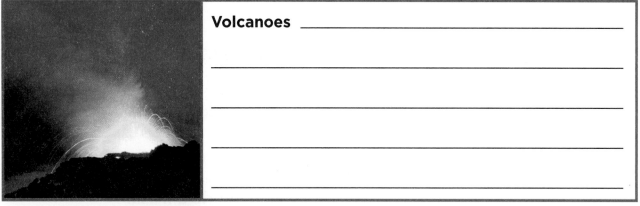

Volcanoes ______________________________

____

____

____

____

Landslides ______________________________

____

____

____

____

Make a FOLDABLES® Study Guide

Make a trifold book. Use it to summarize what you learned about sudden changes to Earth's land.

Think, Talk, and Write

1. **Vocabulary** What is a volcanic eruption?

2. **Summarize** How can Earth's surface change suddenly?

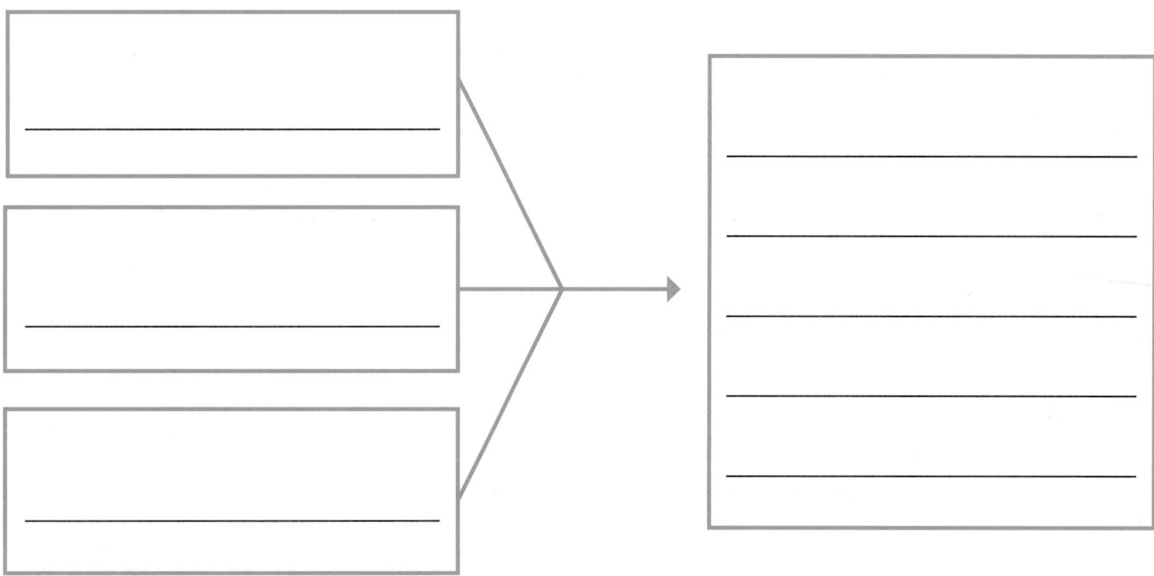

3. **Critical Thinking** What causes earthquakes?

4. **Test Prep** **Which of these is melted rock below Earth's surface?**

   A lava
   B ash
   C crust
   D magma

What causes sudden changes to the land?

Meet Ro Kinzler

▲ Ro's favorite place to collect lava samples is Kilauea volcano in Hawaii.

Ro Kinzler is fascinated by volcanoes and volcanic rocks. She would go just about anywhere to find out more about them. Ro is a scientist at the American Museum of Natural History.

Ro travels to the Cascades in Northern California to collect lava samples from active volcanoes like Mount Shasta and Medicine Lake. She wants to study how magma moves through Earth. Back in the lab, Ro does experiments. She heats and squeezes the lava samples to find out how they formed deep in Earth.

Lava is melted rock that cools at Earth's surface.

4.2.3 Demonstrate and describe how earthquakes, volcanoes, and landslides suddenly change the shape of the land.

You don't find volcanoes only on land. There are lots of them on the ocean floor. Ro and other scientists have gone to the bottom of the ocean to study volcanoes. They use small underwater vehicles called submersibles.

The scientists visited the Mid-Atlantic Ridge, part of the longest volcano chain in the world. Ro is one of the few people to have ever seen it. She peered out the portholes of the submersible *Alvin* with other scientists. They made careful observations. They used these observations to make maps of the ocean floor.

Compare and Contrast

Fill in the chart. When you have finished, you will know how volcanoes on land and in the ocean are similar and different.

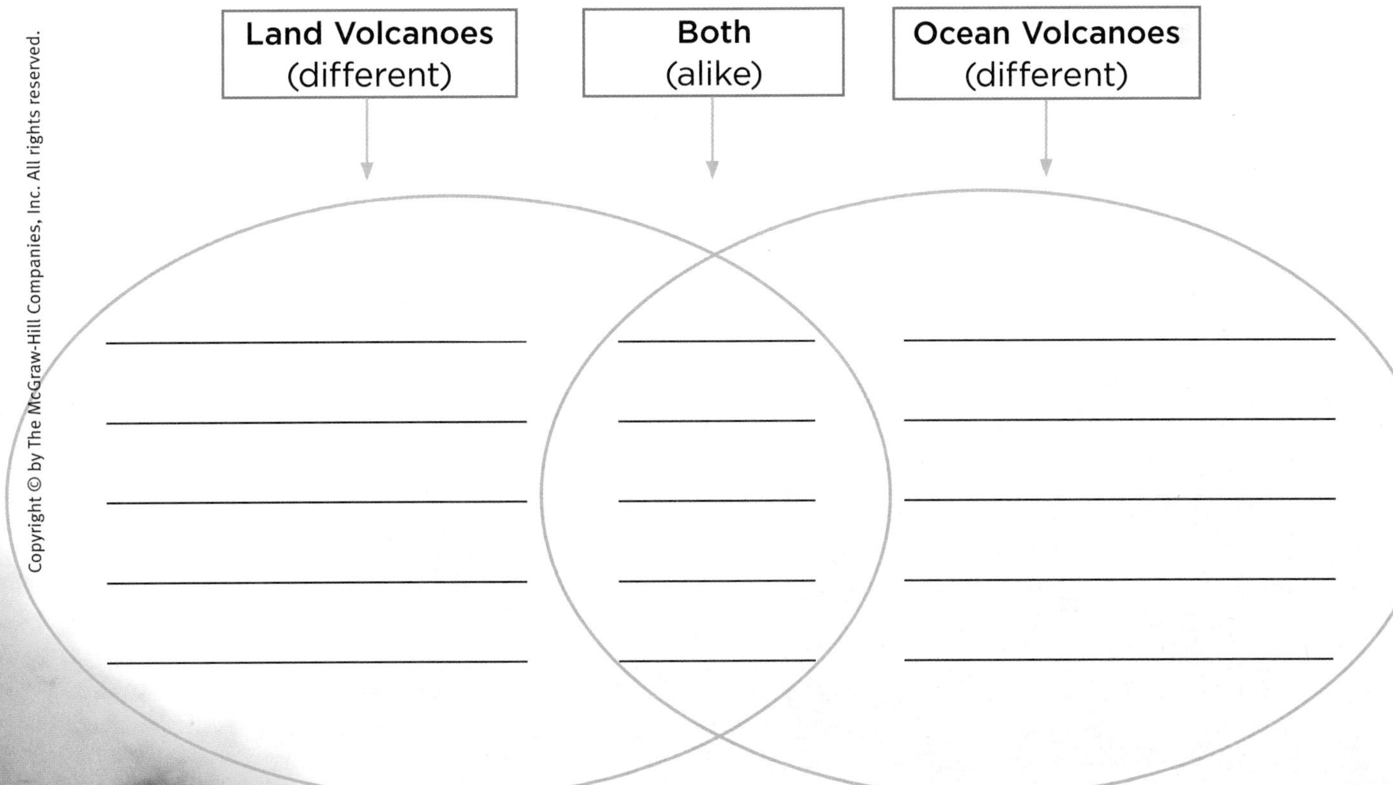

REMEMBERING AN EARTHQUAKE

Sometimes nature can be very violent. I was reminded of this one early Sunday morning in my home town of San Francisco. This is what happened.

First, a deep rumbling sound woke me. I heard things starting to rattle. "It must be an earthquake!" I thought.

Then, the ground began to shake and roll. The earthquake lasted only a minute but it seemed much longer. Finally, the shaking stopped. I reminded myself that life would go back to normal soon.

Next, I began to search for my parents. I found my way through the early dawn light. Mom and Dad had woken up, too. We made our way to the backyard to look at the damage.

A personal narrative

- tells a story from personal experience
- expresses the writer's feelings, using the "I" point of view
- tells where and when the event happened
- uses details that appeal to the reader's senses
- uses time-order words, such as *first*, *next*, *then*, and *finally*, to tell the sequence of events

Write About It

Narrative Writing Write a personal narrative about an event that you experienced. What happened? What did you do? How did you feel? Use the "I" point of view. Include time-order words to show the order of events.

Drafting

Try to grab your reader's interest in the first sentence of your personal narrative. Here are two sentences that Antonio wrote. Circle the one he should use to begin his narrative.

October 15, 2009 is a date I shall never forget.

I had an interesting experience in October.

Glue your Notebook FOLDABLES here. Use Foldable I on page 290.

Now write the first draft of your own personal narrative. Begin with an attention-grabbing sentence. Tell the events in the sequence that they occurred. Use details and end by telling what the event meant to you.

Next, revise and proofread your personal narrative. Ask yourself:

- **Have I used the "I" point of view?**
- **Have I organized the events in sequence?**
- **Have I corrected all grammar errors?**
- **Have I corrected all spelling, punctuation, and capitalization errors?**

ELA 4.4.1 Select a focus, an organizational structure, and a point of view based upon purpose, audience, length, and format requirements for a piece of writing.

UNIT 2 Review

Visual Summary

Summarize each lesson in your own words.

Lesson 1 ______________________________

____

____

____

____

____

Lesson 2 ______________________________

____

____

____

____

____

Make a FOLDABLES® Study Guide

Glue your lesson study guides to a large sheet of paper as shown. Use your study guide to review what you have learned in this unit.

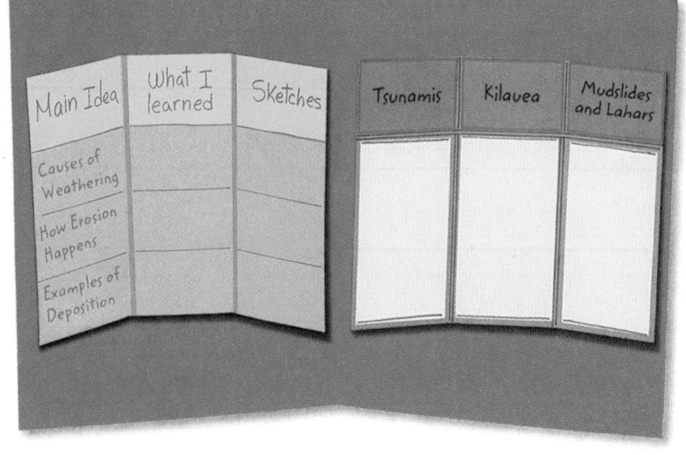

Vocabulary

DOK I

Fill each blank with the best term from the list.

delta, p. 68	**landslide,** p. 86	**volcano,** p. 84
deposition, p. 68	**magma,** p. 84	**weathering,** p. 64
earthquake, p. 82	**sediment,** p. 68	
erosion, p. 66	**tsunami,** p. 83	

1. A(n) ________________ is a mountain made of hardened lava and ash.
2. A giant ocean wave caused by an earthquake is called a(n) ________________.
3. The dropping off of weathered rock, sand, and soil is called ________________.
4. A cavern is formed by the ________________ of limestone.
5. The feature that a river deposits where it enters the ocean is called a(n) ________________.
6. Particles of rock weathered and eroded from larger rocks are called ________________.
7. The sudden movement of rock in Earth's crust causes a(n) ________________.
8. The process that removes rock, sand, and soil is ________________.
9. Any ________________ that reaches the surface is called lava.
10. Rocks and soil move suddenly down a slope during a(n) ________________.

LOG ON e-Glossary Words and definitions online at www.macmillanmh.com

UNIT 2 Review

Skills and Concepts

DOK 2–3

Answer each of the following.

11. **Main Idea and Details** Describe three processes that cause sudden changes to Earth's surface.

12. **Summarize** When does a river deposit its sediment?

13. **Cause and Effect** What pulling effect is needed to cause a landslide?

14. **Critical Thinking** A field is plowed just before a heavy rainstorm. Why will the field be more likely to experience soil erosion?

15. **Classify** What do till and moraines have in common?

Glue your Notebook FOLDABLES® here. Use Foldable I on page 290.

16. **Persuasive Writing** A land developer wants to build homes at the base of a large mountain in an area that is known for earthquakes and flooding. Write a letter to the town board explaining why you think homes should not be allowed to be built there.

17. **True or False** *Canyons form by wind erosion.* Is this statement true or false? Explain.

____

18. **True or False** *Glaciers are partly responsible for the high quality of farmland in Indiana.* Is this statement true or false? Explain.

____

____

19. The Hawaiian Islands were formed by

A volcanoes.
B glaciers.
C earthquakes.
D sediment.

20. How does Earth's surface change?

____

____

____

____

____

____

Test Prep

Circle the best answer for each question.

1. The picture below shows rocks and sand along the side of a stream.

   The settling of rocks and sand is an example of which process?

A deposition
B weathering
C eruption
D landslide
4.2.2 (DOK 1)

2. What MOST LIKELY caused the shape of the land in this desert?

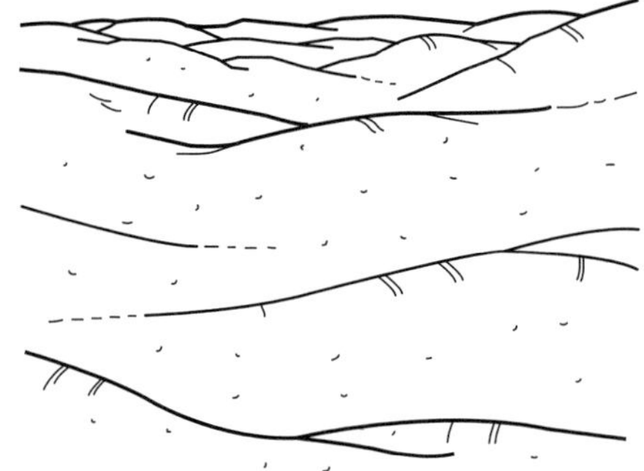

A rain
B wind
C flowing water
D freezing water
4.2.2 (DOK 2)

3. Which of these MOST LIKELY shows the oldest river?

A

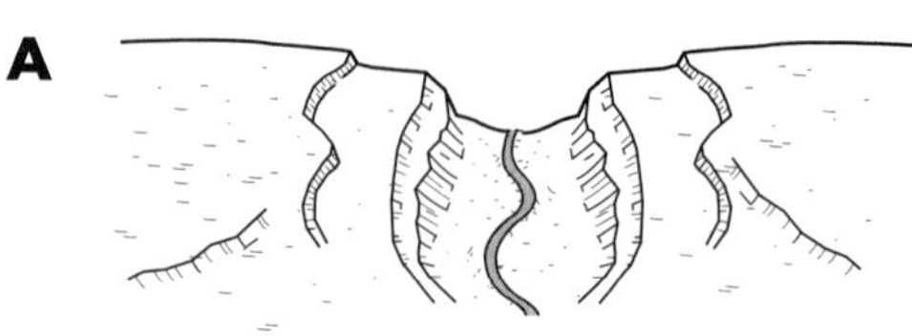

B

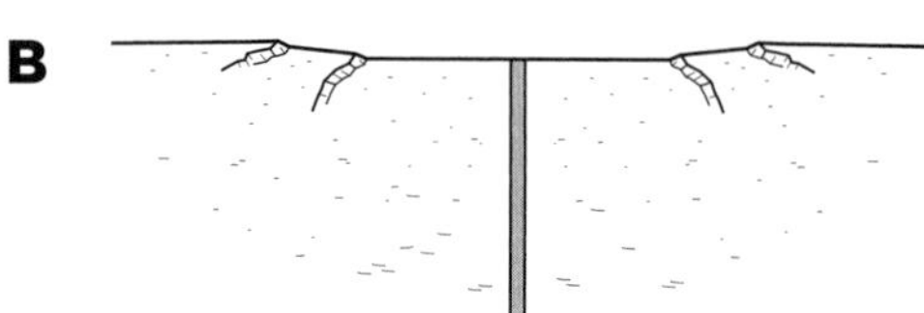

C

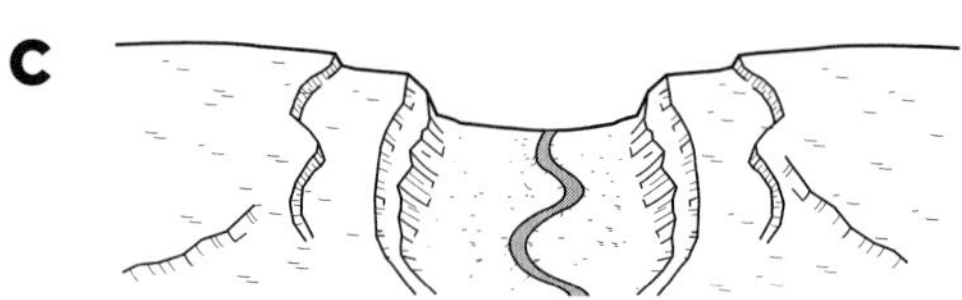

D

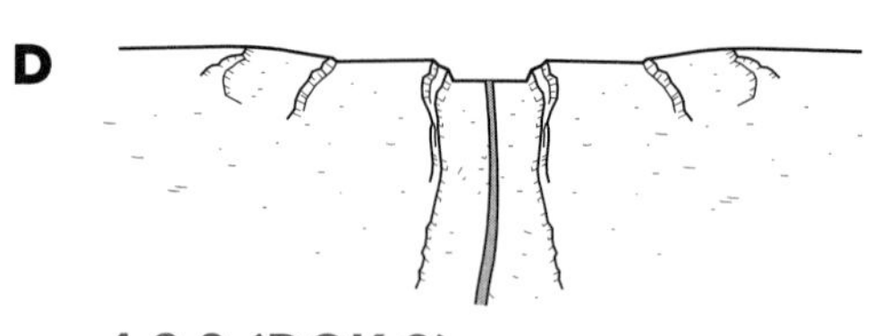

4.2.2 (DOK 2)

4. Which of these is MOST LIKELY a slow process?

A a beach flooding
B a volcano erupting
C a rock weathering
D an earthquake
4.2.1 (DOK 2)

5. Which of these has steep sides and a flat top?

A plateau **C** moraine
B volcano **D** valley
4.2.2 (DOK 1)

6. Compare and contrast erosion and weathering.
4.2.2 (DOK 2)

____

____

7. Describe TWO causes of erosion at Indiana Dunes National Lakeshore.
4.2.2 (DOK 2)

____

____

8. Describe ONE way that landslides can be prevented.
4.2.3 (DOK 2)

____

9. Lava flowed from three vents on a volcano. The table shows the number of hours the lava flowed over a four day period.

Day	North Vent	South Vent	East Vent
1	10 hours	4 hours	5 hours
2	10 hours	10 hours	3 hours
3	6 hours	16 hours	2 hours
4	?	?	?

Which vent had the LONGEST flow of lava over the first three days?
4.2.3 (DOK 1)

____

What sort of data could you expect on the fourth day?
4.2.3 (DOK 3)

____

____

UNIT 3

Investigating Earth's Resources

How do people use and change the land?

____

____

____

____

____

____

Vocabulary

natural resource a necessary or useful material we get from nature

nonrenewable resource a resource that cannot be replaced

renewable resource a resource that can be replaced

pollution a harmful substance in the environment

conservation using resources wisely

recycle use old materials to make new products

As you read the unit, complete the chart about natural resources and our environment.

Our environment...

... provides many natural resources. Natural resources are called __________ if they can be replaced. Those that cannot be replaced, such as coal and oil, are _______________ . Coal and oil are types of __________ .

... can be changed. Sometimes the change is harmful. A harmful change is __________ , which is when something harmful is added to the environment. People can protect valuable land by turning it into parks or _________________ .

... is important to all living things.

People practice ____________ when they use natural resources wisely. Three ways to conserve natural resources and protect the environment begin with the letter R. These three Rs are __________ , __________ , and __________ .

Lesson 1

Natural Resources

limestone quarry near New Amsterdam, Indiana

4.2.4 Investigate earth materials that serve as natural resources and gather data to determine which are in limited supply.

Look and Wonder

The picture shows an Indiana quarry. Workers are removing limestone rock that formed on an ocean floor over 350 million years ago. How will the rock be used? Will we ever run out of limestone?

____

____

____

____

____

Essential Question What materials do we get from Earth and how do we use them?

____

____

____

____

How do we use Earth materials?

Purpose

Classify objects as natural or made by people.

Procedure

Glue your Notebook FOLDABLES here. Use Foldable I on page 290.

1 Observe Look at the objects with a hand lens. Draw and label the objects on a separate sheet of paper.

2 Infer List the four objects made by people. Match each with the natural object from which it is made.

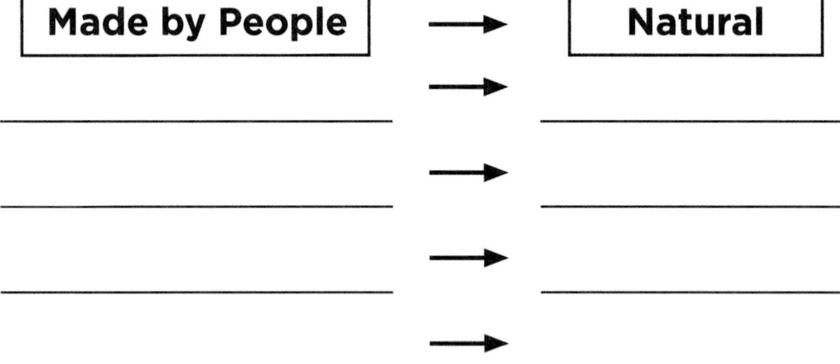

Made by People	→	Natural
	→	
	→	
	→	
	→	

3 Classify Explain why you classified each object as natural or made by people.

Materials

- hand lens 
- chalk
- ceramic pottery  
- clay
- cotton boll  
- fabric 
- limestone 
- pencil
- twig 

The Nature of Science Identify simple patterns in data and propose explanations to account for the patterns.

Draw Conclusions

4 Compare your results with those of your classmates. Did all students get the same results? Explain.

____

____

____

____

Explore More

Gather additional objects, such as coins, buttons, and common classroom objects. How can you identify the materials from which they are made? Make a plan and try it. Describe your results below.

____

____

____

Open Inquiry

Think of your own question about natural objects. Make a plan and carry out an experiment to answer your question.

My question is: ______________________________

____

How I can test it: ______________________________

____

My results are: ______________________________

____

____

Read and Respond

What are natural resources?

Your classroom contains many different objects. How many of them were made from Earth materials? Perhaps you have a wooden pencil at your desk. The pencil came from lumber, or cut trees. Lumber is a natural resource. A **natural resource** is a necessary or useful thing we get from nature. Chances are, most of the objects in your classroom came from natural resources.

Lumber is a natural resource that comes from a living thing.

A natural resource can be a living or a nonliving thing. Plants are living natural resources. They provide food, clothing, and shelter. Rocks and minerals are nonliving natural resources. Most rock and mineral resources come from mines. A mine is a place where natural resources are removed from Earth. The graphite in your pencil came from a mine. Most metals come from mines. So does coal.

Coal is a rock that we burn for fuel. We burn it to *generate*, or produce, electricity. About half of the electricity generated in the United States comes from burning coal.

Coal is a natural resource that comes from a mine. We burn coal to generate much of our electricity.

Quick Check

1. Are air and water natural resources? Explain your answer.

____

____

Indiana Limestone

In Unit 2 you read that Indiana has many limestone caverns. Limestone is an important natural resource that is mined in Indiana. It is used in many products, such as concrete, toothpaste, and medicine. It is used to make steel and paper. Limestone is even added to some flours to make bread. Limestone may have been in the toast you had for breakfast!

Indiana's state stone is a special limestone, known as Indiana Limestone. Unlike some other limestones, it can be removed from mines in very large blocks. It is soft and easily carved when first mined. When it dries, it becomes hard and resistant to weathering. Its light color makes it an attractive building stone. The Empire State Building and the Indiana State Capitol were both built with Indiana Limestone.

Quick Check

2. How might you have used limestone today?

____

____

3. What made Indiana Limestone a good choice for use in the Empire State Building?

____

____

____

The Empire State Building, located in New York City, is made with Indiana Limestone. ▼

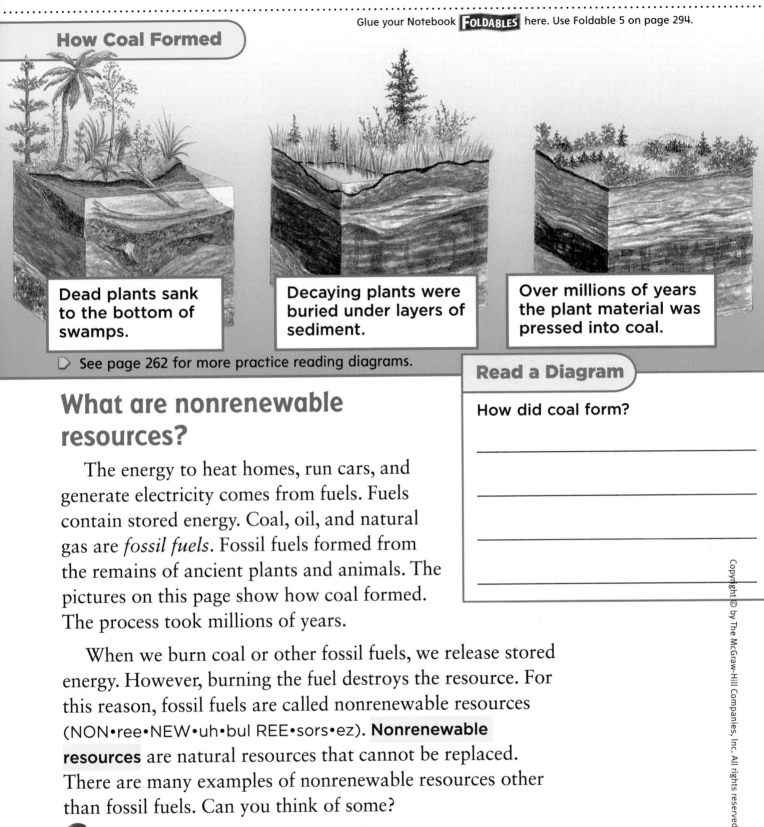

Glue your Notebook FOLDABLES here. Use Foldable 5 on page 294.

How Coal Formed

Dead plants sank to the bottom of swamps.

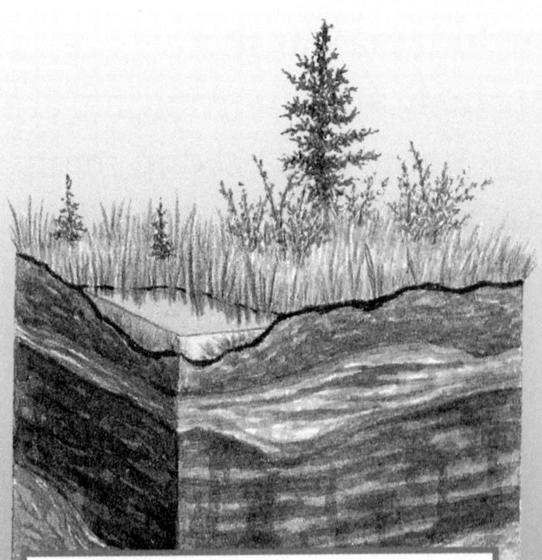

Decaying plants were buried under layers of sediment.

Over millions of years the plant material was pressed into coal.

See page 262 for more practice reading diagrams.

Read a Diagram

How did coal form?

____

____

____

____

What are nonrenewable resources?

The energy to heat homes, run cars, and generate electricity comes from fuels. Fuels contain stored energy. Coal, oil, and natural gas are *fossil fuels*. Fossil fuels formed from the remains of ancient plants and animals. The pictures on this page show how coal formed. The process took millions of years.

When we burn coal or other fossil fuels, we release stored energy. However, burning the fuel destroys the resource. For this reason, fossil fuels are called nonrenewable resources (NON•ree•NEW•uh•bul REE•sors•ez). **Nonrenewable resources** are natural resources that cannot be replaced. There are many examples of nonrenewable resources other than fossil fuels. Can you think of some?

 ***Quick Check***

4. **Name a nonrenewable resource that is not a fossil fuel. Explain why it is nonrenewable.**

____

Fossil Fuel Supplies

One liter of natural gas takes millions of years to form. It burns within a few seconds! As we consume Earth's fossil fuels, it gets harder—and more expensive—to find new supplies.

Searching for new supplies of fossil fuels is a difficult process. To find oil and natural gas, deep holes must be drilled below Earth's surface. Once oil has been found it must be refined, or purified. Then it must be moved to the location where it is needed.

Generating electricity from fossil fuels creates other problems. Power plants are large and expensive to operate. As fossil fuel supplies continue to decrease, we will need to develop other sources of energy.

Drill rigs explore deep into Earth looking for oil and natural gas. ▼

Quick Check

5. What is happening to Earth's supply of fossil fuels?

____

____

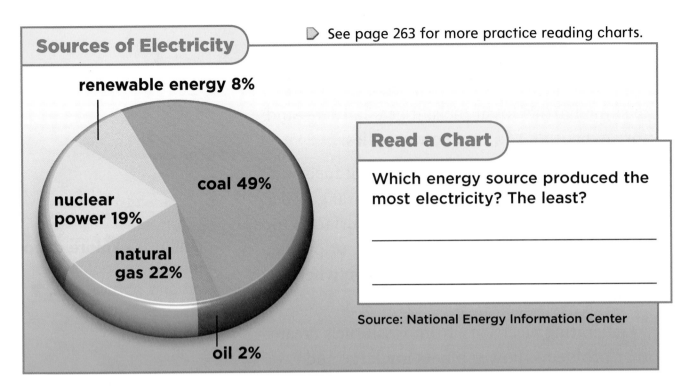

Sources of Electricity

See page 263 for more practice reading charts.

renewable energy 8%

coal 49%

nuclear power 19%

natural gas 22%

oil 2%

Source: National Energy Information Center

Read a Chart

Which energy source produced the most electricity? The least?

____

____

What are alternative energy sources?

Underline four alternative energy sources in the second paragraph on this page.

Scientists are always looking for sources of electricity that do not require fossil fuels. These are called alternative energy sources. Many of these are being used in Indiana.

The Sun provides us with a source of energy every day. A tool called a solar cell can change the energy from sunlight into electricity. The wind is another alternative energy source. Windmills use the energy from wind to produce electricity. Flowing water can be used to generate electricity too. Hydroelectric dams block the flow of rivers. The movement of water through the dam generates electricity. In some places, people generate electricity from the heat inside Earth.

Quick Check

6. **What is the name of the tool used to generate electricity from the Sun's energy?**

____

Renewable Resources in Indiana

Alternative energy sources are renewable resources. **Renewable resources** can be replaced. For example, we will not use up our supply of sunlight or wind. As water flows through a dam to produce electricity, rainwater replaces it.

Indiana has many renewable sources of energy. In Benton County and White County, there are large wind farms. Indiana wind farms generate about enough electricity to power a small Indiana city, such as Richmond. Many new wind farms are being built. The new wind farms will double the amount of electricity generated by wind in coming years.

There are also solar energy and biofuel programs in Indiana. *Bio* means "life." A biofuel is a fuel produced from living things. Switchgrass is a plant that can be burned for energy. Corn can be used to produce ethanol. Ethanol can be used instead of gasoline to power our vehicles.

Quick Lab

Learn more about Earth's renewable and nonrenewable resources by doing the Quick Lab on page 282.

Wind farms gather the energy from wind and turn it into electricity. ▼

Quick Check

7. Name a renewable resource that is not an alternative energy source. Explain why it is renewable.

____

____

____

____

____

____

____

Visual Summary

Summarize the lesson in your own words.

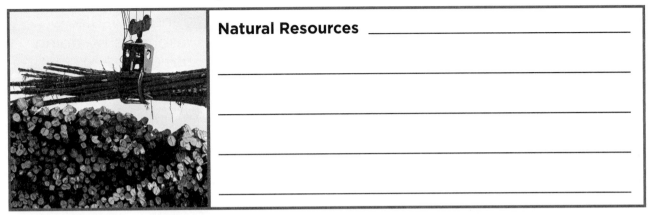

Natural Resources ______________________________

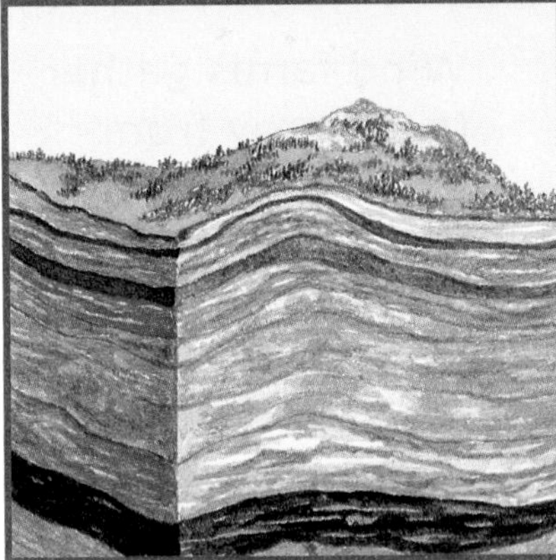

Nonrenewable Resources ______________________________

Alternative Energy ______________________________

Make a FOLDABLES® Study Guide

Make a trifold book. Use it to summarize what you learned about natural resources.

Think, Talk, and Write

1. **Vocabulary** Any renewable energy resource is called a(n)

______________________.

2. **Classify** Give examples of the two classes of natural resources shown below.

Mineral Resource	Energy Resource
______________________	______________________
______________________	______________________

3. **Critical Thinking** Is Indiana Limestone a renewable resource? Explain.

____

____

4. **Test Prep** **Which of the following is a nonrenewable source of energy?**

A wind
B natural gas
C flowing water
D heat inside Earth

Essential Question What materials do we get from Earth and how do we use them?

____

____

____

____

____

LOG ON e-Review Summaries and quizzes online at www.macmillanmh.com

Reading in Science

FINDING ORE

Did you use a metal that came from a mine today? You did if you ate breakfast with a spoon or rode your bike to school. A spoon might contain silver. A bicycle might contain chromium. These metals started out as ores in the ground.

Ores are rocks that have useful minerals. Many ores contain metals, such as silver, chromium, or platinum. Ores can be found in all kinds of places, from old volcanoes to river valleys. The ores are removed from the ground. Then the mineral is separated from the ore.

Scientists travel the world looking for new supplies of certain ores. Platinum, for example, is hard to find. Platinum is used in electrical equipment and jewelry. Platinum is in limited, or short, supply. This makes it valuable.

Do you have any coins in your pockets? What ore do you think they came from? Do you think the ore is in limited supply?

Predict

When you predict,

- you tell what you think might be the answer to a question;
- you research facts about the topic to check your prediction.

Write About It

Predict Pick a certain kind of coin, such as a penny or a nickel. Make a prediction to answer the following question: Is the ore used to make the coin in limited supply? Then write about the answer to your question.

4.2.4 Investigate earth materials that serve as natural resources and gather data to determine which are in limited supply.

Planning and Organizing

Answer the questions to help you write your paragraph.

1. What are ores and how are they used?

____

____

2. Why are some ores in limited supply?

____

____

Drafting

Write a prediction to begin your paragraph.

____

____

Now write your paragraph on a separate sheet of paper.

Glue your Notebook FOLDABLES here. Use Foldable I on page 290.

▲ These rings are made of platinum.

◀ Chromium is used in bicycle frames.

LOG ON e-Journal Write about it online at www.macmillanmh.com

Pollution and Conservation

4.2.5 Describe methods that humans currently use to extend the use of natural resources. 4.2.6 Describe ways in which humans have changed the natural environment that have been detrimental or beneficial.

Look and Wonder

Every day, huge tanker ships carry oil across the ocean. Oil can harm living things in the ocean and along its shores. What happens if oil spills? How can people clean it up?

____

____

____

____

____

Essential Question How can people protect natural resources?

____

____

____

____

Explore

How can you clean an oil spill?

Materials

- plastic container
- water
- cork
- eyedropper
- vegetable oil
- paper towels
- sponge

Make a Prediction

Oil and water do not mix. How could you separate oil from the surface of water? From the surface of a solid? Make a prediction.

___

___

Test Your Prediction

1. Fill a plastic container halfway with water. Float a cork in the water.

2. **Make a Model** Using an eyedropper, carefully drip 6–7 drops of oil onto the water's surface.

3. **Observe** Watch the oil, water, and cork for about 30 seconds. Record your observations.

___

___

4. Based on your observations, make a plan to test your prediction. Use only the materials your teacher gives you.

___

___

5. Carry out your plan to clean the oil from the water and cork. Record your results.

___

___

Nature of Science Make predictions and formulate testable questions.

Draw Conclusions

6 **Communicate** How well were you able to clean the oil from the water? From the cork? Describe your findings.

____

____

7 Was your prediction correct? Explain. What other materials do you think might have worked?

____

____

Glue your Notebook FOLDABLES® here. Use Foldable 3 on page 292.

Explore More

Research the 2010 oil spill from the *Deepwater Horizon* drilling rig in the Gulf of Mexico. How did it affect natural resources there? Report your findings on a separate sheet of paper.

Open Inquiry

Think about how you could remove other substances from water. Design an experiment to test your idea.

My question is: _______________

____

How I can test it: _______________

____

My results are: _______________

____

____

____

Read and Respond

What is pollution?

On April 20, 2010, there was an explosion on the drilling rig *Deepwater Horizon*. The rig sank in the waters of the Gulf of Mexico. For months, oil leaked from the drilling site. The spill was the largest of its kind. It harmed living things in the ocean and along hundreds of miles of coastal areas. The spill had a disastrous effect on the environment. The **environment** is made up of all the living and nonliving things in an area.

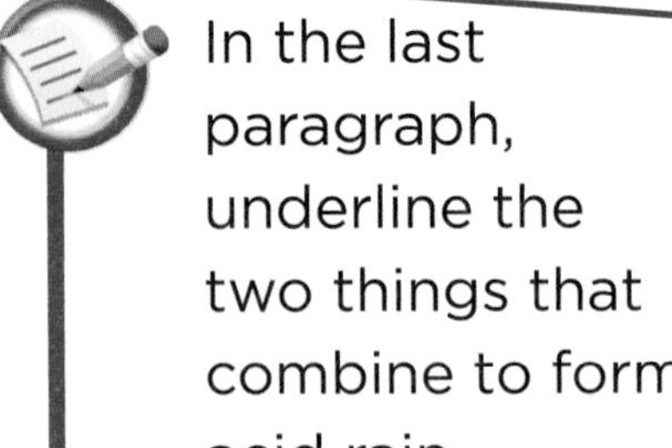
In the last paragraph, underline the two things that combine to form acid rain.

When a harmful substance is added to the environment, it causes **pollution** (puh•LEW•shun). Pollution can harm the environment. Some pollution comes from natural sources, like forest fires and volcanoes. However, most pollution comes from the activities of people.

Acid Rain

When we burn fossil fuels, gases and particles go into the air. Some of the gases combine with water droplets in the air. When this happens, acid rain forms. Acid rain can harm living things, especially certain kinds of trees. It can also damage buildings and monuments.

Acid rain killed the trees in this forest.

Nutrients

Oil spills are not the only way we pollute water. Other types of water pollution begin on land. For example, nutrients from farming and detergents are flushed with waste water into rivers. The rivers flow into lakes and oceans. Extra nutrients cause problems in rivers, lakes, and oceans.

The nutrients are used by tiny living things called algae. The algae grow and make more algae. The algae use up oxygen in the water. This can kill fish and other living things there.

Mining

In Lesson 1 you read that most metals come from ores that are found in mines. An *ore* is a rock that contains a resource, such as metal. To remove the metal from the rock, harmful substances are used. These substances can get into water supplies and harm animals and plants.

When there are too many nutrients in water, the water turns green with algae.

Quick Check

1. How can nutrients harm the environment?

____

____

2. List four ways people pollute the land.

____

____

Contour Plowing

See page 264 for more practice reading photos.

Read a Photo

Why would a farmer use this method of planting?

____

____

____

How can we practice conservation?

Everyone can conserve resources. **Conservation** (kahn•sur•VAY•shun) means using our resources wisely.

Water Conservation

Clean drinking water is a valuable natural resource. Many towns and cities collect waste water from homes and businesses. The collected water goes to a sewage treatment plant. There the water is cleaned and returned to the environment. Cleaning water takes energy.

When you conserve water, you conserve energy. There are many things you can do to help. Turn off the faucet when you are not using it. Run only full loads in laundry machines and dishwashers. Ask your family to fix leaky toilets and faucets. Every bit of conservation adds up!

Soil Conservation

Did you know that it takes hundreds of years for just one inch of soil to form? The soil can be eroded by wind and heavy rain. To conserve soil, farmers practice soil conservation. They plant trees to keep the soil in place and slow down the wind. They may practice crop rotation. Crop rotation is when farmers change crops every year. Crop rotation conserves the nutrients in soil.

Farmers may also use contour plowing to conserve soil. They plow fields in curved rows that follow the shape of the land. This method makes "steps" that channel the flow of rainwater. Without contour plowing, the water runs downhill, carrying loose soil and nutrients with it.

The 3 *R*s

Three ways you can conserve resources start with the letter R. To **reduce** means to use less of something. This is the simplest way to conserve. You can reduce your use of paper by writing on both sides. You can reduce your use of energy by turning off the lights when you are not in a room.

Saving energy is an important part of conservation. It takes energy to make a plastic water bottle. You can reuse a water bottle instead of buying new bottles of water. To **reuse** means to use something over again.

To **recycle** means to make a new product from old materials. Recycling keeps materials out of landfills. A landfill is where trash is buried. Many communities recycle paper, plastic, glass, and metal. This saves energy, but it also saves space.

To learn more about conservation, do the Quick Lab on page 283.

In the last paragraph, underline two ways that recycling helps conserve resources.

Glue your Notebook FOLDABLES here. Use Foldable 5 on page 294.

The 3 Rs in Action

Reusing and recycling water bottles reduces our use of energy.

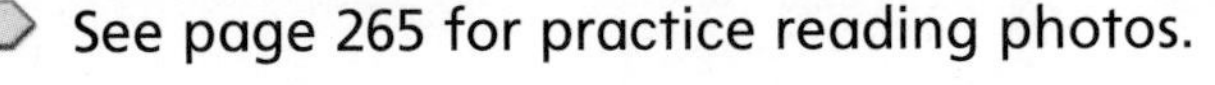

See page 265 for practice reading photos.

Quick Check

3. How can you conserve resources?

____

____

How do people protect the environment?

The picture at the bottom of this page shows old subway cars being lowered into the ocean. These subway cars will provide shelter for fish. A shelter is a safe place. The fish will have a safe place to avoid their enemies. The cars will also provide a place for mussels and shrimp to live. Mussels and shrimp need a hard surface upon which they can attach.

People can help in other ways too. People can clean up damaged environments. Soils and water supplies that have been polluted by mining can be cleaned. The process is expensive, but many efforts such as these are already happening in many areas.

Forests that have been cut down can be replanted. Fisheries that have been overfished can be protected. In many areas, there are laws to protect forests and fisheries from overuse.

✓ *Quick Check*

4. What are some positive ways in which people can affect environments?

____

____

____

These old subway cars will become a home for fish.

Nature Preserves

There are many different kinds of environments in Indiana. There are forests with tall trees. There are prairies with grasses and open spaces. There are wetlands that are home to an astonishing number of different kinds of living things. Each kind of environment has certain plants and animals. Many of these living things can survive nowhere else.

To protect the living things in Indiana, there are many state parks and nature preserves. A nature preserve protects natural areas. It keeps them in their natural condition.

Laws also help protect living things and their environments. The laws prevent people from dumping trash or harmful substances near protected areas. Certain animals and plants have laws that protect them. These animals and plants cannot be harmed.

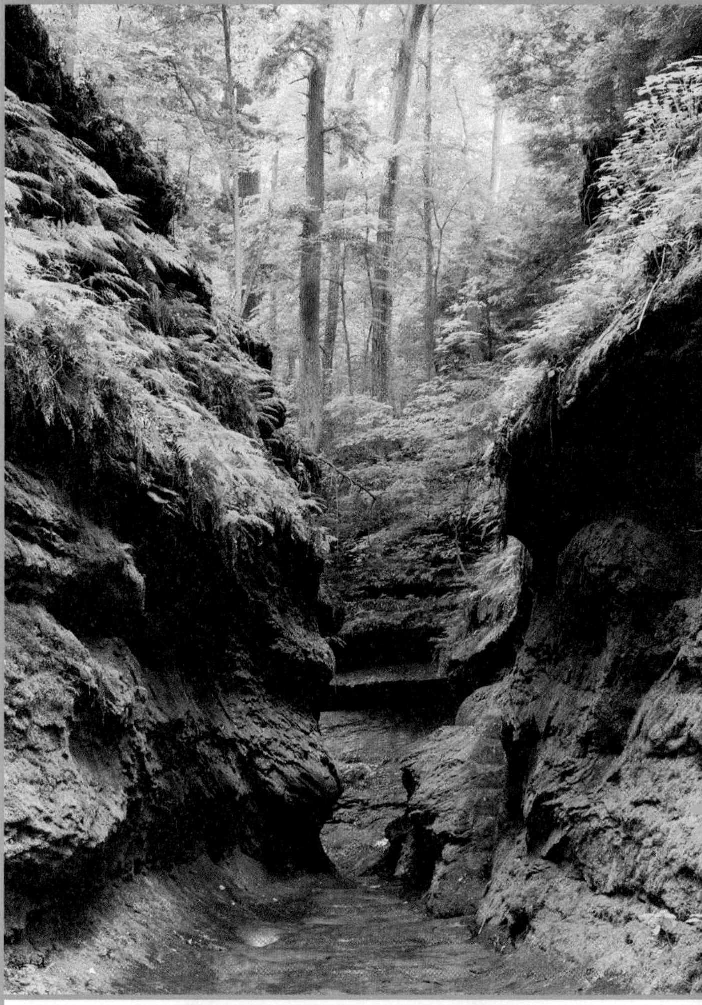

Turkey Run State Park and other Indiana state parks and nature preserves protect natural areas.

Quick Check

5. Why is it important to keep forests, prairies, and wetlands in a natural condition?

____

____

6. How do laws help the environment?

____

____

Visual Summary

Complete the lesson summary in your own words.

Pollution ______________________________

____

____

____

____

Conservation ______________________________

____

____

____

____

Benefits to Environment ______________________________

____

____

____

____

Make a FOLDABLES® Study Guide

Make a trifold table. Use it to summarize what you read about pollution and conservation.

Main Idea	What I learned...	Helps the environment
Harmful to environment		
Saving resources		
Helpful to environment		

Think, Talk, and Write

1. **Vocabulary** A(n) ________________ is made up of the living and nonliving things in an area.

2. **Summarize** Describe how people can help the environment.

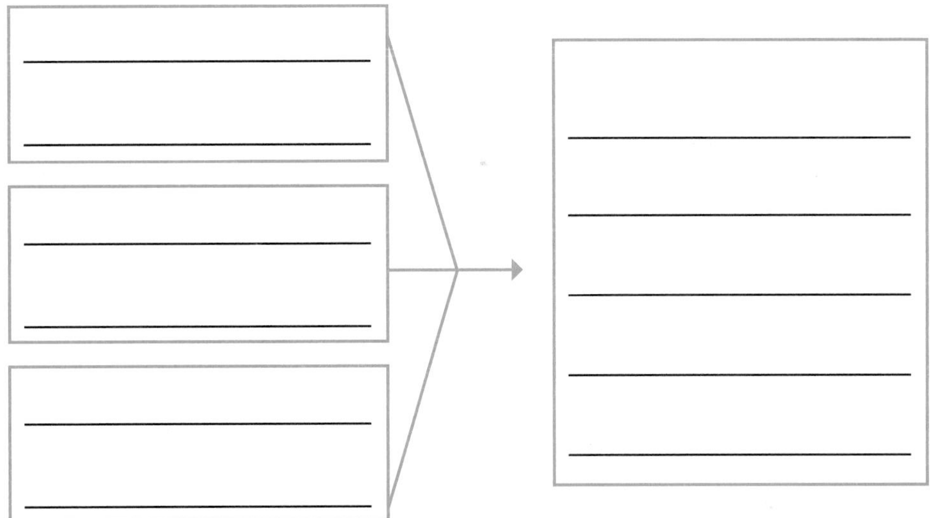

3. **Critical Thinking** Write a plan that your family can follow to conserve water. Which of the steps do you think will help conserve the most water? Explain.

____

____

4. **Test Prep** **The burning of which product causes MOST acid rain?**

A litter
B fertilizers
C pesticides
D fossil fuels

How can people protect natural resources?

____

____

____

____

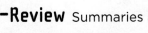

SAVING THE SOIL

Much of the food we eat comes from plants grown in soil. Good soil is important for growing crops. However, sometimes the way we grow our food can harm the soil.

Plowing is pulling a blade through the soil to turn it over. Plowing exposes the soil to erosion.

To prevent erosion, some farmers use a method called *contour plowing*. They follow the curves of a hillside instead of plowing straight up and down. This method stops rainwater from washing soil and nutrients down the slope. The problem is that contour plowing takes longer than plowing in straight lines. It also uses more fuel.

Some farmers plant seeds at the end of a harvest. The plants that grow are called cover crops. When farmers are ready to plant again, they plow the cover crop into the soil. This adds nutrients and protects the soil.

Some farmers do not plow their fields after a harvest. The old crop roots and stems protect the soil through the winter. When it's time to plant, the farmers do not plow. They just dig holes in the field and place seeds in the holes. This method is called no-till planting. No-till planting also has its problems. Farmers may need to use chemicals to kill weeds that plowing would have removed.

Main Idea and Details

The main idea is the focus of the article. Complete the table below about what farmers do to save the soil.

Main Idea	Details
Contour plowing is helpful.	It is used on a __________ to stop __________ from eroding soil and __________ .
Contour plowing is not easy.	It takes more __________ and uses more __________ than straight plowing.
Some farmers do not plow their fields after the harvest.	Instead, they __________ holes in the ground.
After the harvest, some farmers plant cover crops.	This adds __________ and __________ the soil.

Write About It

Main Idea and Details

What are some ways that farmers protect the soil? List the advantages and disadvantages of each method.

4.2.5 Describe methods that humans currently use to extend the use of natural resources.

UNIT 3 Review

Visual Summary

Summarize each lesson in your own words.

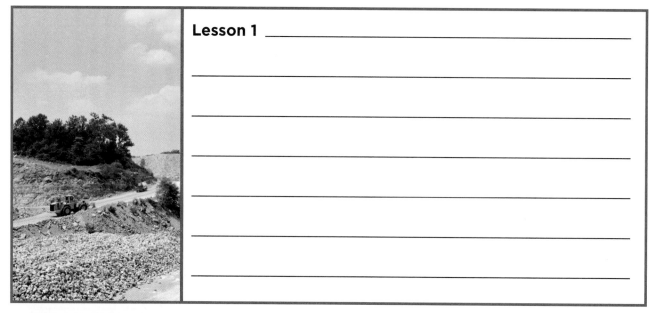

Lesson 1 ______________________________________

Lesson 2 ______________________________________

Make a FOLDABLES® Study Guide

Glue your lesson study guides to a large sheet of paper as shown. Use your study guide to review what you have learned in this unit.

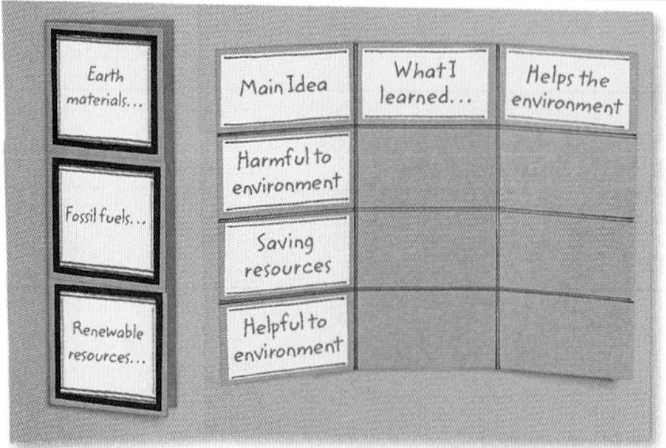

Vocabulary

DOK I

Fill each blank with the best term from the list.

alternative energy, source, p.110

conservation, p. 122

environment, p. 120

fossil fuels, p. 108

natural resource, p. 106,

nonrenewable resource, p. 108

pollution, p. 120

recycle, p. 123

renewable resources, p. 111

reuse, p. 123

1. An Earth material that cannot be replaced is a(n)

__________________________.

2. Anything added to the environment that is harmful is

__________________________.

3. A way to conserve resources and protect the environment is to __________________________ products over and over again.

4. The wise use of natural resources is called

__________________________.

5. Easily replaced materials, such as trees, are __________________________.

6. Wind farms are a(n) __________________________.

7. Energy resources called __________________________ formed millions of years ago from the remains of once living things.

8. We __________________________ when we make new products form old materials.

9. A(n) __________________________ is any necessary or useful thing we get from nature.

10. The living and nonliving things in an area form a(n)

__________________________.

LOG ON e-Glossary Words and definitions online at www.macmillanmh.com

UNIT 3 Review

Skills and Concepts

DOK 2–3

Answer each of the following.

11. **Main Idea and Details** Describe each of the 3 *R*s.

12. **Cause and Effect** When does an environment become polluted?

13. **Summarize** List the ways environments might be protected by laws.

14. **Critical Thinking** Which renewable energy source do you think will be most important in the future? Explain your answer.

15. **Problem and Solution** How can drinking water become polluted? What can be done to keep it safe?

16. **Critical Thinking** How can all of the 3 *R*s help conserve fossil fuels?

____

____

17. **True or False** *Coal is a renewable resource.* Is this statement true or false? Explain.

____

____

18. **True or False** *Ores are a renewable resource.* Is this statement true or false? Explain.

____

____

19. Crop rotation is used to conserve

A plants.
B soil nutrients.
C water nutrients.
D animals.

The Big Idea

____

20. How do people use and change the land?

____

____

____

____

____

____

Test Prep

Circle the best answer for each question.

1. The picture below shows a wind farm.

A wind farm is an example of which of the following?

A fossil fuel
B mineral resource
C alternative energy
D nonrenewable resource
4.2.5 (DOK 1)

2. Which human activity MOST LIKELY harms the environment?

A crop rotation
B reusing water containers
C recycling notebook paper
D burning fossil fuels
4.2.6 (DOK 2)

3. Which of these would MOST LIKELY be protected by a nature preserve?

A a certain kind of animal or plant
B a mineral resource about to run out
C an alternative energy source
D a company that mines and burns fossil fuels
4.2.4 (DOK 2)

4. Indiana's state rock, Indiana Limestone, is an example of which of the following?

A an energy resource
B an alternative energy source
C a renewable resource
D a nonrenewable resource
4.2.6 (DOK 2)

5. Antonio chose to ride his bike to school instead of riding in the family car. This is an example of

A recycling.
B reducing.
C polluting.
D reusing.
4.2.5 (DOK 2)

6. Which of the following belongs in the empty circle?

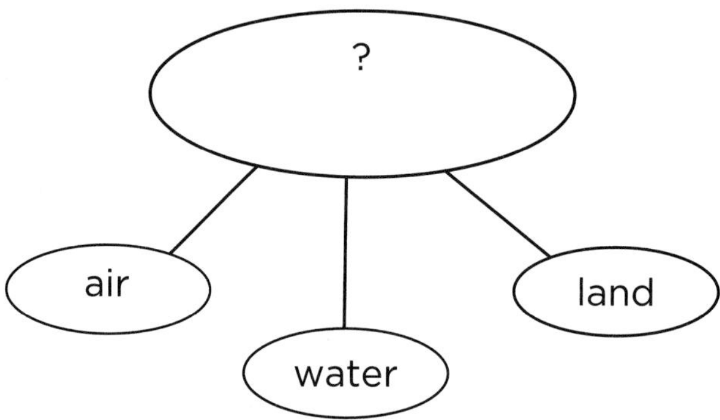

A 3 *R*s
B fossil fuels
C natural resources
D alternative energy
4.2.6 (DOK 1)

Answer the following questions.

7. **Vocabulary** What does recycling mean?
4.2.6 (DOK 1)

8. **Infer** A town burns switchgrass to generate electricity. Is the switchgrass an alternative energy source? Explain.
4.2.5 (DOK 2)

9. **Critical Thinking** Are people always aware of the pollution they cause?
4.2.6 (DOK 2)

10. What natural resource is the arrow pointing to in the picture?
4.2.4 (DOK 2)

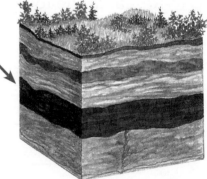

Describe how this resource formed and how it is used.
4.2.5 (DOK 3)

▲ Earth scientists who study volcanoes wear protective suits.

Earth Scientist

If you are curious about planet Earth, you might want to become an Earth scientist. Earth scientists study Earth and other planets.

Not all Earth scientists study rocks. Some work with businesses to locate oil or other resources in the ground. Others work to prevent disasters caused by natural events, such as earthquakes. Earth scientists also look at how Earth has changed over time. They make predictions about the future.

To be an Earth scientist you need a college degree. Most Earth scientists attend school for several more years after college.

Write About It

Research the four branches, or basic areas, of Earth science: geology, meteorology, oceanography, and astronomy. Define each branch. Which branch of the Earth sciences is most interesting to you? Why?

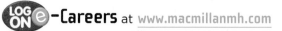

____

____

____

____

____

LOG ON e-Careers at www.macmillanmh.com

INDIANA

Life Science

Academic Standards for Science

Core Standard Observe, describe, and ask questions about structures of organisms and how they affect their growth and survival.

This bird moves up and down trees hunting for insects.

white-breasted nuthatch

Growth and Survival

How do living things survive in their environments?

Vocabulary

offspring the young of living things

inherited characteristic a characteristic passed from parent to young

physical characteristic a body characteristic

population all the members of a species living in an environment

adaptation a characteristic that helps an organism survive

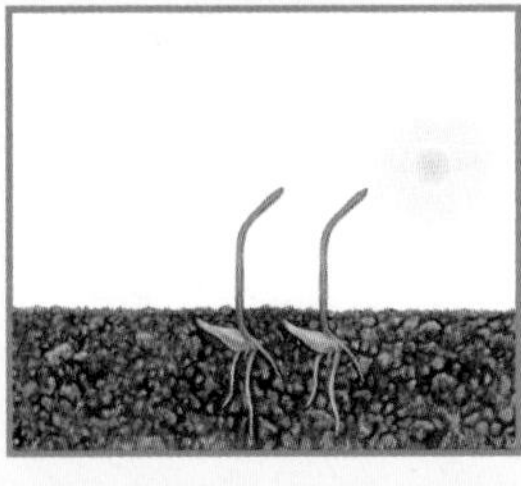

stimuli things in the environment that causes an organism to react

As you read the unit, complete the chart about the growth and survival of living things.

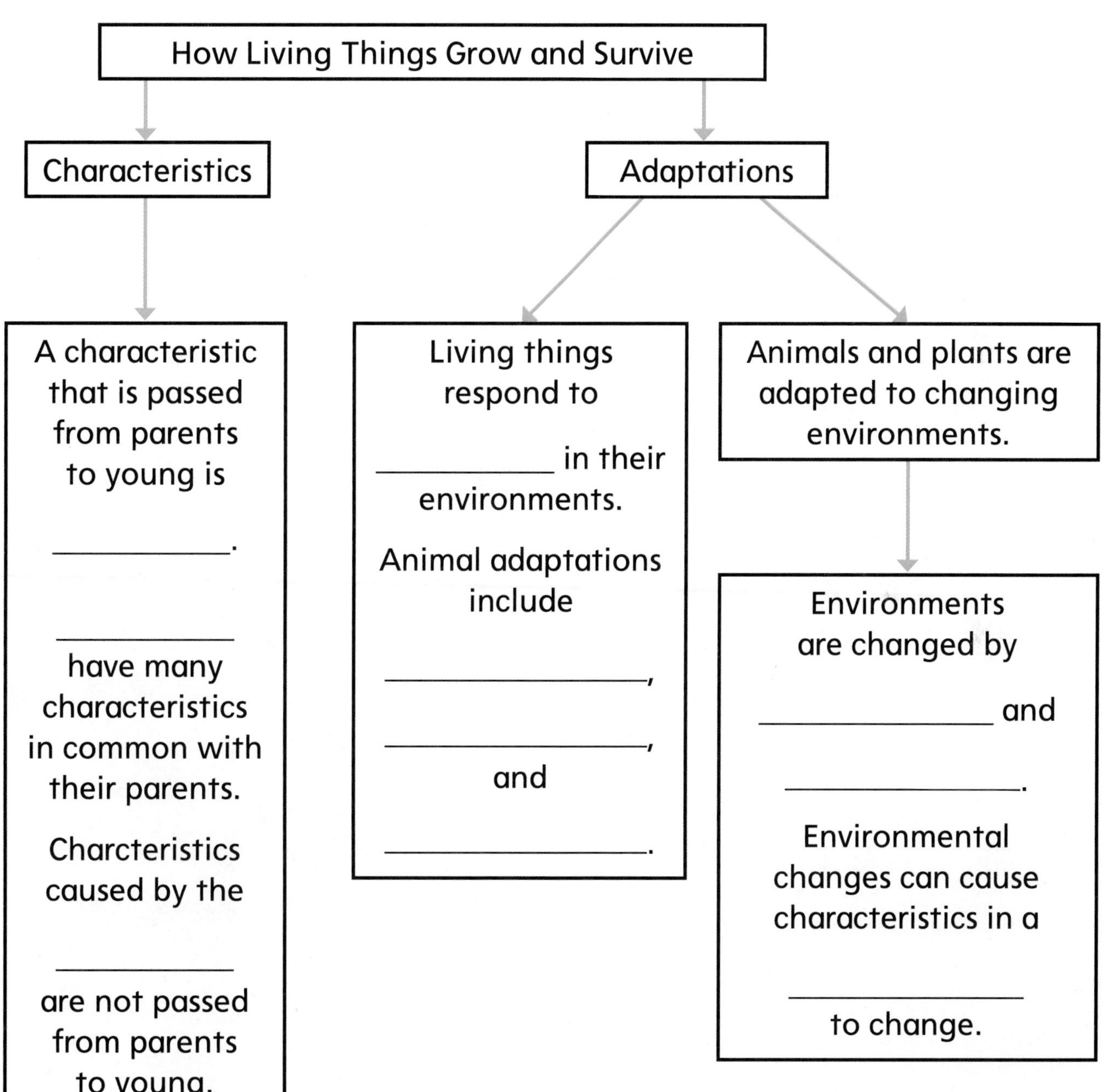
How Living Things Grow and Survive
Characteristics
Adaptations
A characteristic that is passed from parents to young is
__________.
__________ have many characteristics in common with their parents.
Charcteristics caused by the
__________ are not passed from parents to young.
Living things respond to
__________ in their environments.
Animal adaptations include
__________,
__________,
and
__________.
Animals and plants are adapted to changing environments.
Environments are changed by
__________ and
__________.
Environmental changes can cause characteristics in a
__________ to change.

Lesson 1

Parents and Offspring

4.3.1 Observe and describe how offspring are very much, but not exactly, like their parents or one another. Describe how these differences in physical characteristics among individuals in a population may be advantageous for survival and reproduction.

Look and Wonder

The picture shows a young horse and its parents. How are these animals the same? How does the young horse differ from its parents?

Essential Question

What causes living things to look and act the way they do?

Explore

Which characteristics are passed on from parents to their young?

Purpose

To describe and record how parents and their young are alike and different.

young chickens

Procedure

1. **Observe** What characteristics do the young chickens have in common?

___

___

___

guinea pig and young

2. **Observe** Compare the adult guinea pig to its young. Compare the adult elephant to its calf. How are the young animals like the parent? How are they different?

___

___

___

___

___

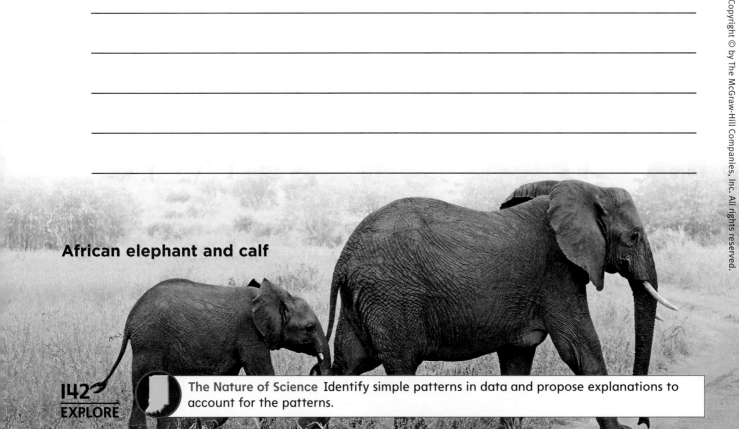

African elephant and calf

The Nature of Science Identify simple patterns in data and propose explanations to account for the patterns.

Draw Conclusions

3 **Infer** Why do you think that the young guinea pigs and elephant look similar to the parent?

____

____

4 **Infer** Why do you think that the young chickens are not identical to each other?

____

____

____

Explore More

Find additional pictures of animals and their young. Do young animals always look like their parents? Explain.

____

____

Open Inquiry

Think of a question about the types of characteristics that are passed from parents to offspring. Make a plan and carry out an investigation to answer your question.

My question is: ____

____

How I can test it: ____

____

My results are: ____

____

Read and Respond

Where do living things get their characteristics?

What do chickens, guinea pigs, and elephants have in common? All these animals reproduce with two parents. To *reproduce* is to make more of one's own kind.

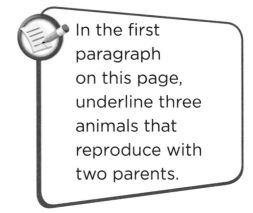

In the first paragraph on this page, underline three animals that reproduce with two parents.

The picture at the bottom of this page shows a mother pig and her offspring. **Offspring** are the young of living things. The offspring have characteristics of their mother. They also have characteristics of their father. Characteristics passed from parents to young are called **inherited characteristics.**

A pig's fur color is an inherited characteristic. So is the shape of its ears. You have inherited characteristics, too. Your eye color and hair color are examples.

Quick Check

1. Name an inherited characteristic in the pigs below. Do not repeat a characteristic already described on this page.

____

Physical Characteristics

Many inherited characteristics we observe are physical characteristics. A **physical characteristic** is a body characteristic. You can observe physical characteristics in animals, plants, and all other living things. Height, weight, and color are examples of physical characteristics. Physical characteristics help you identify and describe different kinds of living things.

Not all characteristics are inherited. Some are caused by the environment. Recall from Unit 3 that the environment consists of the living and nonliving things in an area. The environment can change the physical characteristics of living things. The picture on this page shows a woodpecker and a tree. The woodpecker drills into the tree's bark to find food. This makes holes in the bark.

Physical characteristics caused by the environment are not passed to offspring. An offspring from the tree in the picture will not have holes in its bark. If a tree loses a branch in a storm, this change will not be passed on either.

Quick Check

2. Will a scar be passed from parent to offspring?

____

____

For more practice reading photos, see page 266.

Quick Lab

Investigate inherited characteristics. Do the Quick Lab on page 284.

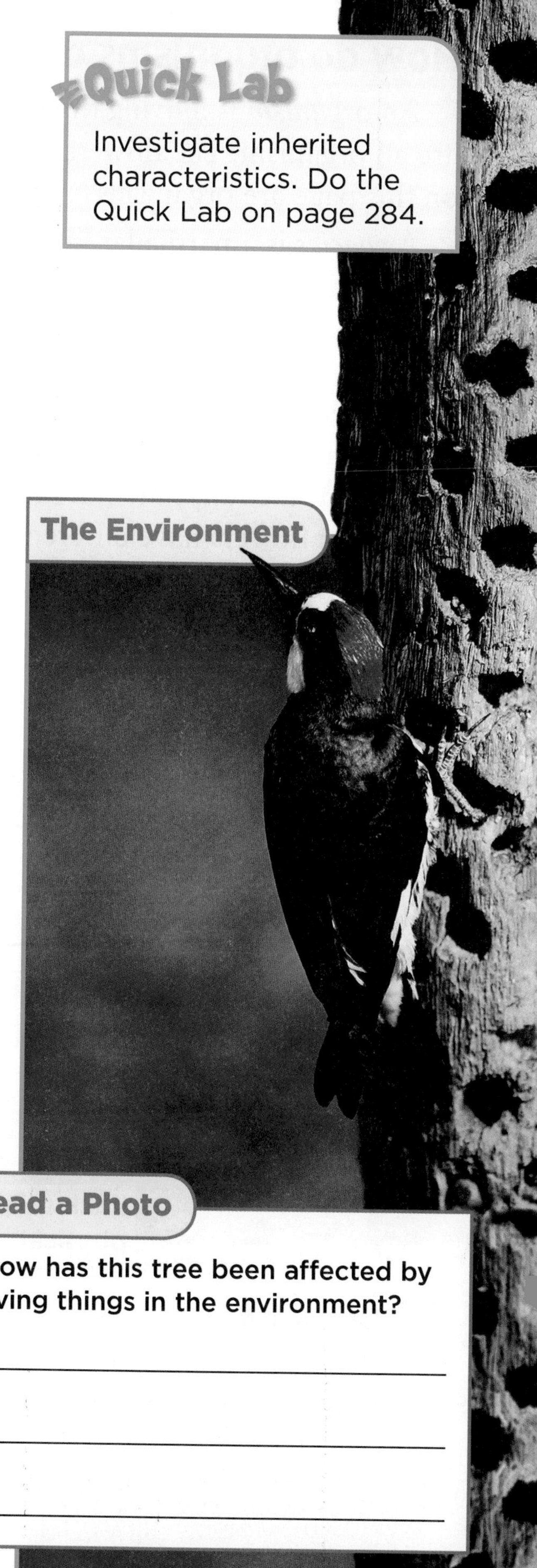

The Environment

Read a Photo

How has this tree been affected by living things in the environment?

____

____

____

How do organisms differ?

An *organism* is a living thing. You are an organism. The flowers shown on this page are organisms.

A *species* is a particular kind of organism. The flowers shown below are tulips. All tulips share certain physical characteristics. For example, their leaves and flowers have similar shapes. However, the picture below shows that the tulips are not all the same. The flowers have different patterns and colors. Some have longer stems than others.

A **population** is all the members of a species that live in an environment. All the tulips that live in a field make up one population.

Certain organisms have physical characteristics that help them survive longer and reproduce more than other organisms. Tulips with longer stems might make more seeds. They might produce more offspring. Over time, there would be more long-stemmed tulips in the population.

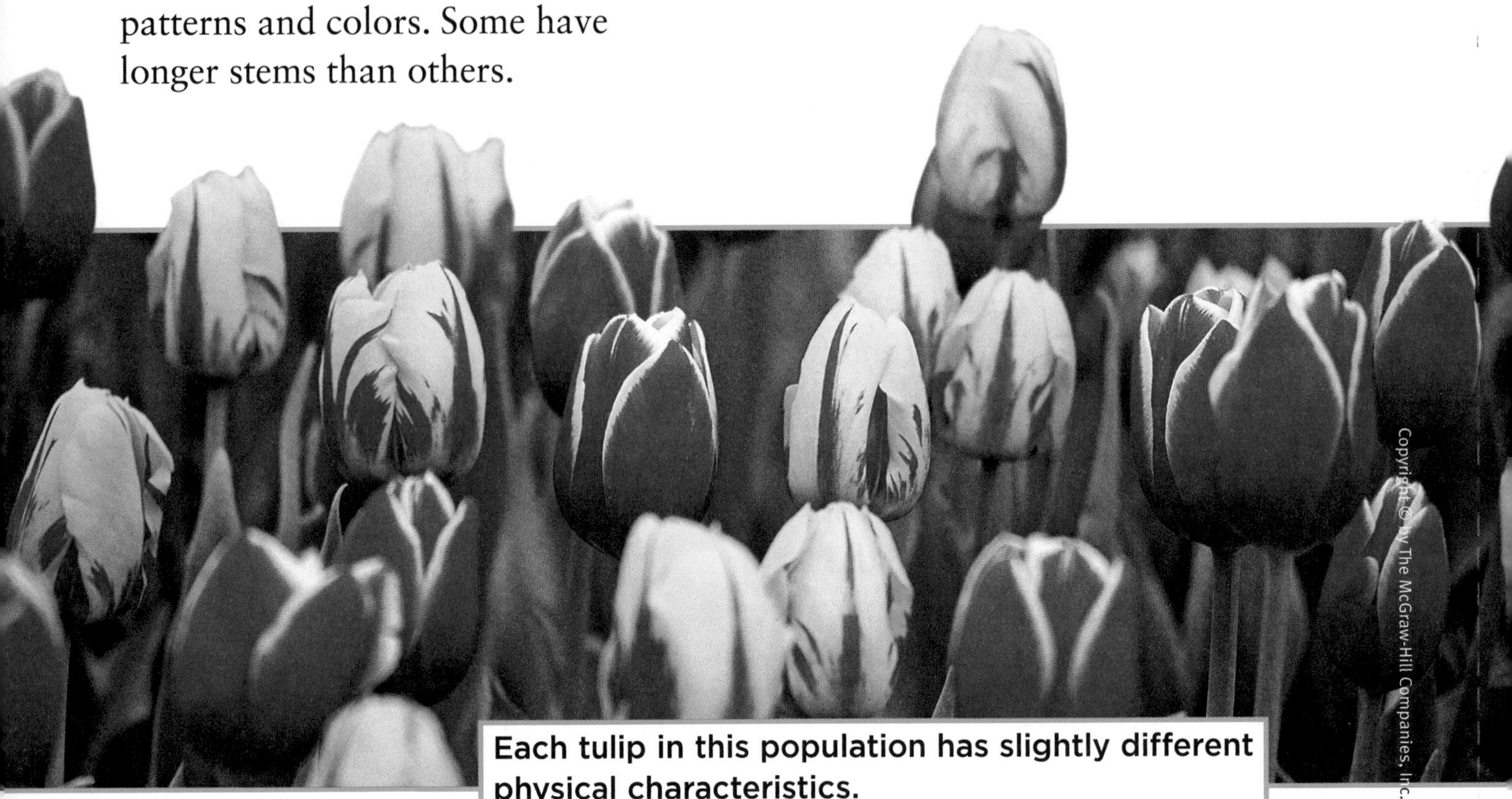

Each tulip in this population has slightly different physical characteristics.

Quick Check

3. Why might tulips with longer stems pass on more of their physical characteristics?

____

____

Different populations of the same species can have different physical characteristics. The photographs on this page show different populations of deer mice. One population lives in sandy environments. The other lives in forests and fields.

The fur color of the two populations is very different. In a sandy environment, white deer mice survive longer and produce more offspring than brown deer mice. In a forest or field environment, the opposite is true.

Quick Check

4. Why might brown deer mice survive longer than white deer mice in a forest?

5. Owls hunt mice. What are some physical characteristics that would help owls to be good hunters?

Glue your Notebook FOLDABLES here. Use Foldable 3 on page 292.

White Deer Mice

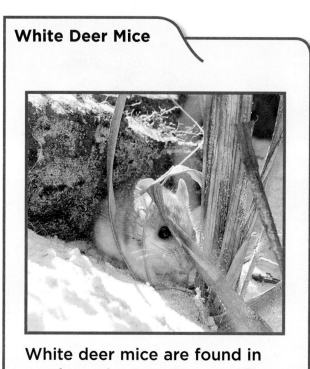

White deer mice are found in sandy environments.

Brown Deer Mice

Brown deer mice are found in forest and field environments.

Migration is an inherited behavior in these geese.

Which behaviors are inherited?

The picture above shows a flock of geese. The geese are flying south for the winter. This helps them find food. Flying south for the winter is an example of a behavior called migration. Behaviors, like physical characteristics, can also be inherited.

Migration is an example of an inherited behavior called instinct. **Instinct** is a way of acting that an animal does not have to learn. Birds build nests, and spiders spin webs, by instinct. Reflexes are also inherited behaviors. Reflexes are reactions. For example, blinking when a piece of dust flies into your eye is a reflex.

✓ *Quick Check*

6. Give an example of an instinct not mentioned on this page. How does the instinct help the animal survive?

____

____

____

Not all behaviors are inherited. Some behaviors are learned. A **learned behavior** occurs when an animal changes its behavior through experience.

Learning can happen when an animal interacts with its environment or with other animals. Do you ride a bicycle? Bicycling is a learned behavior.

Many animals learn to hunt by watching adults. For example, lion cubs watch adults. They practice hunting when they play.

Quick Check

7. A baby crying or a dog barking is an example of a(n) ____________________.

8. A dog doing a trick is an example of a(n) ____________________ behavior.

Sea otters smash clam shells against a rock. This learned behavior helps the otters get food.

Visual Summary

Complete the lesson summary in your own words.

Inherited Characteristics ____________________

____

____

____

____

Characteristics in a Population ____________________

____

____

____

____

Inherited Behavior ____________________

____

____

____

____

Make a FOLDABLES® Study Guide

Make a three-tab book. Use it to summarize what you learned about parents, offspring, and inherited characteristics.

How Offspring Are Like Parents

Characteristics and Survival

Instinct

Think, Talk, and Write

1. **Vocabulary** What is an organism?

____

2. **Main Idea and Details** What are three examples of inherited characteristics?

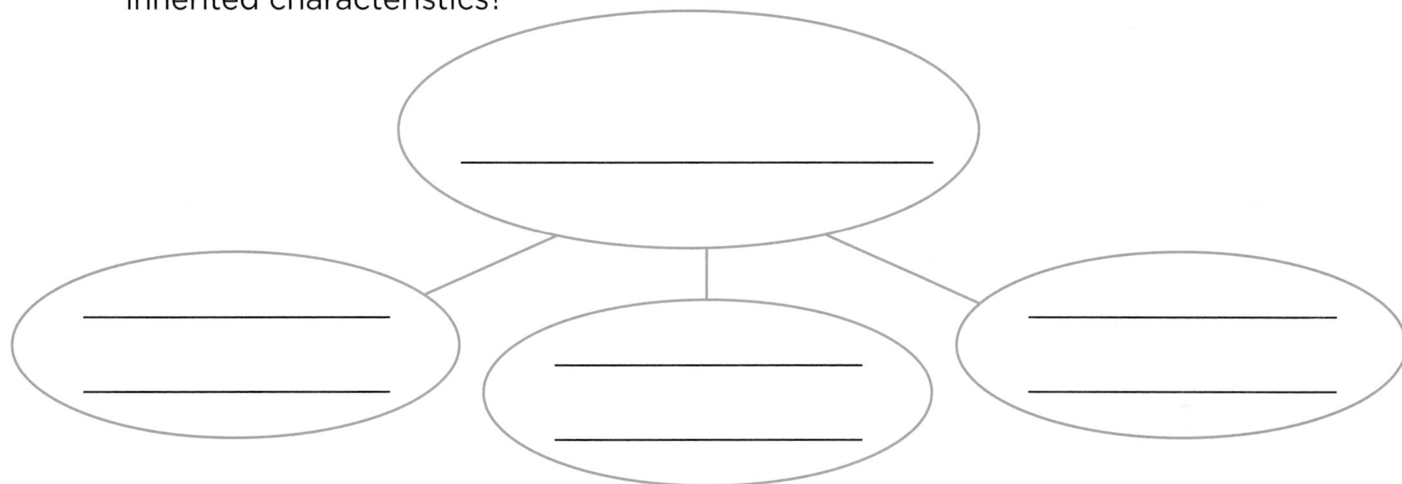

3. **Critical Thinking** A mosquito can fly without having to learn. How does this help the mosquito survive?

____

____

4. **Test Prep** **Which of the following is the BEST example of a learned behavior?**

A spider spinning web
B bird building nest
C blinking
D riding a bike

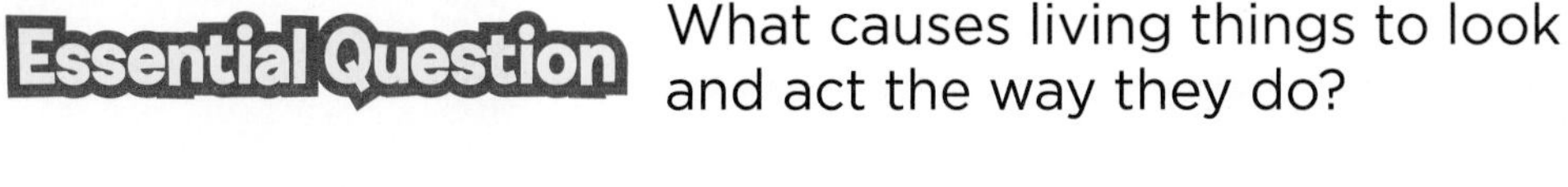

What causes living things to look and act the way they do?

____

____

____

____

Meet Christopher Raxworthy

Chris studies amphibians and reptiles in their environments.

Adult Mantella poison frogs are only about one inch long.

Dwarf dead leaf chameleons grow to about $3\frac{1}{2}$ inches long.

The island of Madagascar lies off the southeast coast of Africa. This island has plants and animals found nowhere else in the world. Chris Raxworthy is a scientist at the American Museum of Natural History. He has spent many years gathering information about these animals and their environments.

On the island, you can find unusual creatures such as the Mantella poison frog. This tiny frog gets its name from its poisonous skin. Its skin is brightly colored which makes it easy to see. This warns its enemies to stay away. Female frogs lay 20–30 eggs on land. After hatching, the tadpoles wiggle to a stream where it takes about one year for them to turn into adults.

The dwarf dead leaf chameleon also makes its home on Madagascar. This unusual animal gets its name because it looks like a dead leaf. During the day, the chameleons hide out among the dead leaves of the rain forest floor. At night, they climb up into the low branches to sleep. Female chameleons lay 2 or 3 large eggs in the leaves on the forest floor. After hatching, it takes about 9 to 12 months for the offspring to grow into adults.

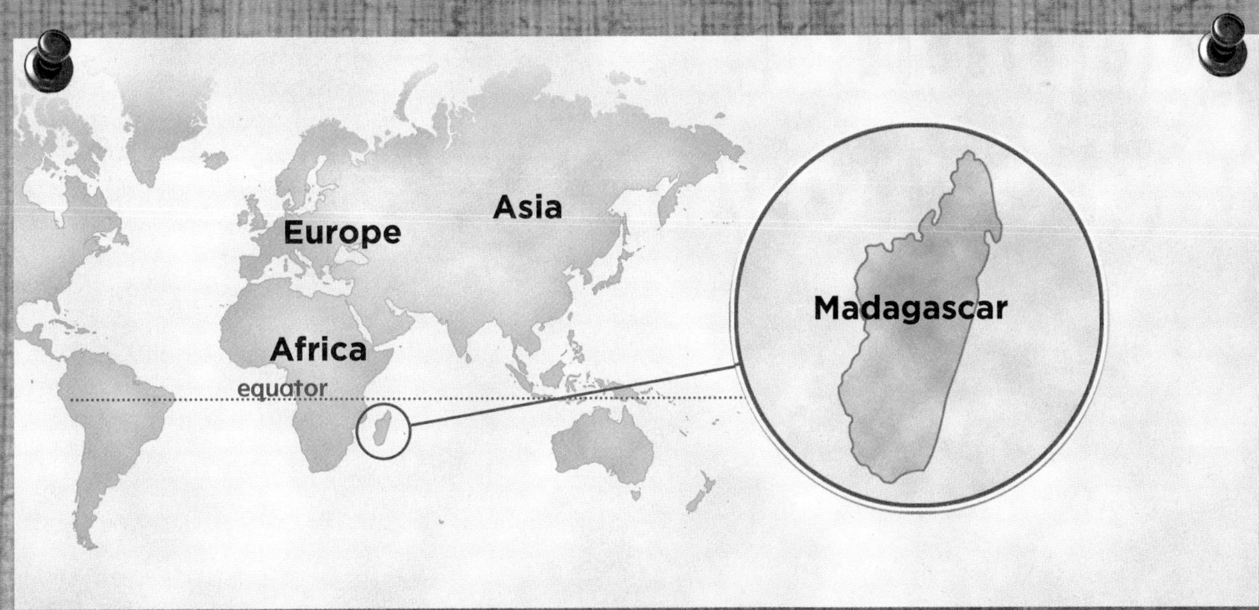

Compare and Contrast Fill in the table below describing the physical characteristics of Mantella poison frogs and dwarf dead leaf chameleons. Tell how the frogs and chameleons are alike and how they are different.

Frog	Chameleon	Frog and Chameleon
It has ________ colors that make it ________ to see.	Its body resembles a(n) ________.	Babies hatch from ________.
Females have ________ offspring.	Its coloring makes it ________ to see.	Young become ________ in about ________.
It has ____________ skin that helps it avoid its enemies.	Females have ________ offspring.	Both organisms have ________ body lengths.

Connect to

at www.macmillanmh.com

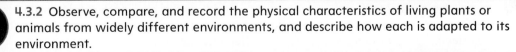

LOG ON e -Journal Write about it online at www.macmillanmh.com

4.3.2 Observe, compare, and record the physical characteristics of living plants or animals from widely different environments, and describe how each is adapted to its environment.

Lesson 2

Adaptation and Survival

4.3.2 Observe, compare, and record the physical characteristics of living plants or animals from widely different environments, and describe how each is adapted to its environment. 4.3.3 Design an investigation to explore how organisms meet some of their needs by responding to stimuli from their environment.

Look and Wonder

The ruby-throated hummingbird feeds on flowers throughout Indiana. How does its long and narrow beak help this bird survive?

______

______

______

______

______

Essential Question How are organisms well-suited for the environments in which they live?

______

______

______

______

Explore

How do plants respond to their environment?

Make a Prediction

Plants need sunlight to live. If the light is blocked, how will a plant respond? Write your prediction.

____

____

Test Your Prediction

1. △ **Be Careful!** Handle scissors carefully. Cut an opening to the side of one end of the shoe box.
2. **Measure** Cut two dividers from the cardboard. Make them as tall as the shoe box but 3 cm narrower.
3. Place the dividers upright along the inside of the box. Tape the first divider to the same side as the opening you cut in step 1. Tape the other divider a few inches away on the opposite side as shown. Put a plant in the end of the box opposite the opening. Put the lid on the box. Turn the opening toward bright sunlight.

Glue your Notebook FOLDABLES® here. Use Foldable I on page 290.

4. **Observe** Every 3–4 days for several weeks, remove the lid to water your plant. Observe and measure its growth. Record your observations in a data table.

- shoe box
- scissors
- cardboard
- ruler
- tape
- potted plant

The Nature of Science Plan and carry out investigations as a class, in small groups or independently, often over a period of several class lessons.

Draw Conclusions

5 **Interpret Data** What happened to the plant? Why?

____

____

6 **Infer** How did the plant get sunlight? How does this model plants that live on the forest floor?

____

____

Explore More

Would a seed grow in the box you made? Design an investigation to find out. Use several lima bean seeds placed in a damp paper towel.

____

____

Open Inquiry

How do seedlings respond to light and dark conditions? Develop a question about this topic or a related topic. Design a fair test to answer your question.

My question is: ____

____

How I can test it: ____

____

My results are: ____

____

Read and Respond

What are adaptations?

Every environment has its challenges. Organisms can meet those challenges with the right set of characteristics.

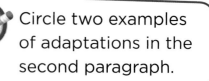

Circle two examples of adaptations in the second paragraph.

Certain kinds of characteristics are adaptations (a•dap•TAY•shunz). **Adaptations** are physical characteristics or behaviors that help a living thing survive in its environment. To survive is to continue to live. The camel can store energy in its hump. Roses have thorns to protect them from being eaten. Can you think of other adaptations?

Organisms have different adaptations depending on the environment in which they live. Some plants in tropical rain forests have leaves with grooves and "drip tips" that help rainwater flow off. These leaves are often large. They catch the little sunlight that shines through the trees. Tropical rain forest trees do not lose their leaves like trees in Indiana. Tropical rain forest trees make food year-round.

Quick Check

1. Name two adaptations of tropical rain forest plants.

____

A camel's hump stores fat for times when food is scarce.

Adaptations in Indiana

Temperatures in Indiana change throughout the year. In summer, the temperature might be 95°F (35°C). In winter, the temperature might be 15°F (-4°C). Indiana organisms must have adaptations to survive these different temperatures.

Indiana bats survive the winter months by hibernating (HI•bur•nayt•ing). When an animal **hibernates**, it goes into a deep sleep. This helps it save energy. Some animals leave the area in the winter. Remember from Lesson 1 that many bird species migrate. In the summer, you might see a bright blue indigo bunting in a field. By winter, the bird has flown south where it can find more food.

Plants in Indiana are also adapted to changing weather. Some trees lose their leaves in the winter. Cold winter air can damage leaves. There is also less water available during winter. When trees lose their leaves, it protects the tree from drying out.

Without leaves, a tree cannot make food. Instead, the tree uses stored food. In spring the tree grows new leaves and begins storing food for the next winter.

Glue your Notebook FOLDABLES® here. Use Foldable 3 on page 292.

▲ This maple tree will soon lose its leaves in preparation for winter temperatures.

Quick Check

2. Name two ways that animals are adapted to changing seasons.

____

____

What are some plant adaptations?

Unlike animals, plants cannot move from place to place. How do they survive when their environment changes?

Stimulus and Response

Things in an environment that cause an organism to respond, or react, are called **stimuli** (STIM•yuh•lye). A single response is a stimulus (STIM•yuh•lus). Plants respond to many different stimuli. The picture on this page shows two plants responding to light. Plants respond to light by growing toward it.

Plants respond to other stimuli as well. Plants respond to water by growing their roots toward the water's source. The roots of most plants grow downward, in the direction of gravity. The stems grow upward, away from gravity.

Quick Check

3. When a flower pot is tipped on its side, the roots grow downward. What is the stimulus in this example?

A sunlight
B water
C wind
D gravity

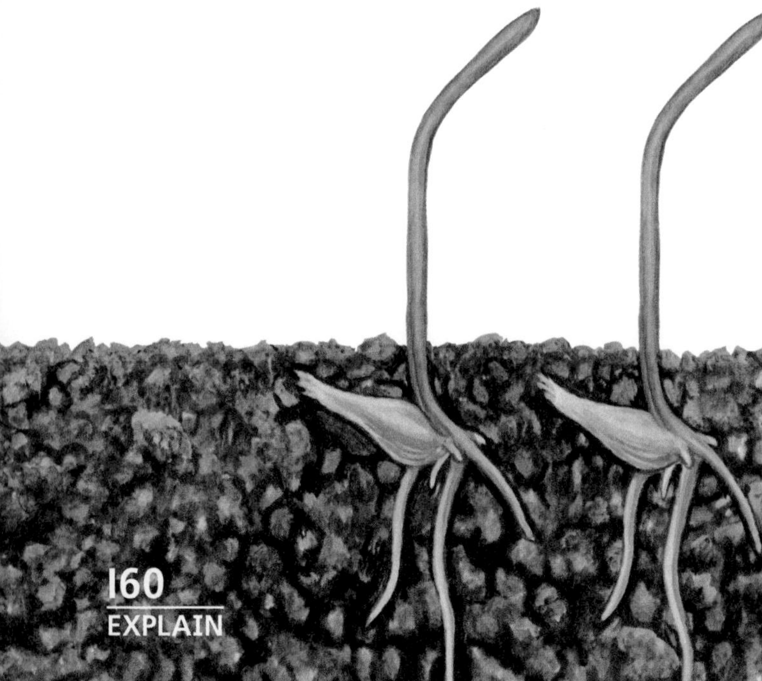

Read a Diagram

In this diagram, what is the stimulus, and what is the response?

____

____

____

See page 267 for more practice reading diagrams.

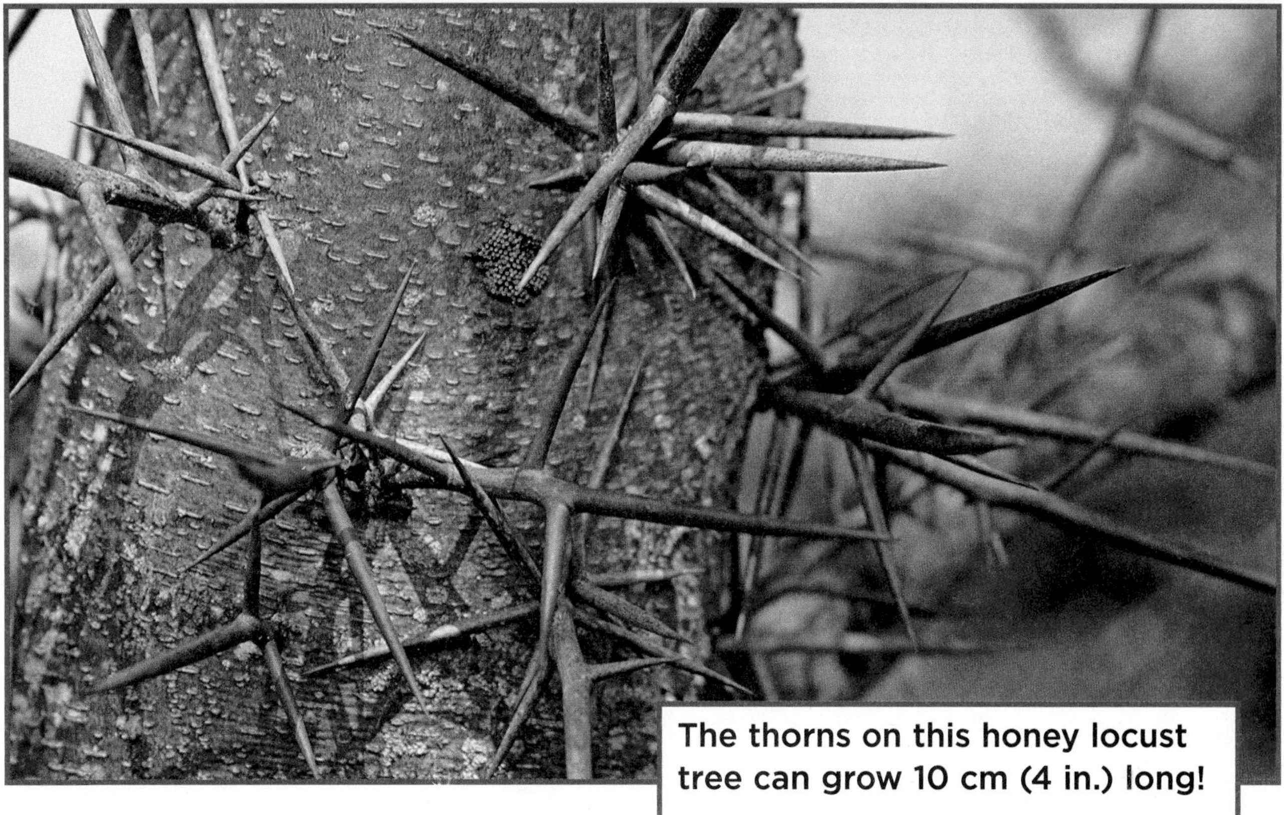

The thorns on this honey locust tree can grow 10 cm (4 in.) long!

Plant Defenses

An animal that eats plants is called a herbivore (HUR•buh•vor). Some plants have structures to protect themselves against herbivores. The honey locust has thorns. Roses also have prickly structures for defense.

You may have encountered stinging nettles or poison ivy in wooded areas. These plants produce poisonous substances for protection. The rash caused by touching these plants is not pleasant! Many plants produce poisons. For example, milkweed is both poisonous and bad tasting for most herbivores. However, the monarch butterfly is one animal that can eat the milkweed. This butterfly can store the poison in its body. It uses the poison for its own protection.

 **Quick Check**

Circle the correct answer.

4. All of the following protect a plant except

   A thorns.

   B poisons.

   C bad-tasting leaves.

   D flowers.

The walking stick uses both body shape and color as camouflage.

What are some animal adaptations?

On pages 158–159 you read about several animal adaptations. Perhaps you have thought of others. On these pages you will see many additional examples. Adaptations are all around us!

Camouflage

A predator is an animal that hunts other organisms for food. The animals predators hunt are called prey. Many prey animals blend in with their environment. This adaptation is called **camouflage** (KAM•uh•flazh). Camouflage helps animals hide.

Bullfrogs have a dark green body to blend in with pond vegetation. Walking sticks have a brown or green body that is shaped like a small branch. Walking sticks blend in with twigs and leaves.

The bullfrog's color helps it blend into lake and pond environments. ▼

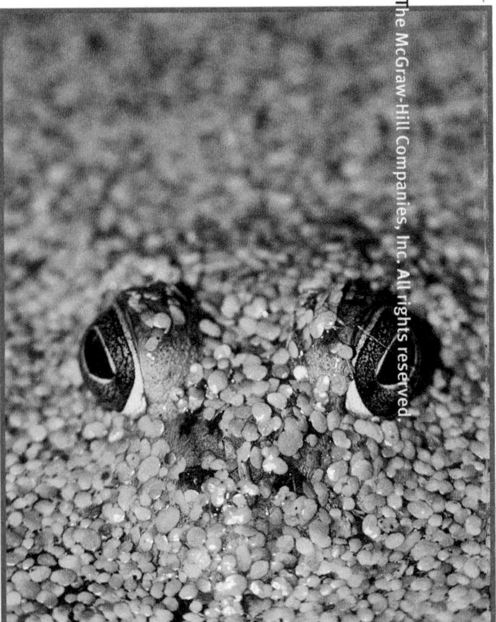

✓ *Quick Check*

5. Could predators use camouflage? Explain your answer.

____

____

Mimicry

Pictured on the right are two insects. One insect is a honey bee. Honey bees defend themselves with stingers. The other insect looks like a honey bee, but it is a hover fly (HUH•vur fleye). Hover flies do not have stingers.

By looking like a honey bee, the hover fly avoids predators. A predator might eat a regular insect but not eat a honey bee. When one kind of living thing looks like another kind, it is called **mimicry** (MIM•i•kree).

Quick Lab

To learn more about mimicry, do the Quick Lab on page 285.

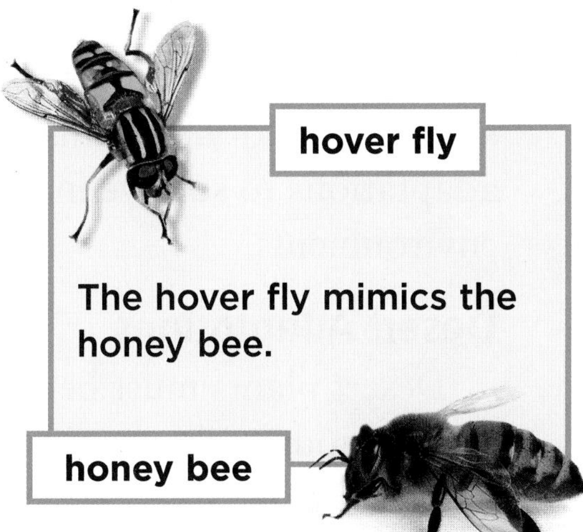

The hover fly mimics the honey bee.

Body Parts

Many animals have body parts to help them hunt or defend themselves. For example, hedgehogs are covered with hard spines. If a predator comes near, hedgehogs curl into a ball. A predator would not want to eat a spiny ball! The stinger of a bee or wasp can also be used for defense.

▲ A hedgehog rolls into a ball when a predator is near.

Quick Check

6. Why do you think a honey bee lacks camouflage?

____

____

How are plants and animals adapted to harsh environments?

Some environments have harsh, or difficult, conditions. Deserts are dry. Some deserts are also very hot during the day and very cold at night. Tundras are cold and dry. Organisms must have adaptations to survive in these harsh environments.

Desert Adaptations

Desert plants must be able to survive long periods without rain. A cactus can hold water just like a sponge. It also has a thick, waxy cover to keep its water inside. Some plants, such as the mesquite tree, grow very long roots to find and absorb water.

Many animals have adaptations for staying cool in hot deserts. The fennec fox has large ears that give off heat. Its fur is thinner than the fur of its relatives in cooler climates.

Camels have many adaptations for life in a sandy desert. Camels can close their nostrils to keep out sand. They have wide hooves that help them walk.

Desert animals can survive with little or no water. A kangaroo rat is an animal that never needs to drink. It gets water from the seeds it eats. A sandgrouse is a desert bird that can soak up and carry water in its feathers.

Desert and Tundra Foxes

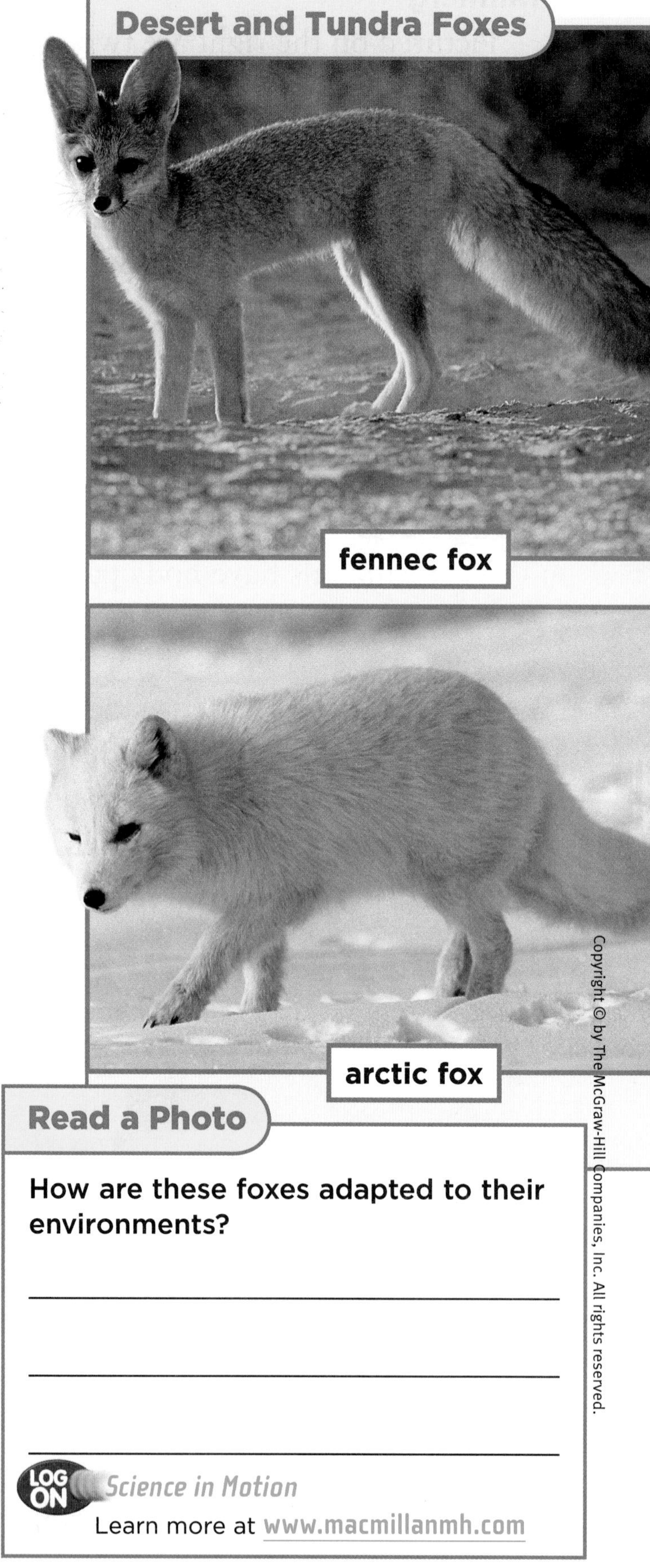

fennec fox

arctic fox

Read a Photo

How are these foxes adapted to their environments?

____

____

____

LOG ON *Science in Motion*

Learn more at www.macmillanmh.com

See page 268 for more practice reading photos.

Tundra Adaptations

At the North Pole, the ground is frozen all year. Winters are long and icy. Summers are short and cool. The winds may blow hard. This is the arctic tundra. Plants and animals must have special adaptations to live here.

Plants in the tundra grow low to the ground. They have shallow roots. There is not much water available for plants. They get most of their water from melting snow.

Most plants grow in clumps, or patches, to keep warm and protect against the wind. They are often dark in color. This helps them to absorb sunlight.

To stay warm, many animals in the tundra have short arms and legs. For example, the arctic fox has shorter ears and legs than the fennec fox. Arctic animals also tend to be larger than animals in warmer areas. This helps them hold in heat.

Sea lions, walruses and polar bears have a layer of blubber, or fat, under their skin. This blubber keeps them warm. These animals have more blubber in winter than in summer.

On this page, underline four physical characteristics of arctic plants. Circle three physical characteristics of arctic animals.

Quick Check

7. Why are there few trees in the tundra?

____

____

____

____

____

Plants in the tundra grow low to the ground. ▼

Visual Summary

Complete the lesson summary in your own words.

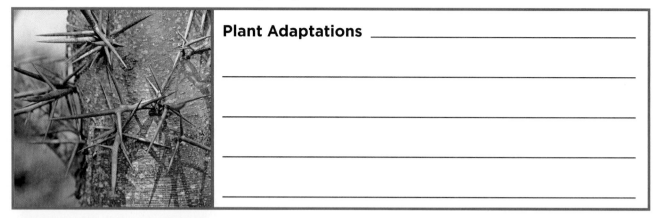

Plant Adaptations ______________________________

Animal Adaptations ______________________________

Harsh Environments ______________________________

Make a FOLDABLES® Study Guide

Make a trifold book. Use it to summarize what you learned about adaptations.

Adaptations	Plants	Animals
Indiana		
Desert		
Tundra		

Think, Talk, and Write

1 **Vocabulary** What is an adaptation?

____

2 **Predict** Suppose someone moved a polar bear to an Indiana forest. What adaptations might the polar bear need to survive there? What might happen to the polar bear?

My Prediction	What Happens

3 **Critical Thinking** How are the adaptations of a tundra plant different from those of a rainforest plant?

____

____

4 **Test Prep** **During cold winters, some animals survive by**

A saving water.
B hibernating.
C shedding their fur.
D scratching at fleas.

How are organisms well-suited for the environments in which they live?

____

____

____

____

LOG ON e-Review Summaries and quizzes online at www.macmillanmh.com

Focus on Skills

Inquiry Skill: Form a Hypothesis

You have learned how adaptations such as camouflage help animals survive in their environments. Consider the skin of the salamander pictured on this page. It lives in Indiana's forests. Its colors and patterns give the salamander camouflage. Scientists study camouflage to learn more about adaptations. They use what they learn to **form a hypothesis** that they can test.

Materials

- tracing paper
- colored pencils or crayons
- scissors
- stopwatch

▶ Learn It

When you **form a hypothesis**, you make a statement about what you think is true. A good hypothesis is based on observations or collected data. It's important that your hypothesis makes sense and can be tested.

▶ Try It

Form a hypothesis about how camouflage affects the ability of a predator to find prey. Will it take more time or less time for the predator to find camouflaged prey? Write your hypothesis in the form, "If an animal is camouflaged, then the amount of time to find it . . ."

___

___

___

◀ **marbled salamander**

The Nature of Science Compare the results of an investigation with the prediction.

1. Choose a photograph of an animal found in Indiana. You may find your own or use one from pages 168–171. Trace its outline on two sheets of tracing paper. Carefully cut out both shapes. △ **Be careful!** Scissors are sharp.

2. Color one copy of your animal to blend in with some visible part of your classroom. Record its physical characteristics in the chart on this page. Do not color the other copy.

Physical Characteristics	
Color	
Shape	
Size	
Pattern	

▼ **fox squirrel**

Focus on Skills

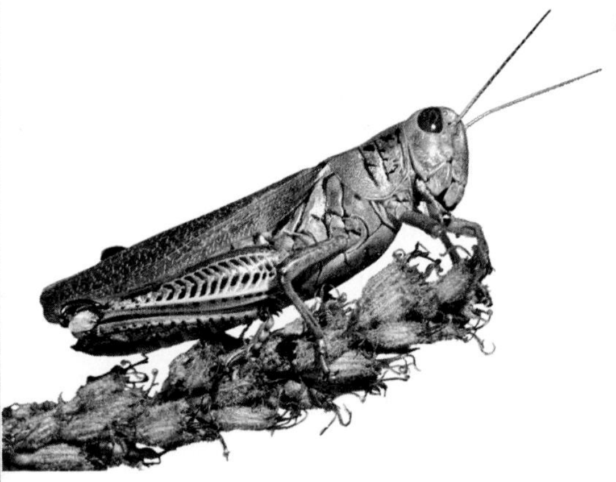

▲ **grasshopper**

3 Predict how long it will take someone to spot the camouflaged outline. Predict how long it will take that person to spot the outline that is not camouflaged. You will not be able to hide the outline.

____

____

____

____

4 Choose four classmates to act as "predators." They will wear blindfolds or leave the classroom while you place your animal outlines in the room. Place the outlines in plain view.

5 Begin with your camouflaged prey outline. Test one predator at a time. Begin timing when your classmate takes off his or her blindfold and returns to the room. Record in the table below how long it takes each predator to find the prey.

Time to Spot Camouflaged Prey	
Predator 1	
Predator 2	
Predator 3	
Predator 4	

6. Now test how long it takes for the predators to find the non-camouflaged prey outline. Repeat steps 4 and 5 using the outline that you did not color. Record how long it takes to find each outline in the table provided.

Time to Spot Non-Camouflaged Prey	
Predator 1	
Predator 2	
Predator 3	
Predator 4	

7. Look at your original hypothesis on page 168. Do your results support your original hypothesis? Explain.

____

____

____

timber rattlesnake ▶

Lesson 3

Changes in the Environment

Petrified Forest National Park, Arizona

4.3.1 Observe and describe how offspring are very much, but not exactly, like their parents or one another. Describe how these differences in physical characteristics among individuals in a population may be advantageous for survival and reproduction. 4.3.4 Describe a way that a given plant or animal might adapt to changes arising from human or non-human impact on the environment.

Look and Wonder

The Petrified Forest National Park is a dry environment for most of the year. During the summer there is a small amount of rainfall. What adaptations allow these saltbrush seedlings to live here? Why don't other plants grow here?

____

____

____

____

____

Essential Question

How are organisms adapted to changing environments?

____

____

____

____

Explore

How can a change to an environment affect living things?

Materials

- 18 green index cards
- 18 yellow index cards
- 18 red index cards

Make a Prediction

How can a period of little to no rain affect living things? Write a prediction.

____

____

Test Your Prediction

1. Write *hawk* on a yellow card, *lizard* on a green card, and *fox* on a red card. These are the predators. Write *prey* on the rest of the cards.

2. Each player takes one predator card. Mix ten prey cards of each color and stack them on the table. Put the other prey cards aside.

3. **Make a Model** Take turns drawing a prey card. Keep only the ones that match the color of your predator card. Return the others to the bottom of the pile. After every three turns, add a new prey card to the deck. This models the growth of the populations in the environment. Play for 12 rounds. Count the cards left in the pile.

4. A long period without rain kills half of the prey. Remove three prey cards of each color. Play again. After every six turns, add a prey card to the deck. Play for 12 rounds. Count again.

The Nature of Science Test predictions with multiple trials.

Draw Conclusions

5 **Use Numbers** How many cards were left at the end of each game?

____

6 **Infer** What did the model in step 3 represent? Did your results match your prediction?

____

____

Explore More

Would your results change if there were fewer predators? Make a prediction and test it.

____

Open Inquiry

How would the animals in an environment be affected by a change that harmed some prey, but favored other prey? Develop your own question about this topic. Then design a fair test to answer this question.

My question is: ______________________________

____

How I can test it: ______________________________

____

My results are: ______________________________

____

____

____

Read and Respond

How do environments change?

Environments are always changing. Some changes are very sudden. Some changes are very slow. Changes make it difficult for living things to survive.

Circle four causes of environmental changes in the second paragraph on this page.

Natural Events

Changes in environments can be caused by natural events. Volcanoes can fill a valley with ash. Hurricanes are large storms that can destroy coastal environments. Too much rain can cause mudslides, turning hills into rivers of mud. Too little rain can cause a drought (DROWT). During droughts, the soil can dry up.

It can take a long time for an environment to recover from such changes. Mount Saint Helens is a volcano in the state of Washington. In 1980, it erupted. Ash killed nearby plants. The environment needed many years to recover.

For more practice reading photos, see page 269.

Read a Photo

How did the environment change in the two photographs?

____

____

____

Natural Change in Environments

Mount Saint Helens in 1980

Mount Saint Helens in 1995

Living Things

Environments can be changed by living things, such as locusts. A locust is a kind of grasshopper. In small numbers, locusts pose little danger. But in some places, giant swarms of locusts can gather in search of food. A swarm can have 50 million locusts in it! The locusts eat any plants along their path. They can leave an entire environment without plants.

A swarm of pink locusts destroyed the plants on this Canary Islands beach.

Some living things can have a helpful effect on an environment. Alligators live in the water, but spend time near the shore. Here, their feet, tail, and snouts churn up the muddy water. These movements create holes. Slowly, these hole fills with water.

Alligator holes help many animals survive periods of drought.

These holes help alligators survive during droughts. The effect does not stop there. Birds and other animals move to the holes when their own environment gets too dry. There they find food, water, and shelter.

Quick Check

1. How might an alligator benefit from a drought?

____

____

2. How can living things change an environment?

____

How are living things adapted to changing environments?

Changes in the environment can occur naturally. They can also be caused by people. How are animals and plants adapted to environments that change constantly?

Quick Lab

Model how changing environments affect animals. Do the Quick Lab on page 286.

Natural Changes

Some prairie environments have frequent fires. Prairies are environments where grasses and wildflowers grow. Fires cause many changes in these environments. Fires create open spaces for smaller plants, trees, and shrubs. The ash that remains after a fire provides nutrients for new plants to grow.

In the last paragraph on this page, underline three ways prairie plants are adapted to fire.

Plants that live in prairies have deep roots. Deep roots help the plants grow back after being burned. Trees in prairies often have thick bark that is not easily burned. The seeds of many prairie plants are adapted to germinate, or sprout, after a fire.

Glue your Notebook FOLDABLES here. Use Foldable I on page 290.

Fire causes a natural change that can benefit living things in an environment.

Changes Caused by People

A species can adapt to changes caused by people. One example was studied in the 1950s by an English scientist named H.B.D. Kettlewell. Kettlewell studied a species of moth called the peppered moth. There are both light and dark forms of this moth in a population. Kettlewell found mostly dark peppered moths in areas with air pollution. Why?

Dark moths are camouflaged when they rest on dark tree bark. The areas with more air pollution had trees with darker bark. Kettlewell found that light moths could not blend in well on dark trees. The light moths were caught more often by birds.

In areas with dark, polluted trees, dark moths survived and reproduced more than light moths. Dark moths produced mostly dark offspring. As a result, polluted areas with dark trees had mostly dark moths.

▲ Light and dark peppered moths on polluted tree bark.

Quick Check

3. What would happen to the moth population if the pollution were cleaned?

____

____

____

Visual Summary

Complete the lesson summary in your own words.

Changes to the Environment ____________________

____

____

____

____

Adaptations to Natural Changes ____________________

____

____

____

____

Adapting to People ____________________

____

____

____

____

Make a FOLDABLES® Study Guide

Make a trifold book. Use it to summarize what you learned about adaptations.

Changes in an environment are caused by...
When environments change, living things...
Physical characteristics in a population...

Think, Talk, and Write

1 **Vocabulary** Too little rain in an environment can cause a

________________.

2 **Cause and Effect** In 1950, air pollution in England increased. How did this affect peppered moths?

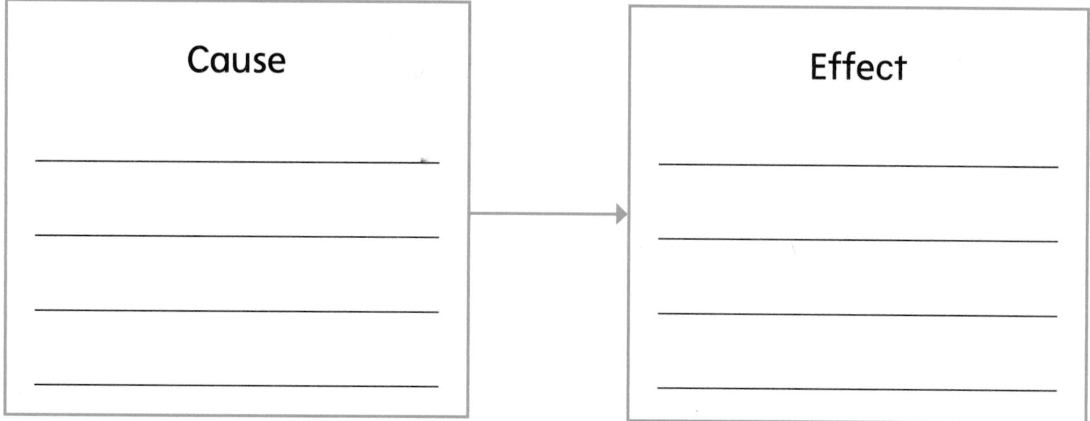

3 **Critical Thinking** A hurricane or a volcanic eruption can cause several changes in an environment. Describe a natural event and explain how it causes changes in the environment.

____

____

4 **Test Prep** **Which of these is MOST LIKELY a natural event that will change an environment?**

A acid rain
B farming
C hurricane
D recycling

How are organisms adapted to changing environments?

____

____

____

____

e-Review Summaries and quizzes online at www.macmillanmh.com

Mail Call

Scientists at the American Museum of Natural History collect stories from people around the world. The stories help scientists learn about local environments.

Dear Museum Scientists,

My name is Clara. I live in California, where the hills are covered with evergreen shrubs. The land is very dry, and there are not a lot of trees. This environment is called a chaparral.

In August, a lightning storm started a wildfire in the chaparral. After the fire, I walked through the area. All I saw were gray ashes.

I walked through the chaparral again in April. It has changed so much! There are fields of wildflowers blooming everywhere. I found a hillside monkey flower and scarlet larkspur. My guidebook told me that these flowers have seeds that may not grow for several years. They need fire, heat, or smoke to sprout and grow.

The wildflowers have attracted insects like honeybees. I also saw a cactus wren and jackrabbits. My guidebook explained that low bushes provide shelter for jackrabbits and nesting cactus wrens. I can't wait to go back to see how the chaparral will change even more!

Your friend,

Clara

a chaparral environment

Write About It

Main Idea and Details Read the letter again. What are the characteristics of plants and animals in the chaparral? Describe how the plants and animals are adapted to this environment.

Main Idea and Details

- A main idea tells what the article is about.
- Details, such as facts and examples, support the main idea.

Connect to AMERICAN MUSEUM OF NATURAL HISTORY at www.macmillanmh.com

LOG ON e-Journal Research and Write about it online at www.macmillanmh.com

4.3.2 Observe, compare, and record the physical characteristics of living plants or animals from widely different environments, and describe how each is adapted to its environment.

Visual Summary

Summarize each lesson in your own words.

Lesson 1 ______________________________

____

____

____

Lesson 2 ______________________________

____

____

____

Lesson 3 ______________________________

____

____

____

Make a FOLDABLES® Study Guide

Glue your lesson study guides to a large sheet of paper as shown. Use your study guide to review what you have learned in this unit.

Vocabulary

DOK 1

Fill in each blank with the best term from the list.

adaptation, p. 158
inherited, p. 144
physical characteristic, p. 145
camouflage, p. 162
mimicry, p. 163
population, p. 146
drought, p. 176
offspring, p. 144
stimuli, p. 160
hibernate, p. 159

1. Things in the environment that cause a living thing to respond are ______________.

2. All the members of a species that live in an area form a(n) ______________.

3. An animal that blends in with its surroundings uses ______________.

4. Fur color is a(n) ______________.

5. When a species has physical characteristics that resemble those of a different species, it uses ______________.

6. A ______________ occurs when an environment experiences very little rainfall.

7. Characteristics that are passed from parent to offspring are ______________.

8. To survive cold winters, some animals ______________.

9. A parent's young are its ______________.

10. A physical characteristic or behavior that helps a living thing survive in its environment is a(n) ______________.

LOG ON e-Glossary Words and definitions online at www.macmillanmh.com

UNIT 4 Review

Skills and Concepts

DOK 2–3

Answer each of the following.

11. **Fact and Opinion** *A desert environment is a bad place for living things to live.* Is this a fact or an opinion? Explain.

12. **Critical Thinking** How do fires help environments?

13. **Form a Hypothesis** Species can die out when their environments change. Choose an animal to research. Form a hypothesis about what might happen to the animal if the environment were to change.

14. **Critical Thinking** How can a living thing's color and shape protect it from predators?.

15. **Critical Thinking** Suppose scientists discovered a new species of plant living in a hot desert. What adaptations might the plant have?

16. What adaptation helps this snow leopard survive in its environment?

A mimicry
B camouflage
C accommodation
D hibernation

17. **Infer** At the zoo, you see an animal that has short legs, thick fur, and small ears. What type of environment do you think this animal is from?

____

____

____

18. Listed below are events that have changed environments. Which of these is not a natural event?

A tornado destroying a prairie
B boat spilling oil into the ocean
C hurricane causing a flood
D lightning strike causing a forest fire

19. **Critical Thinking** Why might a plant mimic poisonous plants?

____

____

The Big Idea

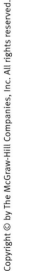

20. What features help living things survive?

____

____

____

____

Test Prep

Circle the best answer for each question.

1. If you visit the arctic tundra, what will you MOST LIKELY observe about the plants that live there?

A leaves are large
B stems are short
C stems are long
D flowers are large

4.3.2 (DOK 2)

2. Which of the following physical characteristics helps the bird obtain food?

A wings
B feathers
C claws
D beak

4.3.2 (DOK 1)

3. A tree's roots grow toward the pipes of a house. The stimulus is MOST LIKELY

A minerals.
B sunlight.
C water.
D gravity.

4.3.3, 4.3.4 (DOK 2)

4. How do many birds survive cold winter temperatures?

A by hibernating
B by migrating
C by digging holes
D by growing fur

4.3.4 (DOK 1)

5. The rose shown below has prickly structures on its stem. How do these structures MOST LIKELY help it to survive?

A They help it obtain food.
B They help it absorb water.
C They help it obtain nutrients.
D They help it stay protected.

4.3.2 (DOK 1)

6. Name ONE reason that many offspring look like their parents. Name ONE reason that many offspring do not look exactly like their parents.
4.3.1 (DOK 3)

____

____

____

____

7. The table below describes some physical characteristics of two different wolf species. Use the table to answer the following questions.

Characteristics	Species 1	Species 2
Fur Color	white	grey
Ear Shape	small, rounded	large, pointed
Leg Length	short	long
Average Weight	100 lbs (45 kg)	79 lbs (36 kg)

Which species is MOST LIKELY found in a cold environment?
4.3.2 (DOK 2)

____

Give TWO reasons for your answer above.
4.3.2 (DOK 3)

____

____

____

____

Nature Photographer

Picture yourself deep in a forest or below the ocean's surface. There is no one else around. You are ready to capture a special moment on film.

To be a nature photographer, you need to take classes in art and photography. You should also enjoy being outdoors.

A nature photographer needs patience. A single shot might take days or even weeks to get. You may face harsh conditions, like swarms of insects or cold rain. But when you capture a perfect photo, it is all worthwhile!

▲ A nature photographer must know about living things and their environments.

Write About It

If you were a nature photographer, in what types of environments would you work? Write a description of the environments you would photograph. What type of adaptations would you expect to see there?

____

____

____

____

____

____

LOG ON e-Careers at www.macmillanmh.com

Science, Engineering and Technology

Academic Standards for Science

Core Standard Design a moving system and measure its motion.

A Grand Prix motorcycle racer can travel at speeds of nearly 350 km/hr (217 mph).

2010 Moto GP at Indianapolis Motor Speedway

UNIT 5

Motion, Forces, and the Design Process

What makes objects move?

____

____

____

____

____

____

Vocabulary

speed how fast an object moves over a certain distance

force a push or a pull

gravity a pulling force between two objects

thrust the force that moves an object forward

lift the force that holds an object in the air

design process a series of steps used to find solutions to problems

As you read the unit, complete the concept map about motion, forces, and the design process.

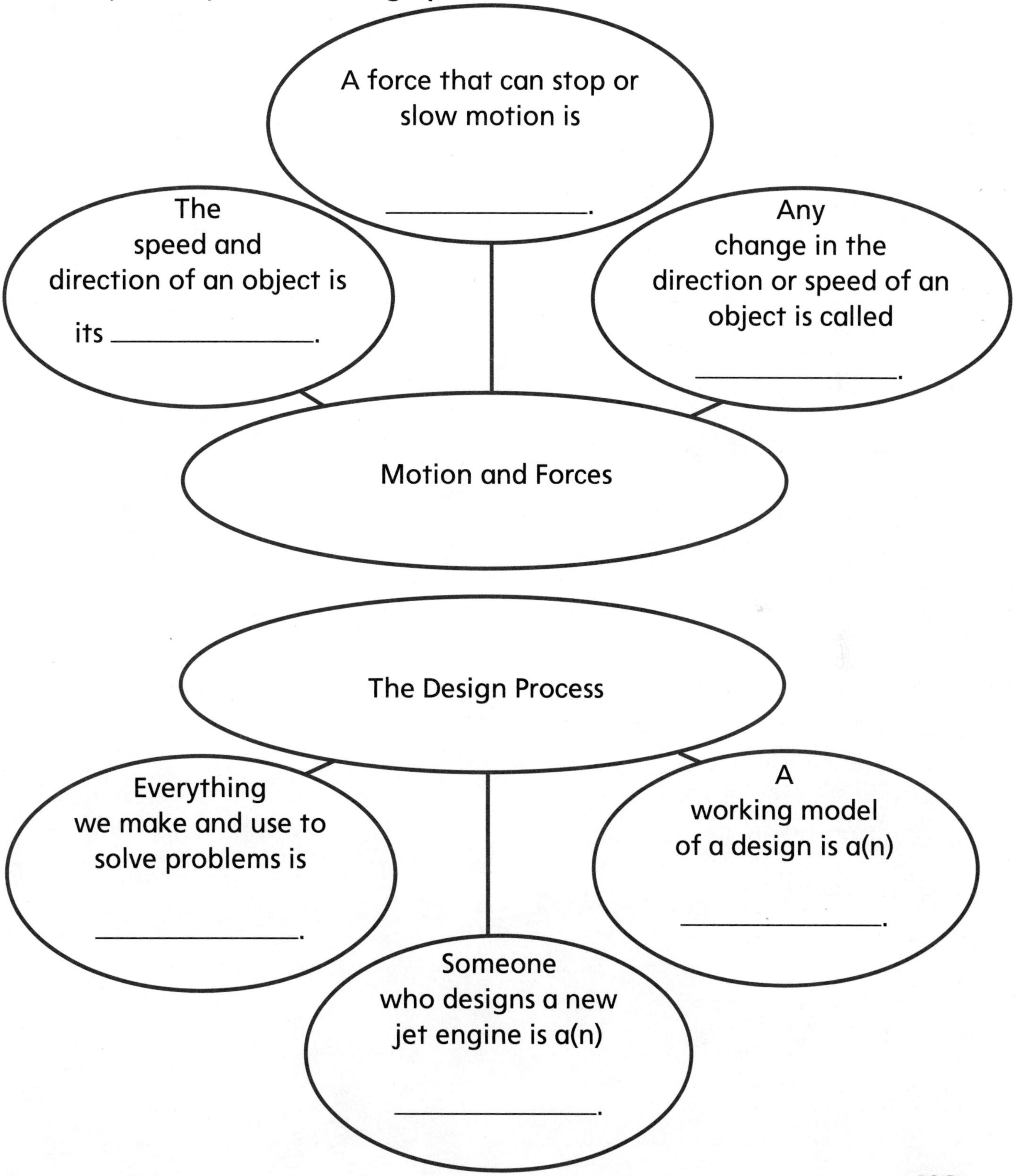

A force that can stop or slow motion is
________________.

The speed and direction of an object is its ________________.

Any change in the direction or speed of an object is called
________________.

Motion and Forces

The Design Process

Everything we make and use to solve problems is
________________.

A working model of a design is a(n)
________________.

Someone who designs a new jet engine is a(n)
________________.

Lesson 1

Changing Motion

the 94th Indianapolis 500, May 30, 2010

Look and Wonder

Have you ever watched race cars speed around a track? The cars are loud and fast! How can you tell how fast a car is moving? What affects the car's speed?

Essential Question How can you compare moving objects?

4.4.2 Make appropriate measurements to compare the speeds of objects in terms of distance traveled in a given amount of time or time required to travel a given distance.
4.4.3 Investigate how changes in speed or direction are caused by forces; the greater the force exerted on an object, the greater the change.

Explore

How fast does it move?

Make a Prediction

In this investigation, you will roll a marble down a sloping path. How will the steepness of the slope affect the marble's motion? Write a prediction.

___

___

Materials

- 4 books
- cardboard tube
- tape
- marble
- stopwatch

Test Your Prediction

1. **Make a Model** Stack three books on top of each other. Place one end of a cardboard tube on top of the stack. Let the other end of the tube touch a fourth book, which is on the table. Tape the tube in place on the outside.

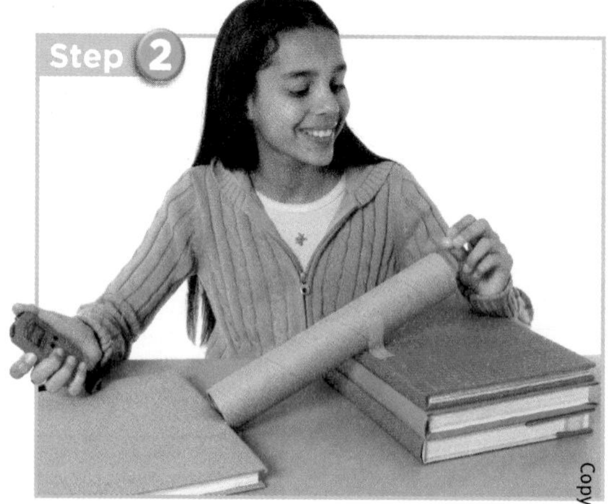

2. Roll a marble down the tube. Start the stopwatch at the same moment that the marble begins to roll. When you hear the marble hit the book, record the time. Repeat this step three times.

	Time 1	Time 2	Time 3	Average Time
Three Books				
Two Books				
One Book				

3. **Use Variables** Repeat step 2 with two books stacked. Then repeat with only one book. Find the average time for each test. To do this, add up the times and divide by the number of trials.

The Nature of Science Test predictions with multiple trials.

Glue your Notebook FOLDABLES® here. Use Foldable 3 on page 292.

Draw Conclusions

4 **Interpret Data** On a separate piece of paper, make a bar graph comparing the average time for three books, two books, and one book. In which setup was the motion fastest?

____

5 Did your results match your prediction? Explain.

____

____

6 **Infer** Why was it important to repeat each test three times?

____

____

Explore More

Would your results change if you used a longer tube? What if you had a higher stack of books? Make a prediction. Try it! Show your results on a separate piece of paper.

Open Inquiry

Think of your own question about the motion of objects. Make a plan and carry out a fair test to answer your question.

My question is: ____

____

How I can test it: ____

____

My results are: ____

____

Read and Respond

What is motion?

When an object is in motion, its location is constantly changing. Think of a race car on a track. It begins and ends a race at the pole position. During the race, the car's location changes as it moves around the track.

At the Indy 500, drivers try to move 500 miles in the shortest amount of time. 500 miles is the distance of the race. **Distance** is how far apart two points or places are. For example, the distance between Evansville, Indiana and Fort Wayne, Indiana is about 400 km (250 mi).

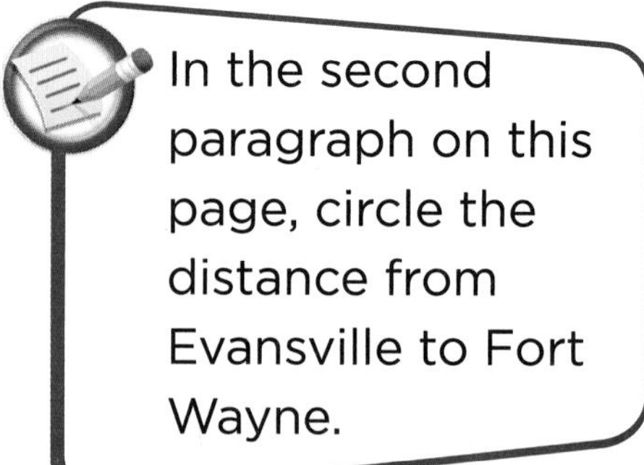

In the second paragraph on this page, circle the distance from Evansville to Fort Wayne.

Glue your Notebook FOLDABLES here. Use Foldable 3 on page 292.

Quick Check

1. A race car driver completes the Indy 500. What distance has the driver traveled?

____

2. A lap around the oval track at Indianapolis Motor Speedway is 2.5 miles. How many laps does an Indy car driver complete during the Indy 500?

____

▼ A trip from Evansville to Fort Wayne is about half the distance of an Indy 500 race.

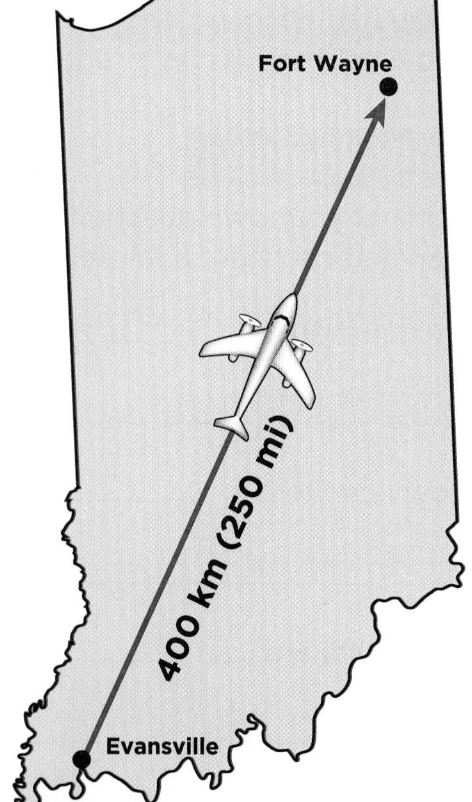

A horse is a fast runner, but a cheetah is faster! What are their speeds?

Speed

All moving objects have speed. **Speed** is how fast an object moves over a certain distance. To know an object's speed, you must know the distance the object moved. You must also know how long it took to go that distance. The speed is the distance traveled divided by the time spent moving.

Suppose that, in one hour, you pedal your bike 20 km (12 mi). Your speed is 20 km/h (12 mph).

If this train's speed is 300 km/h, its velocity is 300 km/h to the east.

Velocity

People sometimes confuse velocity (vuh•LAH•suh•tee) with speed. Speed tells you how fast an object is moving. **Velocity** describes both the speed and the direction of motion. A bicycle rider's speed may be 50 km/h (31 mph). If the rider goes 50 km/h *to the west,* however, that is rider's velocity.

Quick Check

3. Estimate the speed of a cheetah, horse, and elephant.

___

___

___

What are forces?

Objects do not move by themselves. You have to apply a force (FORS) to make them start moving. A **force** is a push or a pull. You use forces to move things all the time. When you pull on a door handle or push a wagon, you apply a force to make something move.

Forces can be large or small. The force a crane uses to lift a truck is huge. The force your hand uses to lift a feather is tiny. It takes more force to move heavy objects than light objects. Forces also affect an object's speed. The more force you use, the faster an object will move.

Friction

An ice hockey player glides on the ice. He slows down and stops. How does this happen? A force called friction (FRIK•shun) is acting on him. **Friction** is a force that occurs when one object rubs against another. It pushes against moving objects and causes them to slow down.

Different surfaces produce different amounts of friction. Rough surfaces, such as sandpaper, usually produce a lot of friction. Smooth surfaces, such as ice, produce less friction. Why do you need to put oil on the moving parts of a bicycle? The oil reduces friction. It helps the parts work smoothly together.

Quick Check

4. How can friction help keep you safe?

____

____

◀ The sharp, metal blades of a hockey player's skates reduce friction on the ice.

Gravity

You can not see gravity (GRA•vuh•tee), but it is what pulls a roller coaster down a slope. **Gravity** is a pulling force between two objects. Without gravity, your roller coaster car would float away into space!

Gravity pulls objects together. The pull of gravity depends on two things. One is the amount of matter, or material, in the objects. The other is the distance between the objects. Earth contains a lot of matter. Its gravity pulls strongly on objects near its surface.

How much gravity does it take to keep you on Earth? The answer is your weight (WAYT). An object's weight is a measure of the pull of gravity on it. When you weigh yourself, you measure the force of gravity in pounds. Scientists measure forces in SI units called newtons (N).

Quick Lab

To learn more about friction and motion, do the Quick Lab on page 287.

Quick Check

5. The Sun is much larger than Earth. Why don't we feel the pull of the Sun's gravity?

____

____

Read a Diagram

At which spot is friction most likely at work? Gravity?

____

____

See page 270 for more practice reading diagrams.

Forces at Work

1

2

WELCOME

AMUSEMENT

ROCKET RACER

What is acceleration?

As race car drivers race around a track, they change speeds. They speed up when they move in a straight line. They slow down when they turn. These are examples of acceleration (ik•sel•uh•RAY•shuhn). **Acceleration** is any change in the speed or direction of a moving object.

The size of a force affects an object's acceleration. A greater force causes more acceleration. The weight of the object matters too. If you apply the same force to an object with more weight, that object accelerates more slowly. The diagram below shows this.

In the second paragraph, underline two things that affect the acceleration of an object.

See page 271 for more practice reading diagrams.

Read a Diagram

In which drawing is the wagon accelerating fastest? Slowest?

____

____

LOG ON *Science in Motion* Watch accelerating objects at www.macmillanmh.com

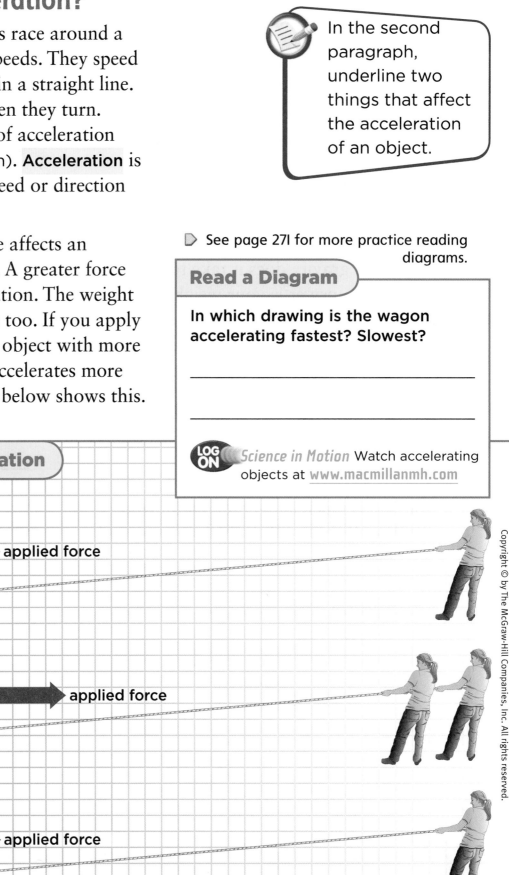

Force and Acceleration

If all the racers apply equal forces, who will win? The racer that weighs least will win. She accelerates fastest.

Forces Add Up

The diagram on page 202 shows the acceleration of a wagon. When one person pulls the wagon, the wagon accelerates. When two people pull the wagon, the wagon accelerates twice as much.

What happens in the third drawing? As before, one person pulls the wagon. This time, however, the wagon weighs twice as much. The wagon accelerates half as fast as in the first picture.

In the first paragraph, underline what happens when two people pull the wagon. In the second paragraph, circle what happens when the wagon weighs twice as much.

Quick Check

6. It takes 5 N to lift an empty backpack. It takes 15 N to lift a textbook. How much force will it take to lift both objects?

____

Visual Summary

Complete the lesson summary in your own words.

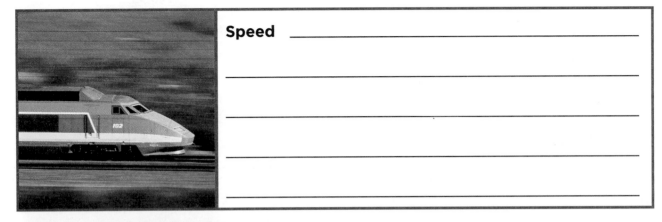

Speed ____________________

____

____

____

____

Forces ____________________

____

____

____

____

Acceleration ____________________

____

____

____

____

Make a FOLDABLES® Study Guide

Make a three-tab book. Use it to summarize what you learned about motion, speed, and forces.

Think, Talk, and Write

1. **Vocabulary** An object has motion if there is a change in

   its ____________.

2. **Summarize** List three words that describe how objects can move. How are the words different from one another?

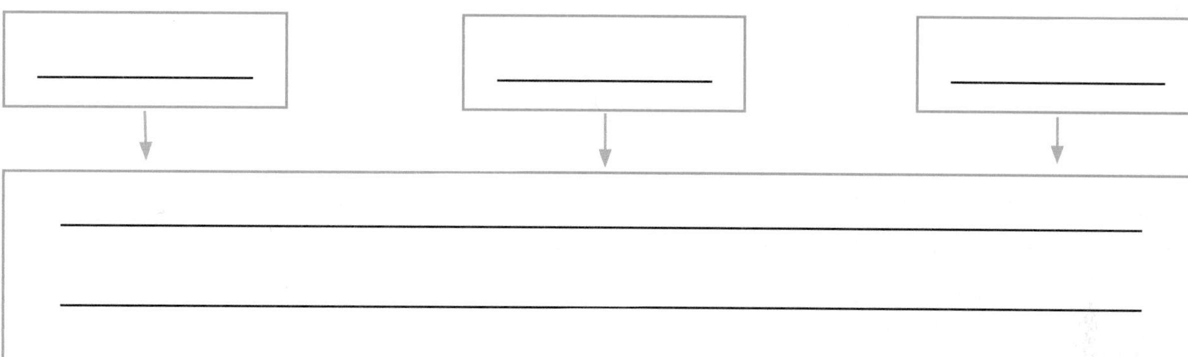

3. **Critical Thinking** Bowling balls and soccer balls are about the same size. Why is a bowling ball harder to throw?

   ____

   ____

4. **Test Prep** **What happens as you apply your bicycle brakes?**

   A You accelerate.
   B You speed up.
   C You increase gravity.
   D You decrease friction.

How can you compare moving objects?

____

____

____

____

Focus on Skills

Inquiry Skill: Use Numbers

You know that gravity affects objects on Earth and elsewhere. Scientists can measure the motion of an object to learn how gravity affects its acceleration. To interpret the data, you may need to do some math or make a graph. You **use numbers** to measure, record, and interpret data.

▶ Learn It

When you **use numbers**, you order, count, add, subtract, multiply, or divide them. This is an important skill for a scientist to have. It is easier to use numbers if you organize them in a table, chart, or graph. That way, you can interpret your results more easily.

▶ Try It

When an object rolls downhill, gravity makes it accelerate. **Use numbers** to learn how quickly gravity makes objects accelerate.

Materials **long table, ruler, masking tape, four books, soup can, stopwatch, graph paper**

1. Using the ruler and tape, divide the table into sections. Make each section 25 centimeters in length.
2. Place two books under each leg at one end of the table.
3. Make a data table like the one shown. Add enough rows for each line of tape in step 1. The number of rows on your data table may be different from the one shown.

Glue your Notebook FOLDABLES here. Use Foldable I on page 290.

Distance	First Test	Second Test
	Time (in seconds)	Time (in seconds)
Start	0	0
Line 1		
Line 2		
Line 3		
Line 4		
Line 5		

The Nature of Science Test predictions with multiple trials.

Focus on Skills

4. Place the soup can on its side at the raised end of the table. Start the stopwatch as you release the can. As the can rolls past each line of tape, record the time. Use the column labeled *First Test*. Have your partner catch the can before it rolls off the table!

5. Repeat step 4. Record the times under *Second Test*.

Apply It

Now **use numbers** to make a line graph on graph paper.

1. First, label the bottom line *Time (seconds)* on the graph below.

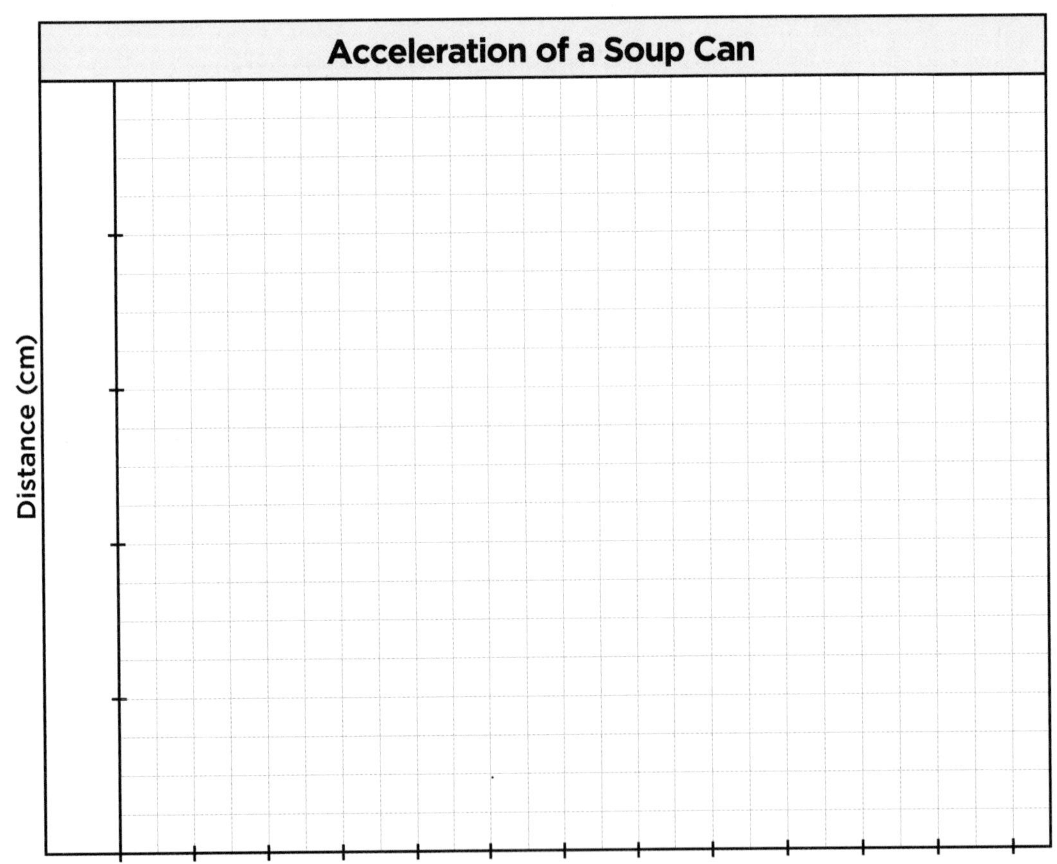

4.4.2 Make appropriate measurements to compare the speeds of objects in terms of distance traveled in a given amount of time or time required to travel a given distance.

2. Next, mark off equal spaces along the left side in units of 25 cm (0, 25, 50, and so on). End this scale with the distance of the last line of tape on the table. Mark off the bottom in units of seconds.

3. Using the data from your first test, write ordered pairs in the form (25, 1) and so on. For each ordered pair, place a point on the graph. You may need to estimate for fractions of seconds. Connect the points. Do the same for your second test, but use a different color for the points and lines.

4. What does each ordered pair tell you? Where is the can moving slowest? Fastest? Did the can accelerate? How could you tell?

____

____

____

____

5. How would adding a book affect the acceleration of the cans? How would removing a book affect acceleration? How could you test this?

____

____

____

____

Lesson 2

Forces and Transportation

Madison, Indiana, along the Ohio River

4.4.1 Investigate transportation systems and devices that operate on or in land, water, air and space and recognize the forces (lift, drag, friction, thrust and gravity) that affect their motion.

Look and Wonder

Barges are constantly moving up and down the Ohio River. What forces cause boats to move? What forces slow the movement of boats?

Essential Question How do we move people and things?

Explore

How can you make a balloon move faster?

Purpose

Investigate forces that affect motion.

Materials

- string 
- plastic drinking straw
- tape 
- 2 chairs
- 3 balloons of different sizes and shapes

- binder clip 
- measuring tape 
- stopwatch 

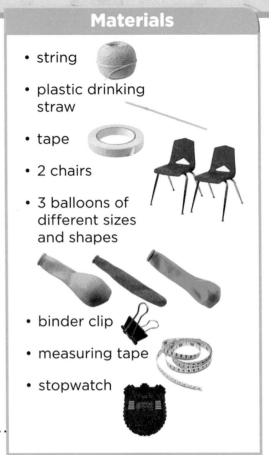

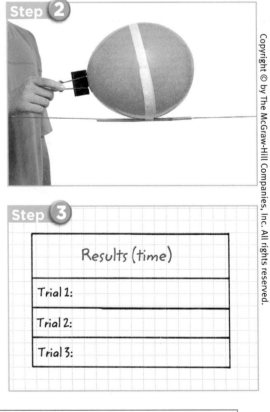

Procedure

1. Run a 10 m length of string through a drinking straw. Tape each end of the string to one of the chairs. Inflate a balloon, and pinch it shut with a binder clip to keep the air in. Use the measuring tape to find the circumference of the balloon. Tape the balloon to the straw. Record the circumference and shape of the balloon on the line below.

   Trial 1 ____________________________________

Glue your Notebook FOLDABLES here. Use Foldable I on page 290.

2. **Experiment** Move the balloon to one end of the string. Have a partner ready with the stopwatch. Your partner should begin timing as soon as you release the balloon. Your partner should stop the timer as soon as the balloon reaches the other end of the string.

Step 2

3. Make a data chart like the one shown on this page. Record the time in your data chart.

Step 3

Results (time)
Trial 1:
Trial 2:
Trial 3:

4. **Use Variables** Repeat steps 1 and 2 with two different balloons. The balloons should be different sizes or shapes.

   Trial 2: ____________________________________

   Trial 3: ____________________________________

The Nature of Science Test predictions with multiple trials.
The Design Process Evaluate and test the design using measurement.

Draw Conclusions

5 **Interpret Data** How do you think the shape or size of the balloons affected how fast they moved? Explain.

____

____

6 **Use Numbers** Calculate the speed of each balloon. Show the steps you used to do each calculation.

_______________________ [ ]

_______________________ [ ]

_______________________ [ ]

Experiment How would another type of string or wire affect the speed of a balloon? How could you find out? Make a plan and try it.

____

____

Open Inquiry

Design your own experiment to investigate the motion of a balloon.

My question is: ____

____

How I can test it: ____

____

My results are: ____

____

Read and Respond

How do rockets fly into space?

It takes a lot of force to send a rocket into space. Rockets use a special force called thrust. **Thrust** is the force that moves an object forward. It can be a pushing or a pulling force. The rocket's engine provides the thrust to push the rocket.

The rocket's thrust must be stronger than gravity for the rocket to fly into space. However, gravity is not the only force working against the rocket's motion. Drag also works against it. **Drag** works against the motion of an object moving through a liquid or a gas. Like thrust, drag is also a force.

In the first paragraph on this page, circle the force that lifts up a rocket. In the second paragraph, underline two forces that slow down a rocket.

thrust

The thrust from the rocket engine pushes the rocket forward.

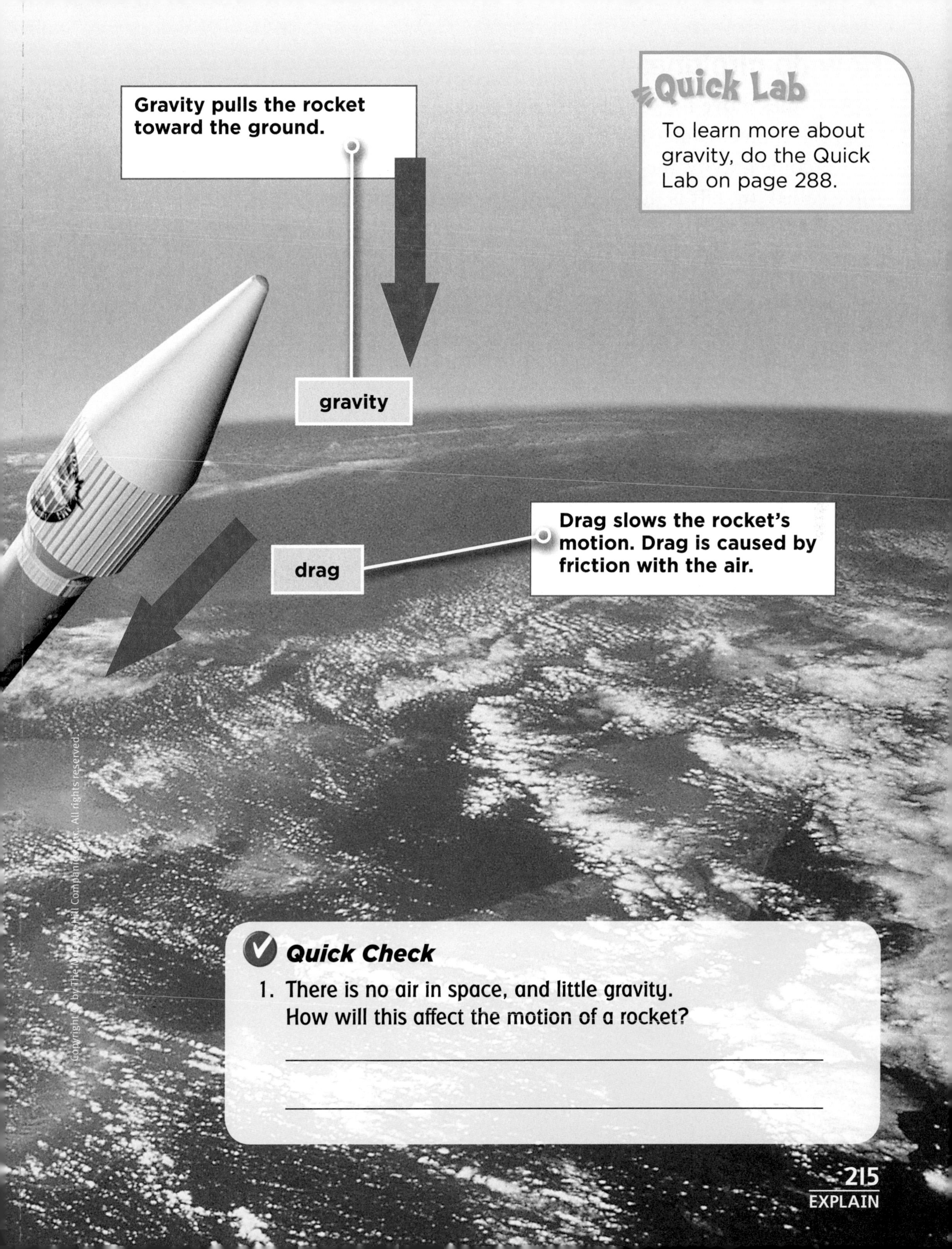

Gravity pulls the rocket toward the ground.

gravity

drag

Drag slows the rocket's motion. Drag is caused by friction with the air.

Quick Lab

To learn more about gravity, do the Quick Lab on page 288.

Quick Check

1. There is no air in space, and little gravity. How will this affect the motion of a rocket?

___

___

How do airplanes fly?

Airplanes move forward because of thrust from the engine. Unlike a rocket that uses thrust to overcome gravity, the airplane uses a different force called lift. **Lift** is the force holds an object in the air. Lift works against gravity. It raises the airplane into the air and keeps it from falling.

There are two things needed for an airplane to have lift. First, the plane must be moving forward through the air. In other words, the plane must have thrust. Second, the moving air must push against the bottom of the wing. The shape of the plane's wings helps create lift.

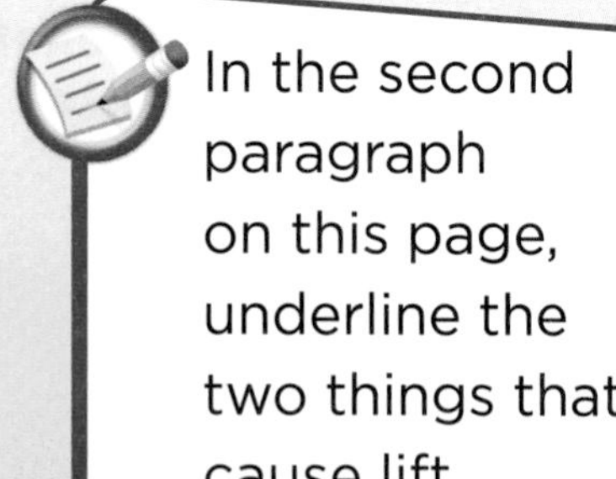

In the second paragraph on this page, underline the two things that cause lift.

What forces slow an airplane? Gravity slows the takeoff of the plane. Drag also affects the plane's motion. Broad, flat surfaces of the plane hit the air and slow the plane's motion.

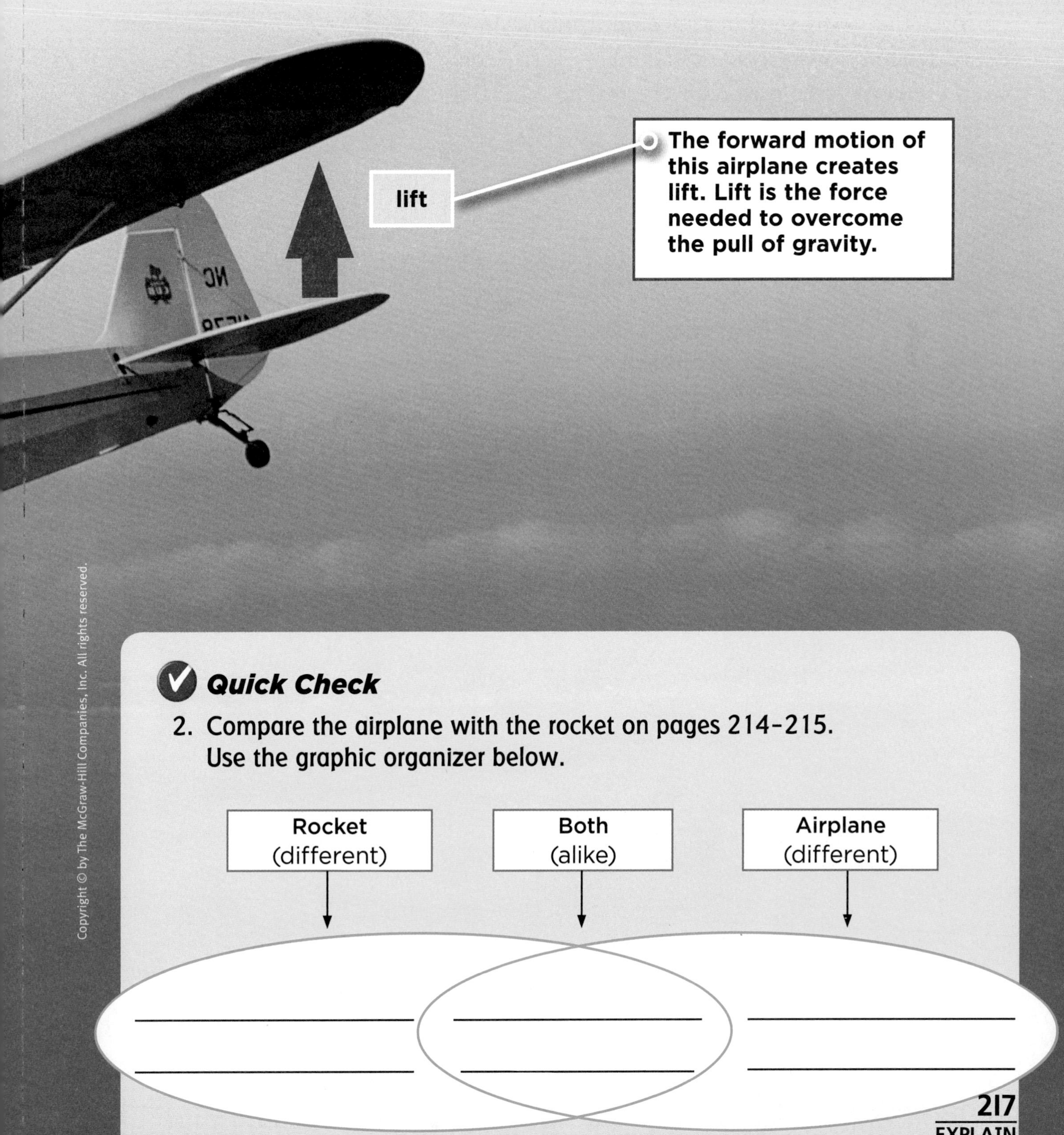

lift
The forward motion of this airplane creates lift. Lift is the force needed to overcome the pull of gravity.

Quick Check

2. Compare the airplane with the rocket on pages 214–215. Use the graphic organizer below.

Rocket (different)	Both (alike)	Airplane (different)
______________	______________	______________
______________	______________	______________

How do we use friction to stop and go?

What happens when you stop pedaling a bicycle? You will coast to a stop. What makes you stop? The answer is friction. You read in Lesson 1 that friction is a force that works against motion. Friction is caused when two objects are in contact with each other. On your bike, these objects are the wheel, the axle and the tire, and the surface.

In the first paragraph on this page, circle the name of a force that stops your bike.

a view from Falls of the Ohio State Park, Indiana

Although friction works against motion, it is also needed for motion. Without friction the train would never be able to move. The wheels would spin on the track. The friction between the wheels and the rails moves the train. This type of friction is called traction (TRAK•shun).

Quick Check

3. Identify the main idea and details about friction and motion. Use the graphic organizer below.

▼ Friction helps stop the train. It also helps the train move.

How do boats float?

Some boats are so large that they are like floating cities. An aircraft carrier is large enough for airplanes to take off and land on the deck. Yet these boats float because a force is pushing them up. This force is called buoyancy (BOY•un•see). **Buoyancy** is the upward force that a liquid or gas has on an object.

Gravity is the force that works against buoyancy. If the force of gravity is greater that the buoyancy force, the object will sink. If the buoyancy force equals or exceeds the force of gravity, then the object will float.

Draw an arrow to show the direction of the force of gravity on the boat.

The Force of Buoyancy

See page 272 for more practice reading photos.

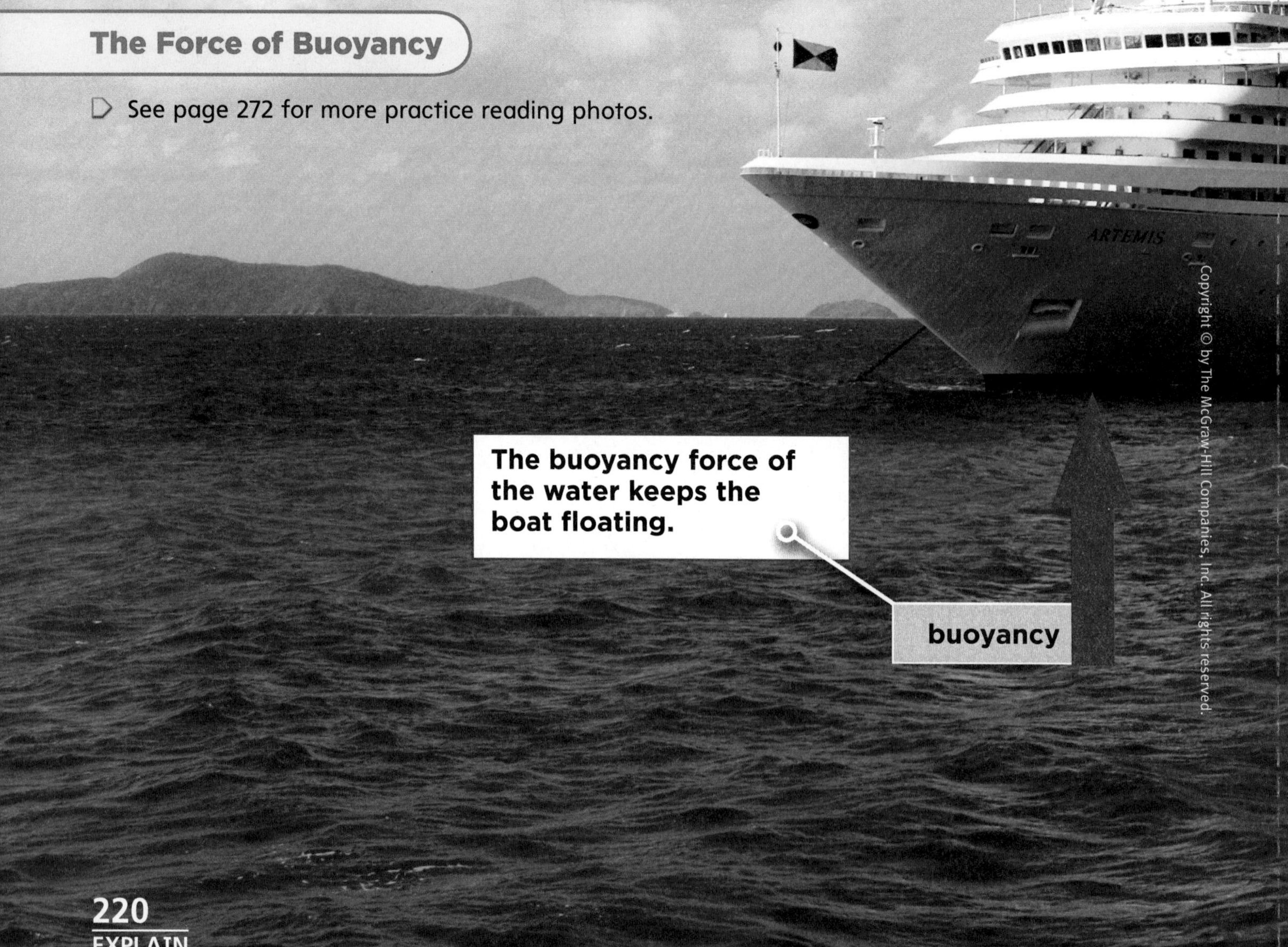

The buoyancy force of the water keeps the boat floating.

An empty steel boat has lots of air space. As cargo is added, the air space decreases and the weight of the boat increases. The boat sits lower in the water. Should too much cargo be loaded into the boat, the force of gravity will become greater than the buoyancy force. Then the boat will sink.

Read a Photo

How does the buoyancy of a boat compare to the lift of a plane?

____

____

How do planes, boats, and cars control their motion?

The same forces used to make a vehicle move also change the speed and direction of a vehicle. To increase the lift of an airplane, a pilot increases the thrust. The pilot also adjusts the flaps on the wing. The airplane rises. Lowering the thrust can cause the airplane to lose altitude, or height.

Draw arrows to show thrust and drag on the pictures of the boat and car. Label the arrows.

A boat's propeller provides thrust to move it forward. A part of the boat called the rudder steers the boat. It does this by changing the direction of the thrust. Suppose the captain steers the boat to the right. The rudder deflects the propeller's thrust to the right. This pushes the back of the boat left and points the front of the boat to the right.

When the driver of a car turns the steering wheel to the left, the wheels point to the left. Traction with the road turns the car in that direction. With all vehicles, the forces that cause motion also control it.

Quick Check

4. Name a force that acts on the boat but not on the car.

____

Visual Summary

Complete the lesson summary in your own words.

Rockets and Forces ______________________________

____

____

____

____

Airplanes and Forces ______________________________

____

____

____

____

Boats and Forces ______________________________

____

____

____

____

Make a FOLDABLES® Study Guide

Make a layered-look book. Use it to summarize what you learned about transportation and forces.

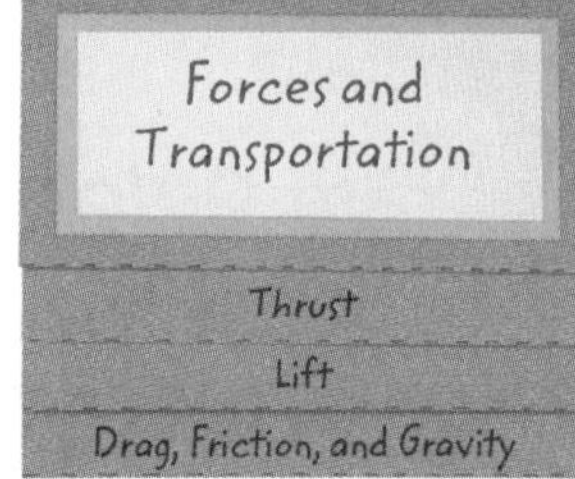

Think, Talk, and Write

1. **Vocabulary** Which force helps a train stop and go?

____

2. **Compare and Contrast** Compare and contrast friction and drag. Use the graphic organizer below.

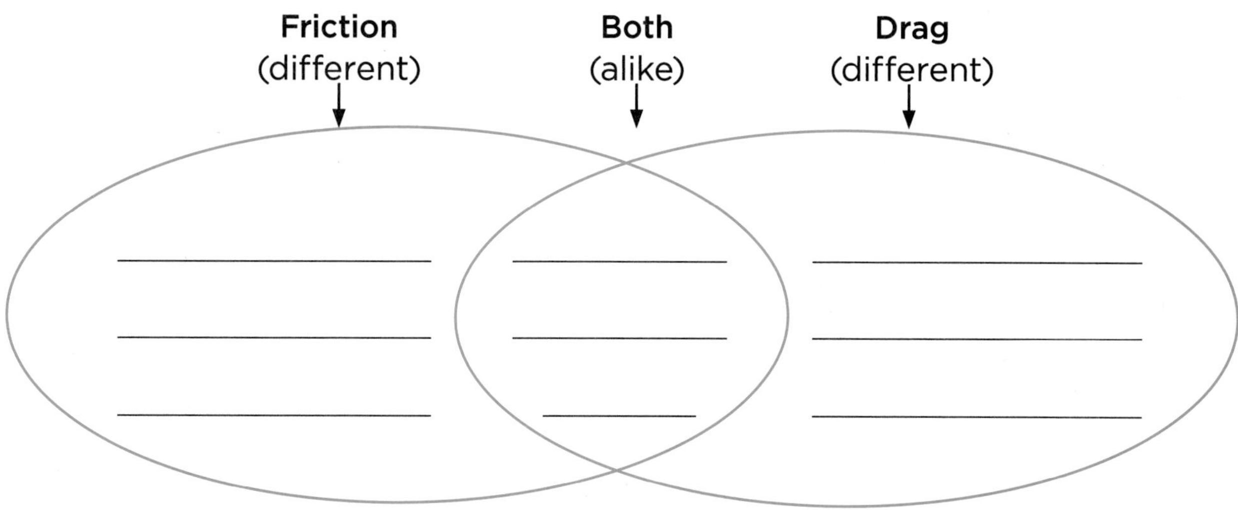

3. **Critical Thinking** Name two places on a train where there is friction.

____

____

4. **Test Prep** **What slows down the movement of a plane?**

A thrust
B drag
C buoyancy
D lift

Essential Question How do we move people and things?

____

____

____

____

LOG ON e-Review Summaries and quizzes online at www.macmillanmh.com

Wheels in Motion

For thousands of years, people have been using the wheel to move things around. You might think that wheels help us move things by reducing friction. Did you know that without friction, wheels would not work?

You use wheels when you ride a bike. The pedals are attached to the rear wheel. When you push the pedals, the wheels turn. Without friction, the wheels would spin but you wouldn't move.

Explanatory Writing

Good explanatory writing

- describes how to complete a task or how something works;
- gives clear details that are easy to follow.

Write About It

Explanatory Writing Research how the brakes on a bike work. Write a description that explains how friction helps the bike stop moving.

Research and write about it online at www.macmillanmh.com

Getting Ideas

First find out how bicycle brakes work. Then fill out the chart below. Write the steps in the process.

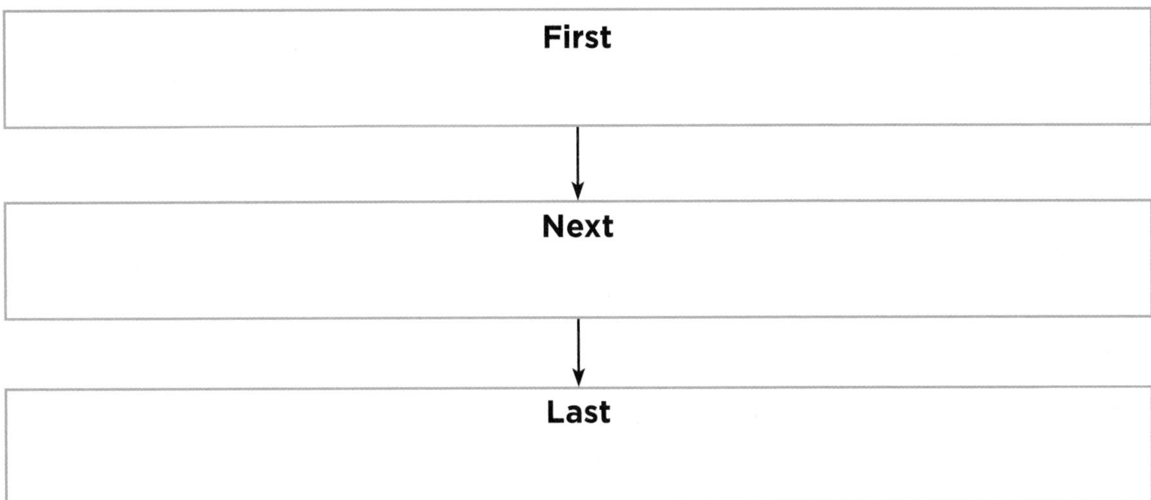

Drafting

Begin your explanation. Write a topic sentence. Tell what your explanation is about.

____

____

____

Glue your Notebook FOLDABLES here. Use Foldable I on page 290.

Now write your explanation. Use a separate piece of paper. Start with the sentence you wrote above. Write easy-to-follow details to tell how the brakes on a bicycle work.

Now revise and proofread your writing. Ask yourself:

- Did I describe how the brakes on a bicycle work?
- Did I give clear, easy-to-follow details?
- Did I correct all mistakes?

4.4.1 Investigate transportation systems and devices that operate on or in land, water, air and space and recognize the forces (lift, drag, friction, thrust and gravity) that affect their motion.

Graphing a Rocket's Acceleration

3, 2, 1 . . . Blast Off! The rocket engines fire, and the rocket moves away from the ground. How does the rocket's speed change as it accelerates? One way to show acceleration is to make a graph. Use the data in the table.

Make a Line Graph

- Label the bottom of the graph *Time (seconds)*.
- Label the left side of the graph *Distance (meters)*.
- Plot the coordinates on the graph and connect the dots.

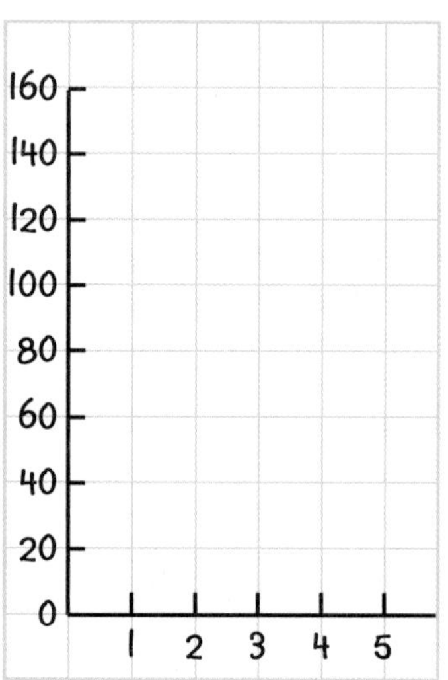

Time (seconds)	Distance (meters)
0	0
1	20
2	40
3	60
4	100
5	160

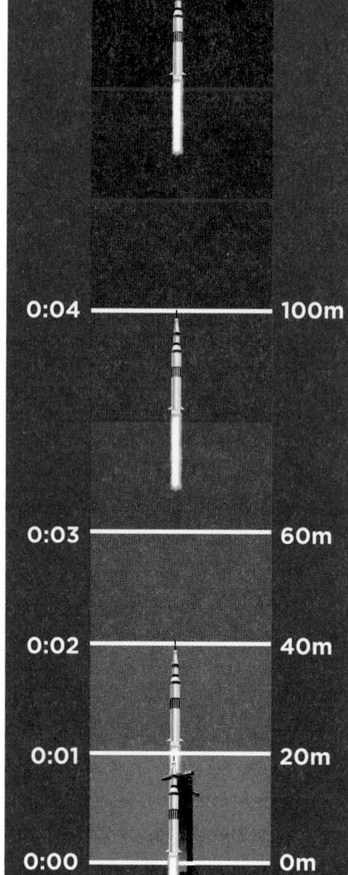

Solve It

1. Does the rocket's speed change? Does its direction change? Explain your answers.

2. When does the rocket start to accelerate? How do you know?

Try It Again

Using a ruler and masking tape, divide the floor into sections. Make each section 25 cm in length. Push a toy car fast enough to cross all the lines. Use a stopwatch to record the time that the car passes each line. Record your data in the chart. Then graph your data. Include a title for your graph and label the bottom and left side of the graph.

Time (seconds)	Distance (meters)
	25 cm
	50 cm
	75 cm
	100 cm
	125 cm

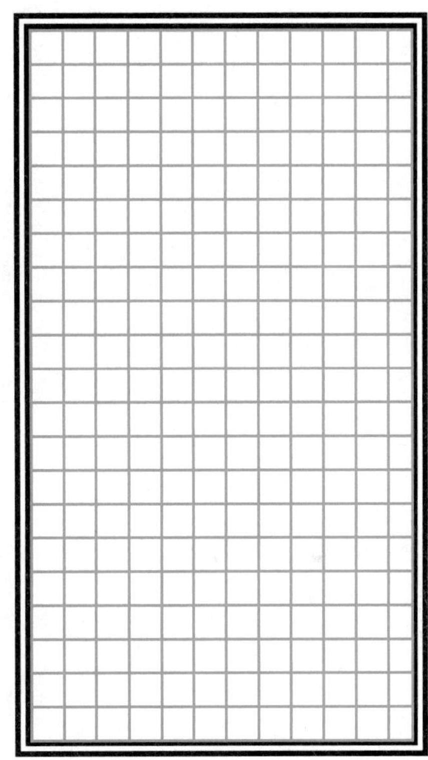

Answer the following questions about the graph.

1. Did the car accelerate? How do you know?

____

2. Would the toy car accelerate if it rolled down a slope? Explain.

____

____

The Design Process Present evidence using mathematical representations (graphs, data tables).

Lesson 3

Technology and Design

solar-powered race cars, Indianapolis Motor Speedway

4.4.4 Define a problem in the context of motion and transportation and propose a solution to this problem by evaluating, reevaluating and testing the design, gathering evidence about how well the design meets the needs of the problem, and documenting the design so that it can be easily replicated.

Look and Wonder

These strange-looking cars do not have gasoline engines. Instead they have solar-powered electrical motors. Why do you think they were built?

Essential Question How do things get designed?

Explore

How can you make a rocket car?

Purpose

Design and test a balloon-powered car.

Procedure

1. You will work on a team with several of your classmates. Your challenge is to build and test a balloon-powered car.

2. Get the materials you will use to make the car. Cut out the frame of the car using a piece of cardboard. The rectangle will be the frame of the car. Use the compass to draw circles for the tires and hubcaps.
   △ **Be Careful!** The scissors and compass are sharp.

3. **Make a Model** Now put the car together. The picture on this page shows you how. Tape the balloon to the short end of a bendable drinking straw. Tape the straw to the rectangle. Attach the hubcaps and wheels. Push thumbtacks through the hubcaps and wheels into the rectangle.
   △ **Be Careful!** Use sharp materials safely.

4. **Measure** Inflate the balloon. Hold it closed with your fingers. Place the car on the starting line. Test the car by letting go of the balloon. Measure the distance traveled by the car (in cm). Record your measurement. Then, repeat your test. Find the average distance traveled by your car. (Hint: To find the average distance, add the two distances together and then divide your answer by two.)

Distance—Trial One: ______________________________

Distance—Trial Two: ______________________________

Average Distance: ______________________________

Materials

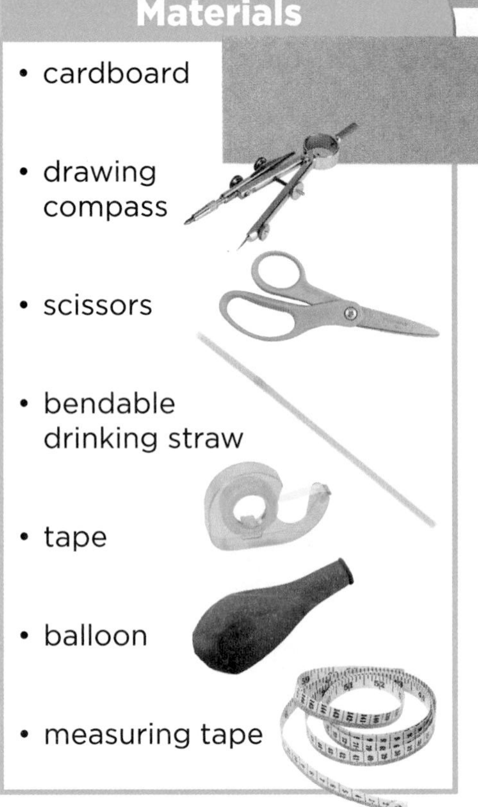

- cardboard
- drawing compass
- scissors
- bendable drinking straw
- tape
- balloon
- measuring tape

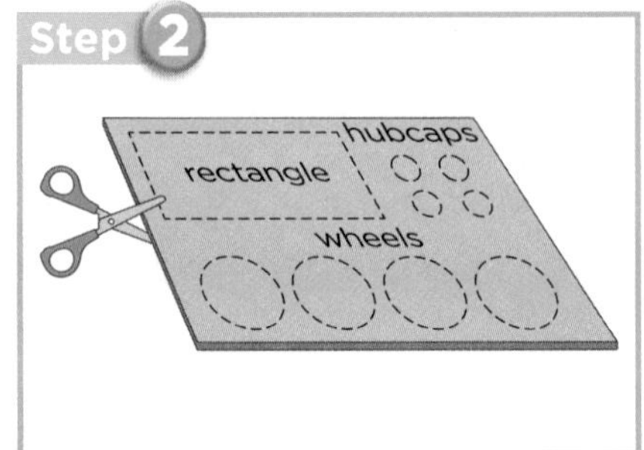

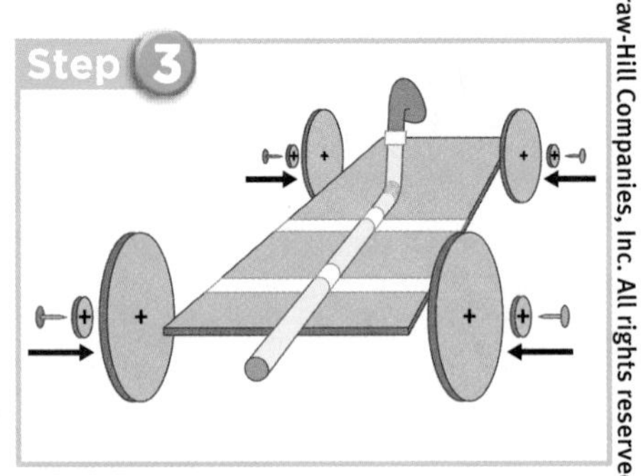

Draw Conclusions

5 **Interpret Data** How could the design of your car be improved? Brainstorm ideas with your group. Write your ideas below.

____

____

____

Put your Notebook FOLDABLES here. Use Foldable I on page 290.

Explore More

Experiment Choose a new design. Draw your design on a separate sheet of paper. Then build it. Design a fair test to compare the new design with the original design. Then try it. Describe your results.

____

____

Open Inquiry

Can you design a car that uses another power source, such as rubber bands, for movement?

My question is: _______________

____

How I can test it: _______________

____

My results are: _______________

____

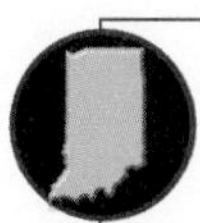

The Design Process As citizens of the constructed world, students will participate in the design process. Students will learn to use materials and tools safely and employ the basic principles of the engineering design process in order to find solutions to problems.

- Identify a need or problem to be solved.
- Brainstorm potential solutions.
- Select a solution to a need or problem.
- Select the materials to develop a solution.
- Create the solution.

Read and Respond

What is technology?

When people have a problem to solve, they often use technology. **Technology** is everything we design, make, and use to solve problems. Technology can be as simple as a pencil or a screwdriver. It can be as complex as a solar cell. A solar cell changes sunlight into electricity. The electricity can be used to power a calculator—or even a car or a plane.

▲ solar cell

Quick Check

1. **Name something that has changed because of new technology.**

____

This team designed a solar-powered car. They raced their car in Indianapolis in 1995.

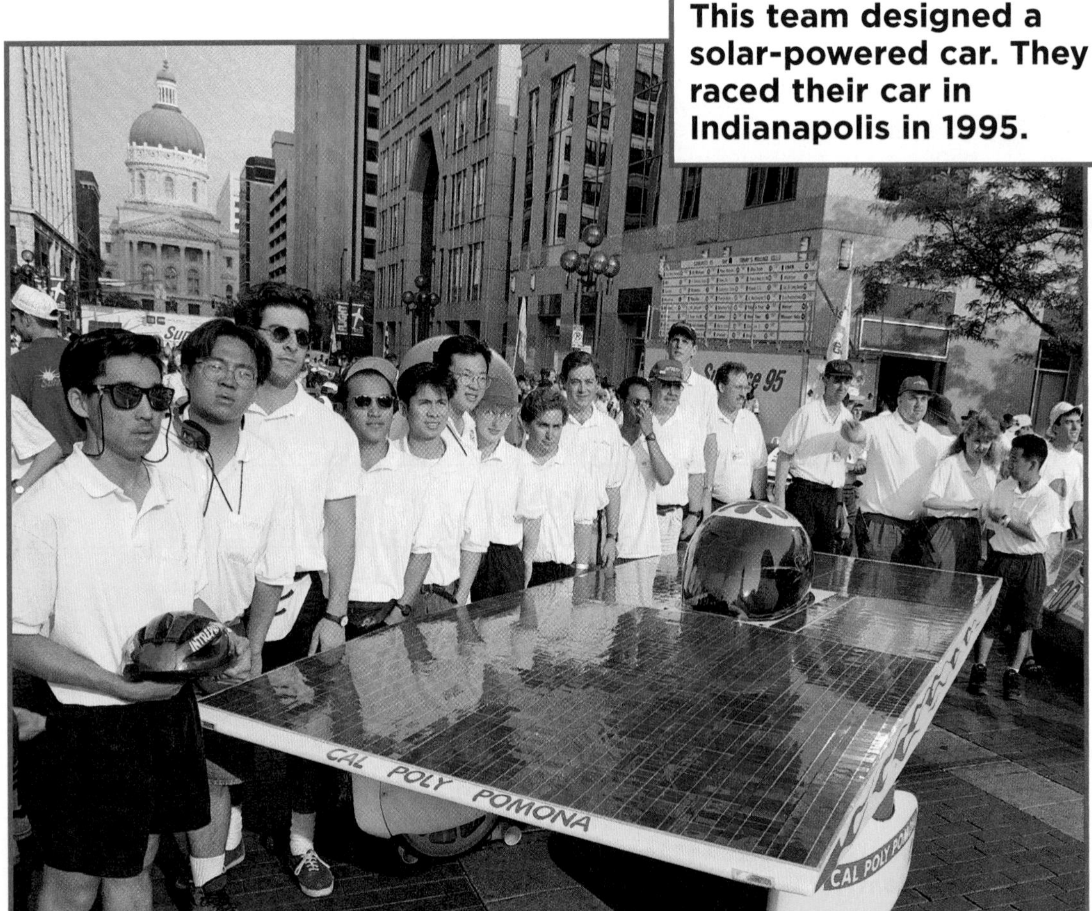

Glue your Notebook FOLDABLES here. Use Foldable I on page 290.

solar-powered airplane

Why We Create Technology

Most technology is created to meet a demand. A demand is a need or a want. For example, one basic human need is food. Another is shelter. Think about a problem you had. The problem created a demand for a solution.

If you designed a solution to your problem, you did the job of an engineer. An **engineer** is a scientist who designs new technology and modifies old technology.

Quick Check

2. How could we use technology to make a new type of car? Give an example.

____

____

____

How fast can an airplane fly?

Imagine flying an airplane into space. One day it might be possible. From 1996–2004, engineers built and tested a rocket plane. It was called the X-43A. Engineers developed new technologies that could one day lead to the design of space planes.

Circle the name of the rocket plane in the first paragraph on this page.

The Need for Speed

The design and testing of the X-43A is shown on these pages. First, the engineers brainstormed ideas for new designs. They chose the best design and built a model. Then, they built a prototype. A **prototype** is a working model that can be tested. The X-43A was tested three times. On the third trial, it broke all aircraft speed records.

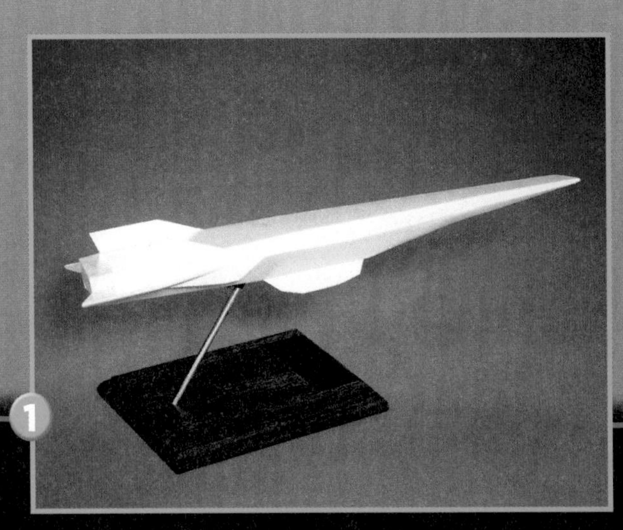

1

2

Faster Than a Speeding Bullet

On November 16, 2004, the X-43A flew at a speed of about 11,000 km/h (7,000 mph). This is nearly 10 times the speed of sound! How could it fly so fast?

Solving Problems

Engineers who worked on the X-43A had studied earlier planes and rockets. They knew that rocket engines need lots of oxygen to burn rocket fuel. That is why rockets carry their own oxygen tanks onboard. The X-43A was designed to burn rocket fuel using oxygen from the air. This made the X-43A much lighter—and safer—than regular rockets.

Quick Lab

To design your own model plane, do the Quick Lab on page 289.

The X-43A accelerates with the help of a booster rocket.

3

testing the prototype

 ***Quick Check***

3. What new technology was used to make the X-43A rocket plane?

____

____

____

What is the design process?

The designing and building of the X-43A shows the design process in action. The **design process** is the series of steps used to find solutions to problems.

The design process begins when a problem, or challenge, is identified. For example, a challenge in the design of airplanes is to make them lighter. The picture on this page shows one way to make a lightweight airplane!

the *Gossamer Penguin* in flight, 1980

The Design Process

See page 273 for more practice reading diagrams.

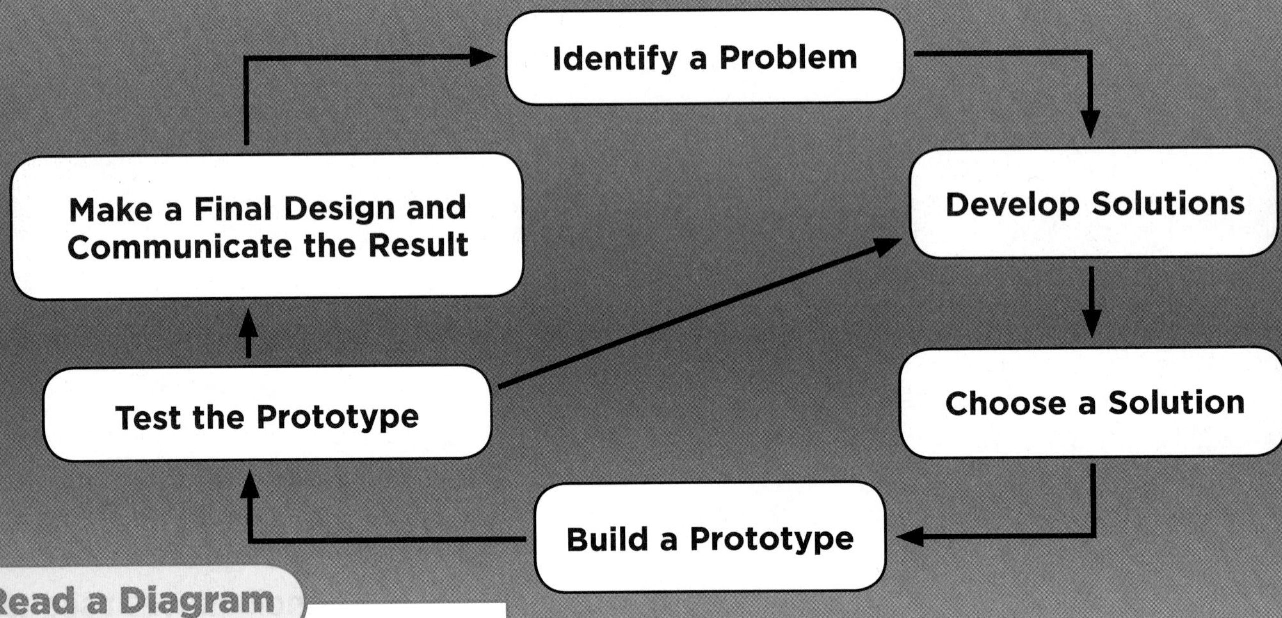

Read a Diagram

What happens if a prototype fails its first test?

____

____

The Gossamer Albatross

In 1979, an airplane called the *Gossamer Albatross* crossed the English Channel. It completed a flight of 36 km (22 mi). For most airplanes this would be a very short distance. However, the *Gossamer Albatross* was no ordinary airplane. It was powered by a bicyclist! A later version of this plane was called the *Gossamer Penguin*. This plane had a solar-powered engine, in addition to a pedaling pilot.

Quick Check

4. Match the step of the design process with the steps needed to design a new airplane.

1. Identify a Problem	• Replace the engine with a bicyclist.
2. Develop Solutions	• Use a new engine. Replace the engine with a bicyclist. Use a solar panel.
3. Choose a Solution	• The *Gossamer Penguin*
4. Build a Prototype	• An airplane needs to be lighter.
5. Test the Prototype	• The *Gossamer Albatross*
6. Make a Final Design	• Fly the *Gossamer Albatross* across the English Channel.

Visual Summary

Complete the lesson summary in your own words.

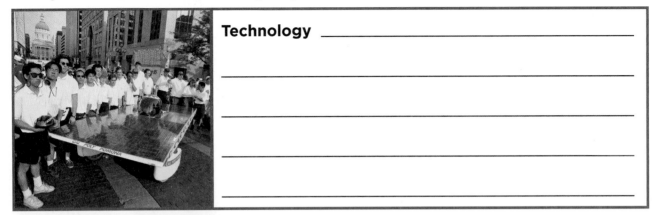

CAL POLY POMONA

Technology ____________________

____

____

____

____

Engineers ____________________

____

____

____

____

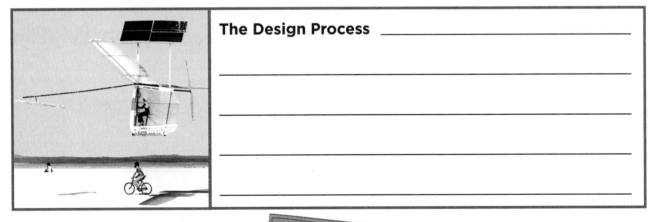

The Design Process ____________________

____

____

____

____

Make a FOLDABLES® Study Guide

Make a layered-look book. Use it to summarize what you learned about technology and design.

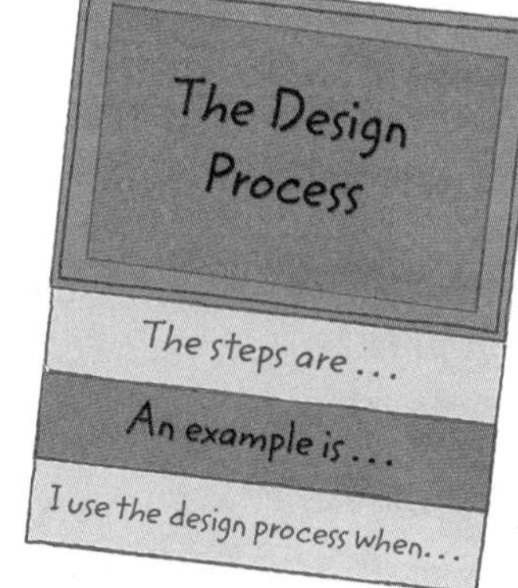
The Design Process
The steps are . . .
An example is . . .
I use the design process when . . .

Think, Talk, and Write

1. **Vocabulary** What is the design process?

2. **Sequence** How does the design process work?

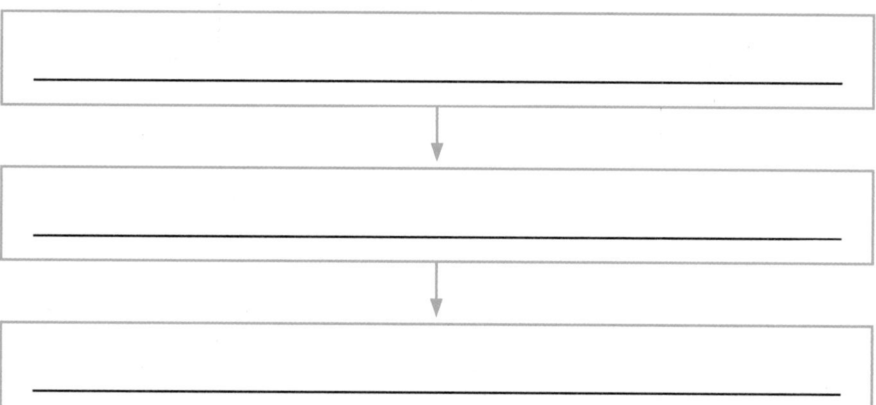

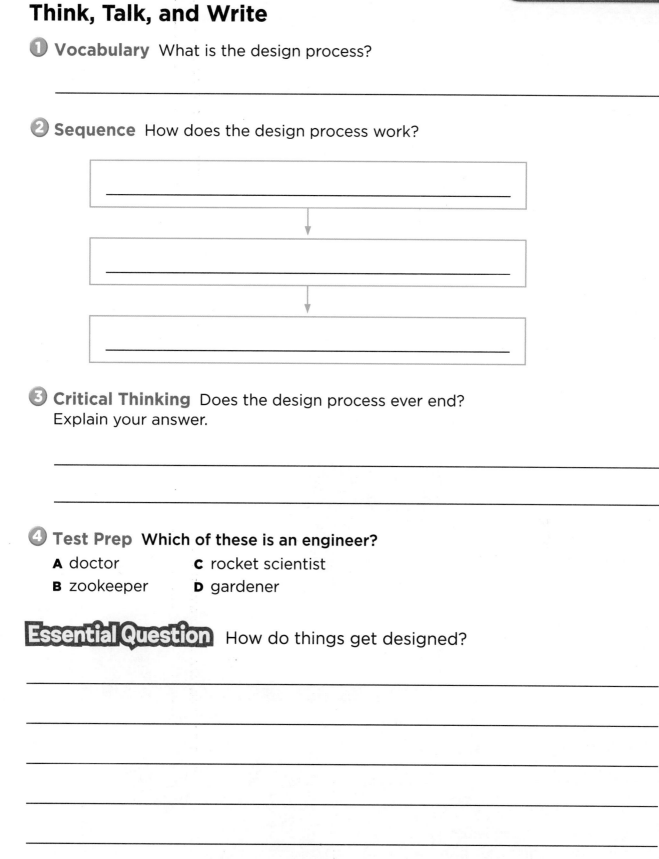

3. **Critical Thinking** Does the design process ever end? Explain your answer.

4. **Test Prep** **Which of these is an engineer?**

A doctor
B zookeeper
C rocket scientist
D gardener

Essential Question How do things get designed?

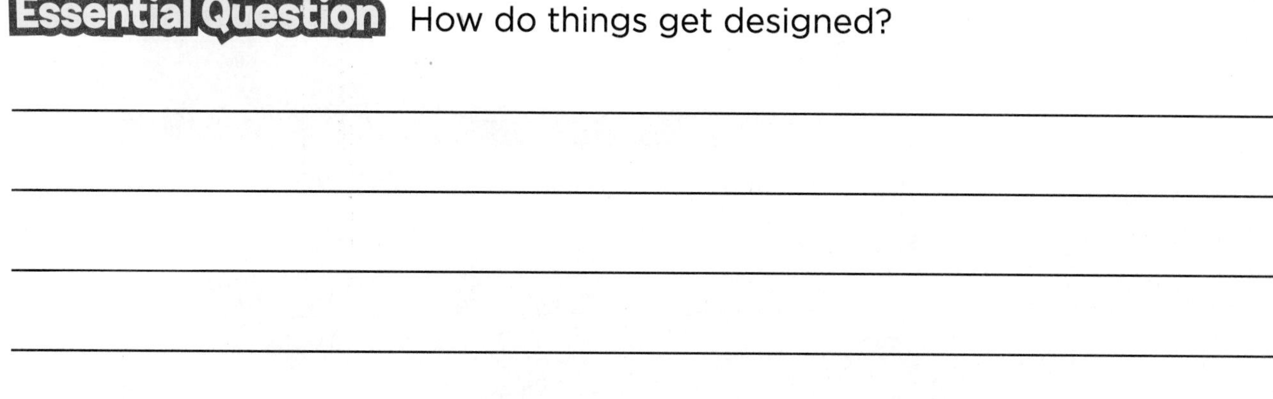

-Review Summaries and quizzes online at www.macmillanmh.com

Focus on Skills

Inquiry Skill: The Design Process

Scientists and engineers rarely design perfect technological solutions on their first attempt. They use the **design process** to improve upon existing designs. They sometimes compare different designs. You use the **design process** too. Any time you experiment with different solutions to a problem, you are using the **design process**.

▶ Learn It

In this investigation, you will design a boat that can hold the most possible cargo. The cargo will be represented by paper clips. You will test two different designs. Then you will use the **design process** to improve upon and communicate your design.

▶ Try It

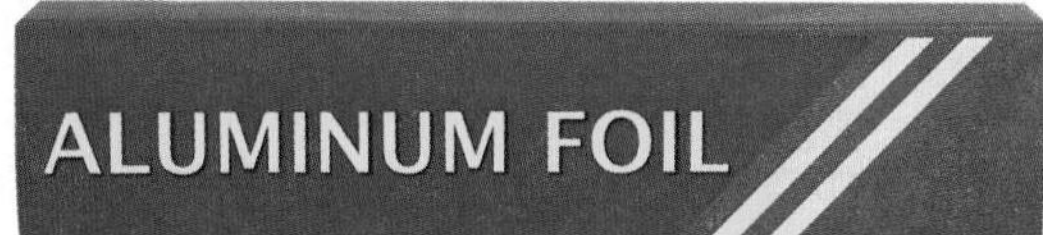

Design an aluminum foil boat. Then use the **design process** to improve upon your original design.

Materials **aluminum foil, container of water**

1. Fold two identical aluminum foil squares into two different boat shapes. Both boats should be capable of holding "cargo" (paper clips). Test both "boats" in a container of water to make sure that each can float. In the chart below, describe your boats in words and in writing.
2. Add paper clips to your first boat design. When the boat can no longer float, record the number of paper clips in the *Results* section of your chart. Repeat this step for your second boat design.

	Description	Drawing	Results
Design 1			
Design 2			

The Design Process As citizens of the constructed world, students will participate in the design process. Students will learn to use materials and tools safely and employ the basic principles of the engineering design process in order to find solutions to problems.

Focus on Skills

Glue your Notebook FOLDABLES® here. Use Foldable I on page 290.

3 Which boat shape held the most paper clips? Describe its shape. What would be the advantages to using this boat to ship cargo? What would be the disadvantages?

____

____

____

____

____

4 Design a new boat that can hold a bag of marbles. You may use any materials. Draw your boat on a separate sheet of paper. Include detailed directions, including the materials you used and the dimensions of the boat.

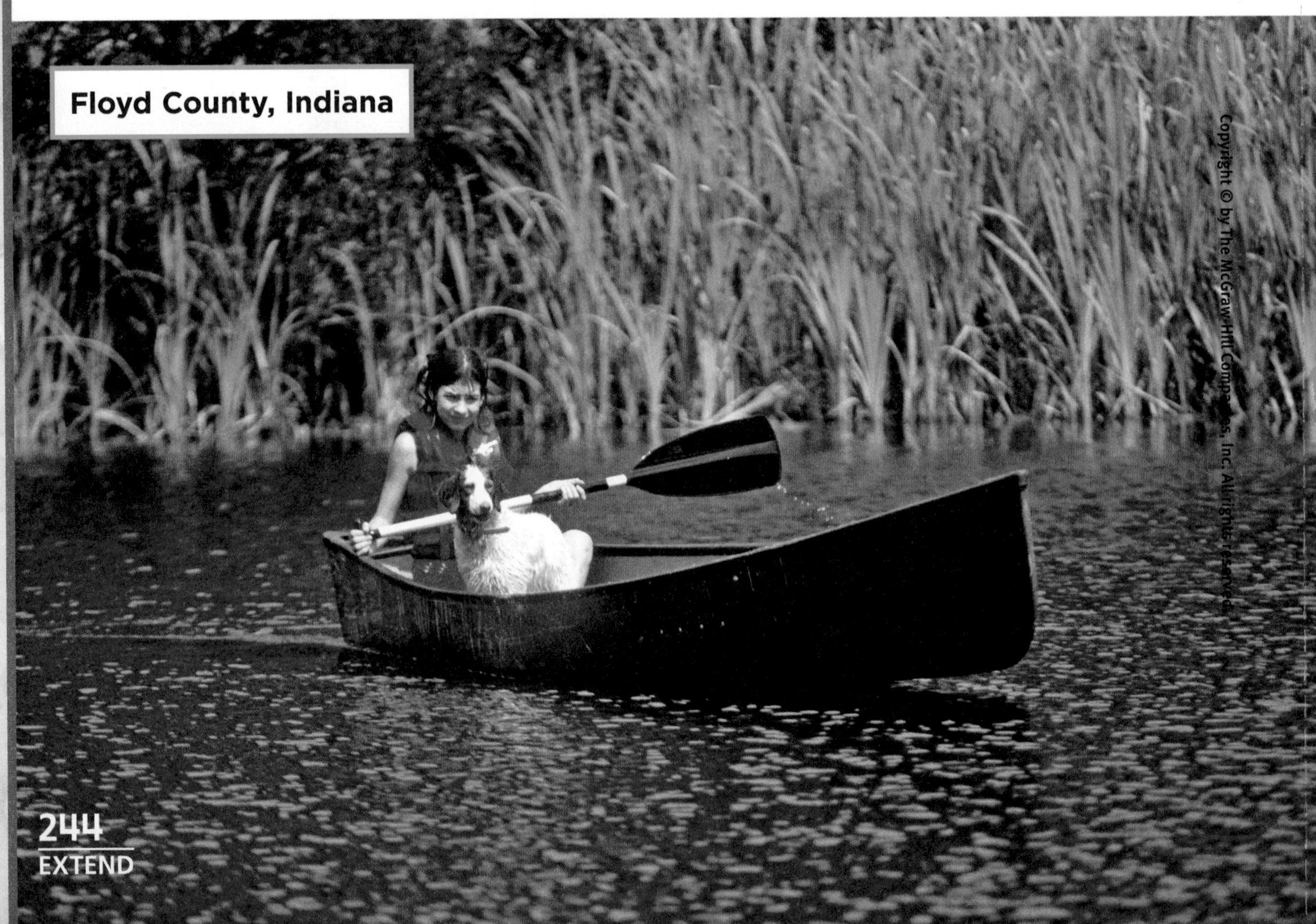

Floyd County, Indiana

Apply It

Describe how you used the **design process**.

1. Is your boat well designed for speed? Explain your answer.

2. How could you modify your boat design to make it faster? How could you test your modified boat design?

3. How does the shape of a boat affect the way it is used?

4. Compare and contrast two different automobile designs. What are the advantages and disadvantages of each?

UNIT 5 Review

Visual Summary

Summarize each lesson in your own words.

Lesson 1 ______________________________

____

____

____

____

Lesson 2 ______________________________

____

____

____

____

Lesson 3 ______________________________

____

____

____

____

Make a FOLDABLES® Study Guide

Glue your lesson study guides to a large sheet of paper as shown. Use your study guide to review what you have learned in this unit.

Vocabulary

DOK I

Fill each blank with the best term from the list.

accelerates, p. 202	**force,** p. 200	**technology,** p. 234
design process, p. 238	**gravity,** p. 201	**thrust,** p. 214
drag, p. 214	**lift,** p. 216	
engineer, p. 235	**speed,** p. 199	

1. The force that slows a vehicle as it moves through a liquid or a gas is called ________________.

2. The power that sends a rocket forward is called ________________.

3. The distance an object travels in a certain period of time is its ________________.

4. A scientist that designs new cars is a(n) ________________.

5. The force that makes an airplane rise is called ________________.

6. To invent a solution to a problem, you use the ________________.

7. A push or a pull is a ________________.

8. The solution to a problem is ________________.

9. The force that pulls objects toward Earth is ________________.

10. When an object changes speed or direction it ________________.

-Glossary Words and definitions online at www.macmillanmh.com

UNIT 5 Review

Skills and Concepts

DOK 2–3

Answer each of the following.

11. **Infer** Why do engineers sometimes test a prototype more than one time?

12. **Compare and Contrast** How are drag and friction similar? How are they different?

13. **Critical Thinking** The Sun is very large. Why don't we feel the effects of its gravity?

14. **Experiment** Does gravity affect all objects the same way? Describe an experiment you could do to find out.

15. **Summarize** How does friction both start and stop the movement of a train?

16. **Main Idea and Details** What is the process that engineers use to create new technology? Give an example.

17. **Draw Conclusions** Will you find more gravity on the Moon or on Earth? Why?

18. **True or False** *Drag speeds up the motion of a rocket.* Is this statement true or false? Explain.

19. **True or False** *Velocity is the speed and force of a moving object.* Is this statement true or false? Explain.

The Big Idea

20. What makes objects move?

Circle the best answer for each question.

1. The picture below shows an airplane rising into the air.

Which two forces slow the airplane's motion?

A thrust and lift
B thrust and drag
C drag and lift
D drag and gravity
4.4.1 (DOK 1)

2. A team of engineers has chosen a solution to a design problem. What should the team do next?

A communicate the design
B identify the problem
C build and test a prototype
D discuss the solution
4.4.4 (DOK 1)

3. Maureen knows the distance a car traveled. What else does she need to know in order to calculate the car's speed?

A its time
B its velocity
C its acceleration
D its mass
4.4.2 (DOK 2)

4. Which of these would MOST LIKELY stop the motion of a train?

A thrust
B heat
C friction
D electricity
4.4.1 (DOK 1)

5. The diagram below shows students playing a tug-of-war game.

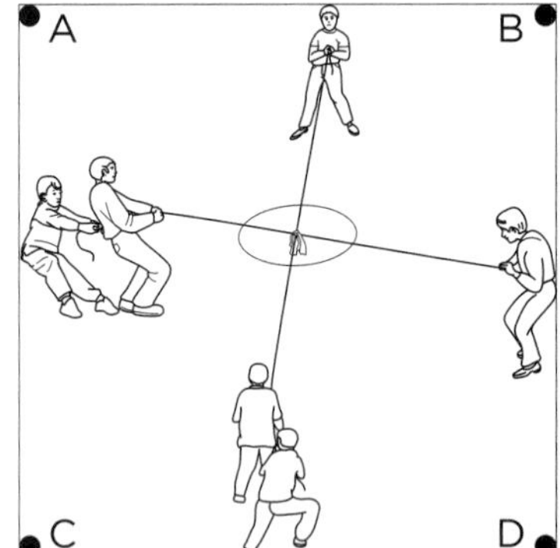

If each student is pulling with the same force, toward which dot will the flag move?

A dot A
B dot B
C dot C
D dot D
4.4.3 (DOK 2)

Answer the following questions.

6. Sean and Matt have two different kinds of bicycles. They want to know which is faster. Describe a fair test they could do to find out.
4.4.2 (DOK 3)

____

____

____

____

7. Describe how you could use the design process to design a faster bicycle.
4.4.4 (DOK 3)

____

____

____

____

8. The graph shows the speeds of a cheetah, a horse, and a bicycle. Which is FASTEST?
4.4.2 (DOK 1)

____

In the time it took the cheetah to travel 1,000 meters, how far did the horse travel? The bicycle?
4.4.2 (DOK 2)

____

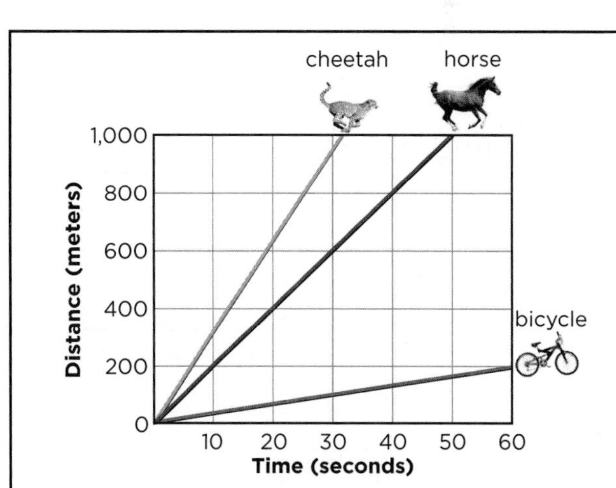

Careers in Science

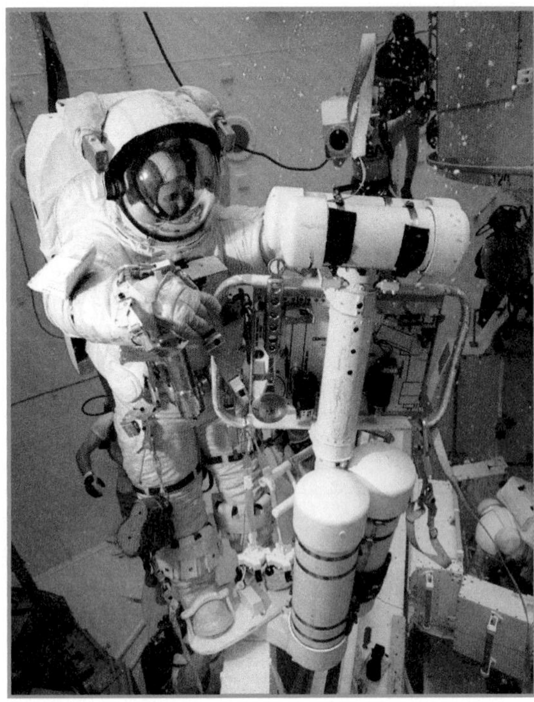

▲astronaut Kathryn Thornton training underwater

Astronaut

Have you ever wondered what it would be like to travel in space? If so, then astronaut is the career for you! Some astronauts are pilots. Others do research while in space.

To become an astronaut, you need to study math and science in school. Astronauts have college degrees in science or engineering. They must also be in excellent physical shape. As part of their training, astronauts must complete some very hard exercises. For example, they must swim three lengths of a swimming pool in their space suit.

Write About It

If you were an astronaut, what might you do in space? Would you like to pilot a spacecraft, work in a space station, or explore the surface of a planet? Write a journal entry about the discoveries you might make.

___

___

___

___

___

LOG ON e-Careers at www.macmillanmh.com

Visual Literacy Skills Practice

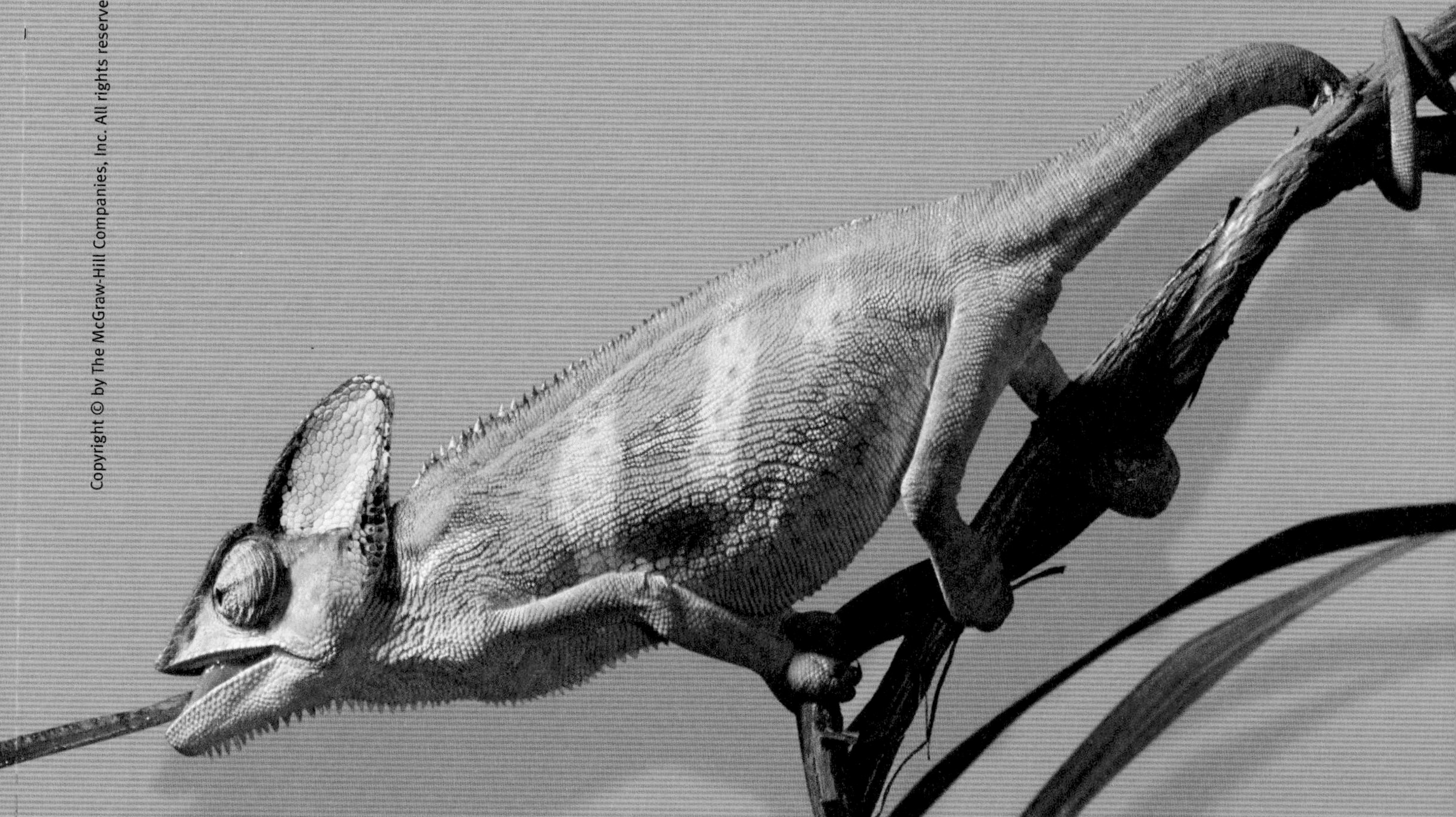

Contents

Visual Literacy

What is heat?

The diagram below shows sources of heat that we come in contact with every day.

Heat All Around

Answer these questions about the diagram.

1. Name an example of heat moving through solids.

____

2. Name two examples of heat moving through a gas.

____

____

____

Read a Diagram

How does heat move?

This diagram shows how heat is transferred from the burner to the water.

Heating Water

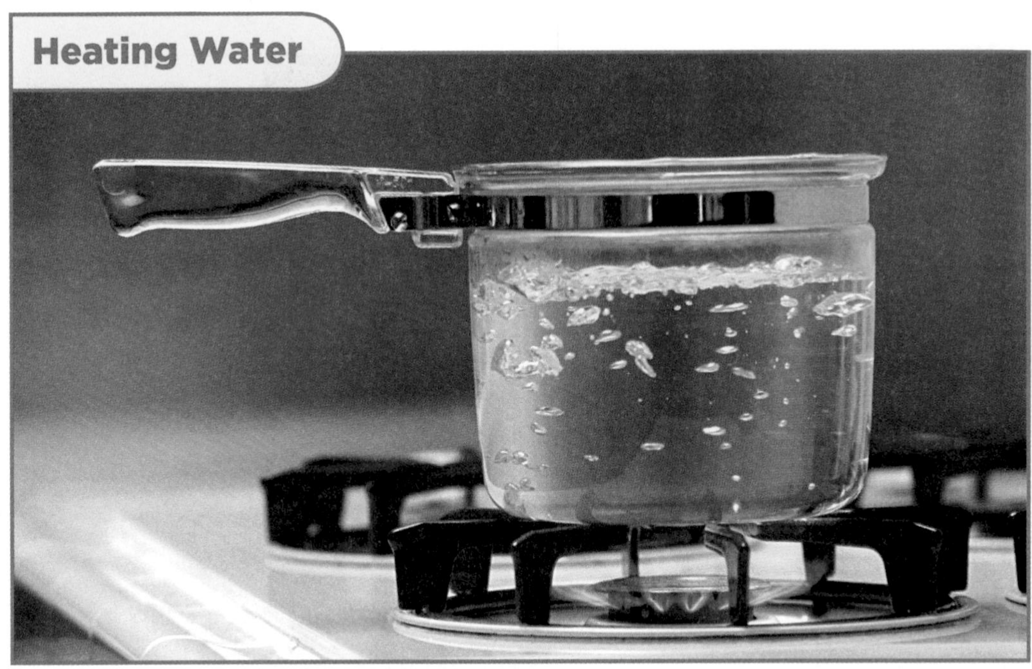

Answer these questions about the diagram.

1. Where is conduction occurring? Explain.

____

____

2. Where is convection occurring? Explain.

____

____

3. How do the particles in the water change as they are heated?

____

____

What is electrical current?

The diagram below shows both a complete and an open circuit. How are they different?

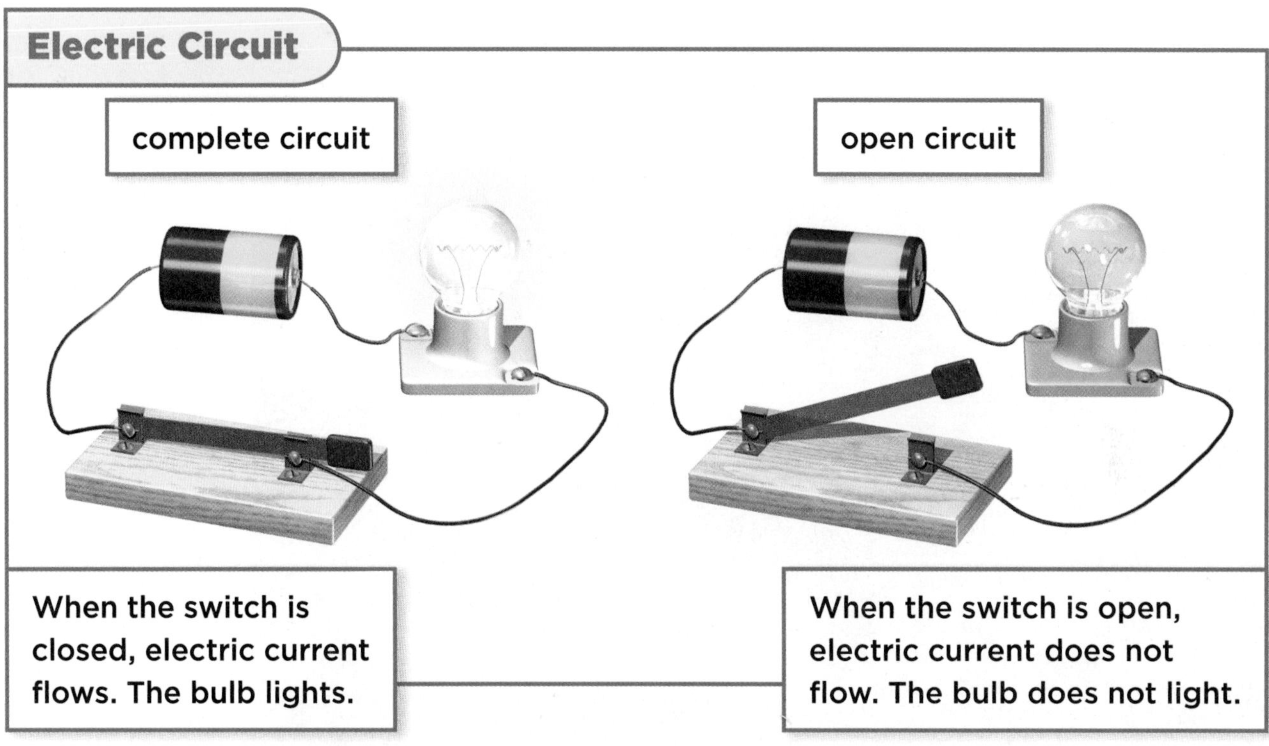

Electric Circuit
complete circuit
open circuit
When the switch is closed, electric current flows. The bulb lights.
When the switch is open, electric current does not flow. The bulb does not light.

Answer these questions about the diagram.

1. How does the circuit on the left look different from the circuit on the right?

____

____

2. Why is the circuit on the right called an open circuit?

____

____

3. How could you light the bulb in the open circuit?

____

____

Read a Photo

What is erosion?

The photograph below shows a river running through a canyon in Utah. It also illustrates the effects of weathering. Look carefully at the shape and location of the river. Study the shading and texture of the cliffs.

Rivers Shape the Land

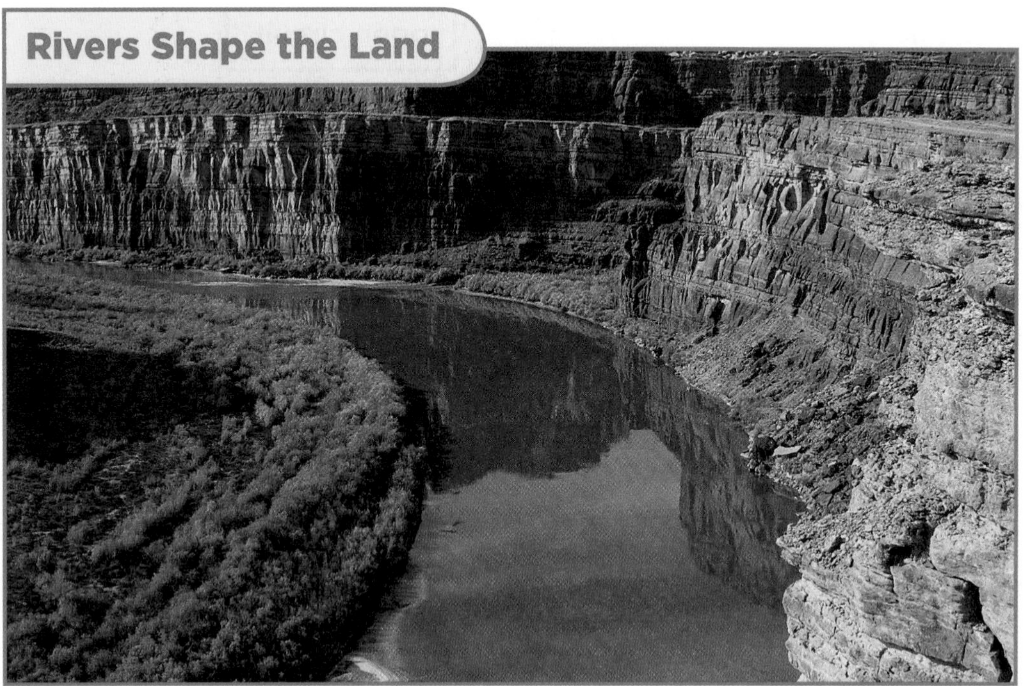

Answer these questions about the photograph.

1. What evidence of erosion do you see in the photograph?

____

2. What do you think caused the erosion?

____

3. What details suggest that it took thousands of years for the canyon to form?

____

____

What are some features of Indiana's land?

A map can display different things about a place. This map uses different colors to represent different areas in Indiana. Each region has features that characterize it. These regions were shaped by deposition and erosion.

Answer these questions about the map.

1. Where in Indiana are sand dunes found?

____

____

2. In which region of Indiana are caverns found?

____

____

3. What two areas were not covered by glaciers during the last ice age?

____

____

4. What land feature extends across Indiana from Michigan and Ohio to Illinois?

____

____

Shapes of the Land in Indiana

Read a Diagram

What are earthquakes?

An earthquake is a movement of the rocks that make up Earth's crust. This diagram will help you understand how earthquakes affect Earth's surface.

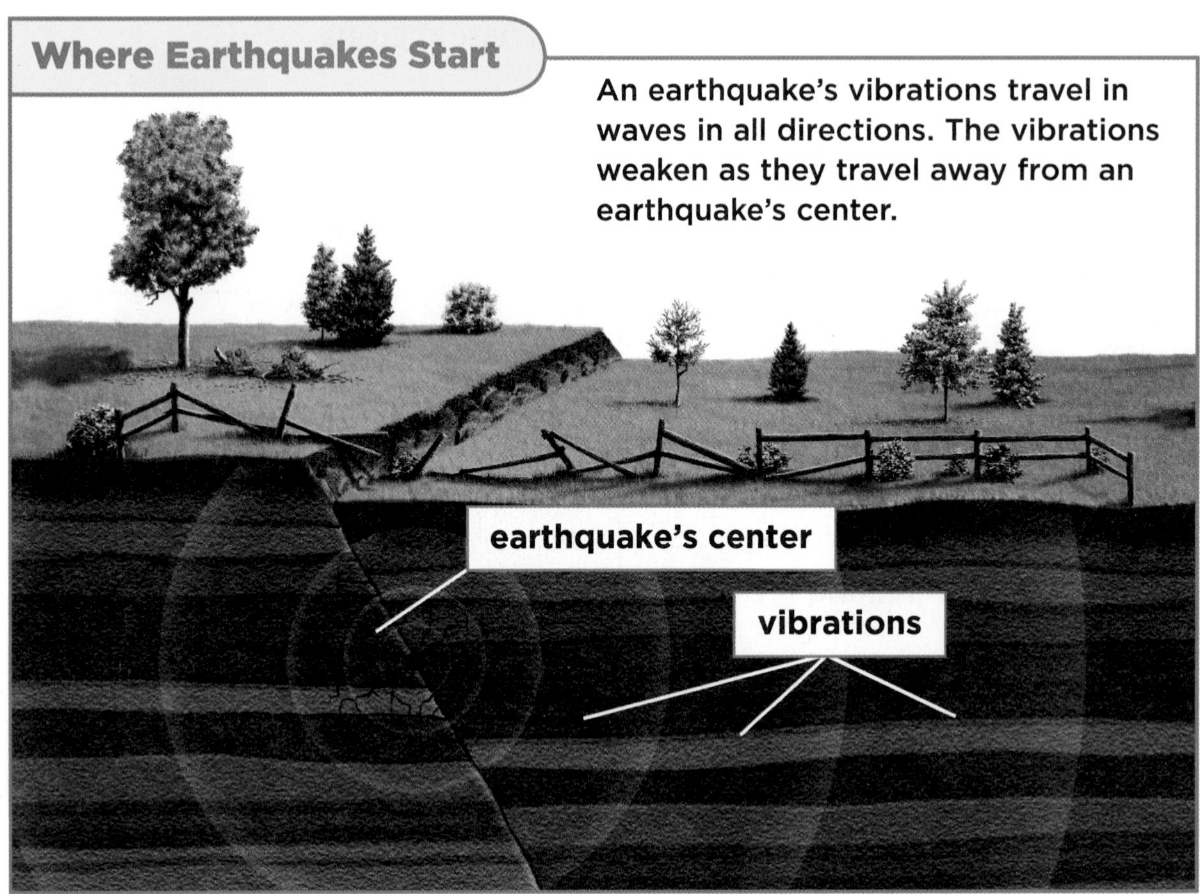

Where Earthquakes Start
An earthquake's vibrations travel in waves in all directions. The vibrations weaken as they travel away from an earthquake's center.
earthquake's center
vibrations

Answer these questions about the diagram.

1. What damage did the earthquake do?

____

____

2. What to do the circles in the rock represent?

____

____

What is a volcano?

Volcanoes are made of melted rock from deep below the surface. Each time a volcano erupts, melted rock pours out. Look at the diagram below to understand more about how a volcano forms.

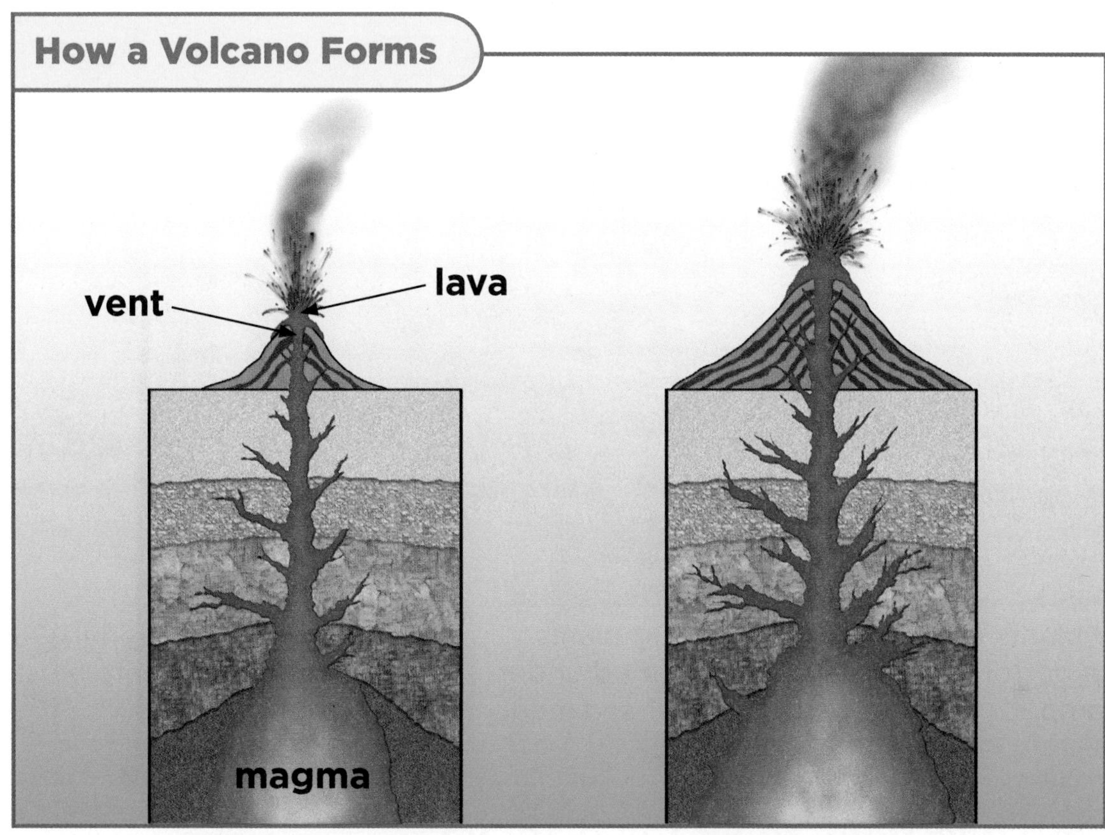

Answer these questions about the diagram.

1. Lava is melted rock that flows on land. What part of the diagram represents lava?

___

___

2. How does the volcano get larger?

___

___

Read a Diagram

What are nonrenewable resources?

Much of the energy that we use comes from fossil fuels. Look at the steps in the diagram below to see how coal was formed.

How Coal Formed

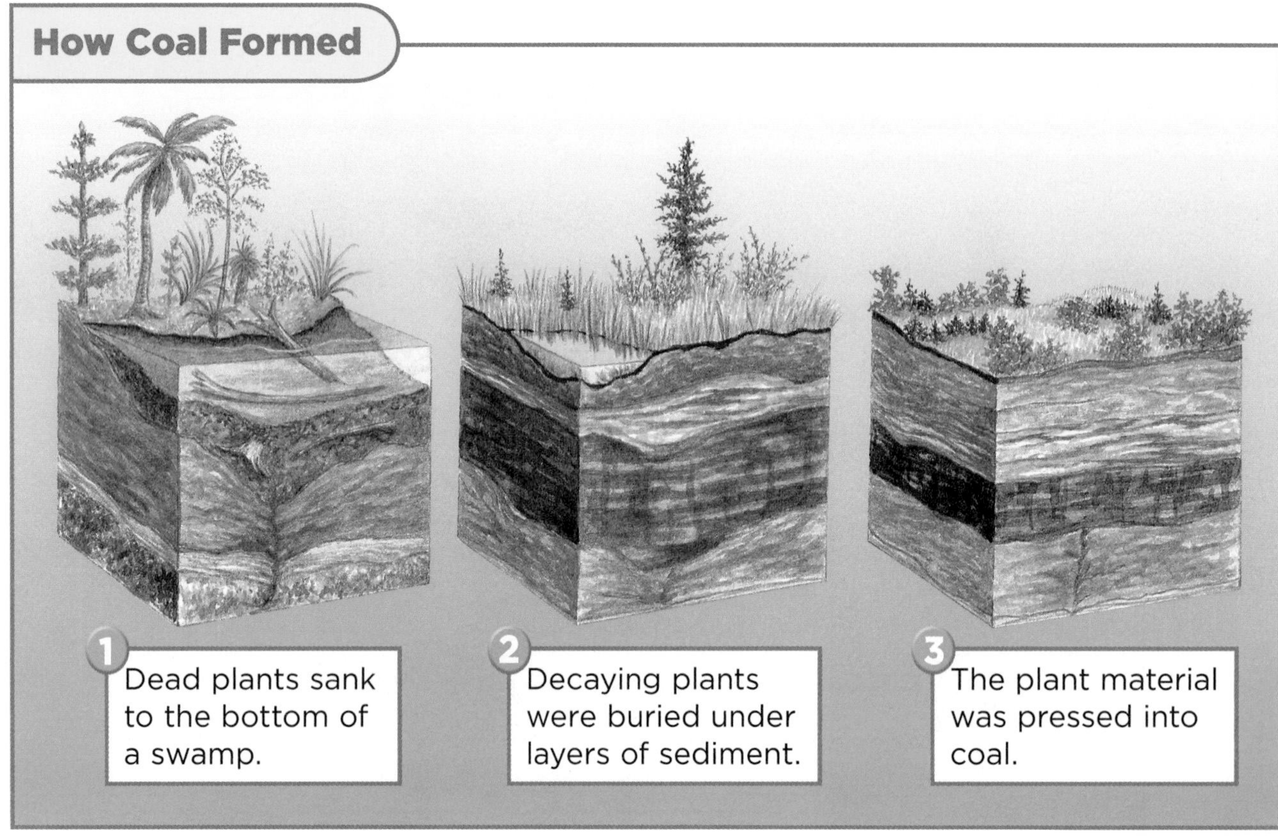

1 Dead plants sank to the bottom of a swamp.

2 Decaying plants were buried under layers of sediment.

3 The plant material was pressed into coal.

Answer these questions about the diagram.

1. What makes up coal?

____

2. What turns this material into coal?

____

3. How is the coal removed?

____

What are alternative energy sources?

Fossil fuels are a nonrenewable source of energy. The Sun, wind, and other sources provide us with renewable sources. The chart below shows the percentage of renewable and nonrenewable sources of electricity that we used in 2005.

Answer these questions about the chart.

1. What percentage of electricity came from renewable energy in 2005?

____

____

2. Did more electricity come from renewable or nonrenewable resources?

____

____

3. Which sources of electricity are not fossil fuels? What percentage of electricity comes from these sources?

____

____

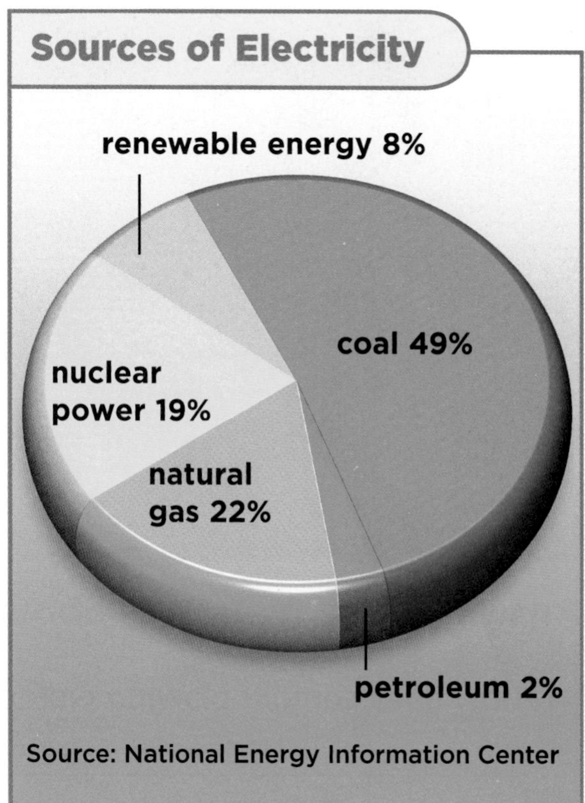

Read a Photo

How can we practice conservation?

Some farmers have always used contour plowing to grow better crops. Study the plow lines in the photograph below.

Contour Plowing

Answer these questions about the photograph.

1. How does contour plowing protect the soil?

____

____

2. How does contour plowing conserve water?

____

____

____

____

What are the 3 Rs?

The photographs below show examples of the 3 Rs. As you look at the photographs, think about other ways to conserve resources.

The 3 Rs in Action

Answer these questions about the photographs.

1. Which photograph shows a material being reused? How is it reused?

____

____

____

2. How is reducing different from recycling?

____

____

____

Read a Photo

Where do living things get their characteristics?

The woodpecker shown below is looking for insects to eat inside the tree. The photograph displays some traits that are inherited and some that are not inherited.

The Environment

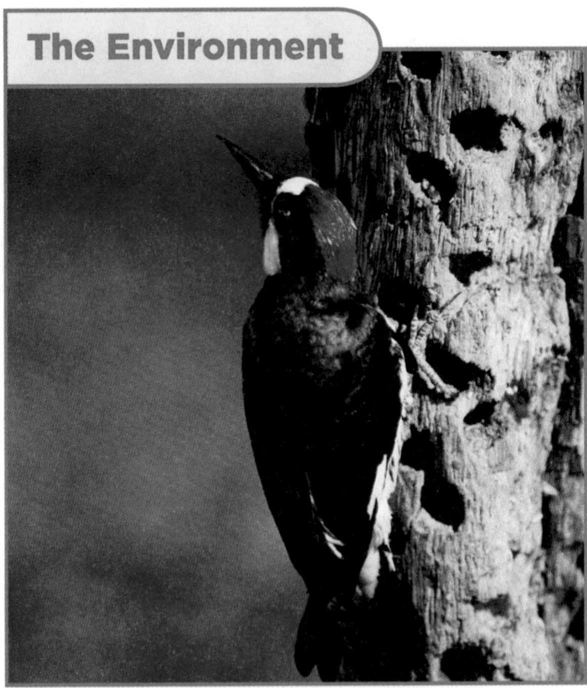

Answer these questions about the photograph above.

1. Are the holes made by the woodpecker in the tree inherited characteristics?

____

2. Can these holes be passed on to its offspring?

____

3. What inherited characteristics do you see in this picture?

____

____

What are some plant adaptations?

This diagram shows two plants responding to stimuli in their environment. Study the diagram and answer the questions below.

Plant Response

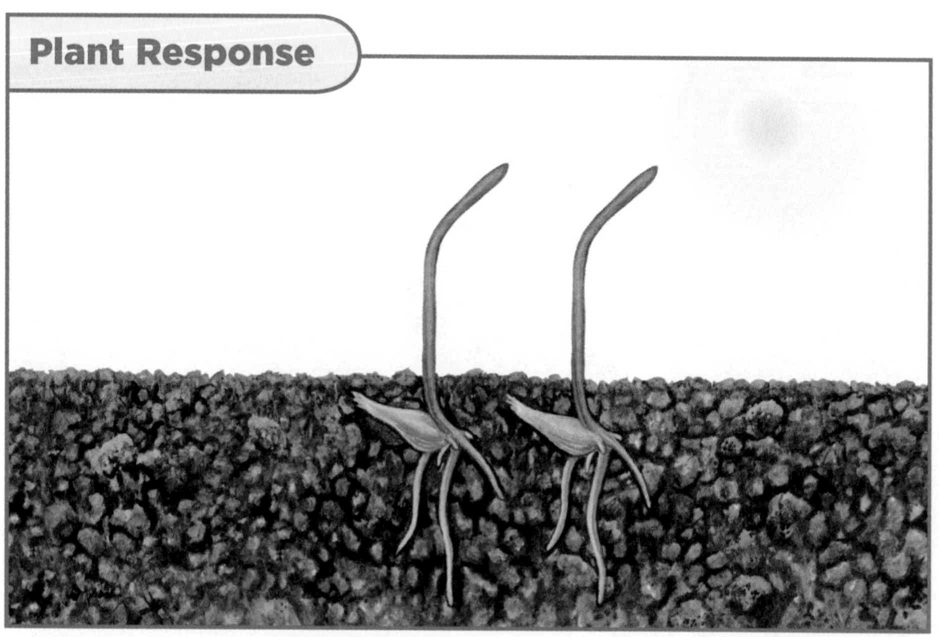

Answer these questions about the diagram.

1. How are these plant shoots responding to the light?

____

____

2. How are these two plants responding to gravity?

____

____

3. What is an example of another stimulus a plant may respond to?

____

____

Read a Photo

How do plants and animals adapt to harsh environments?

Look at the animals' bodies to see how they are adapted to their environments.

Desert and Tundra Foxes

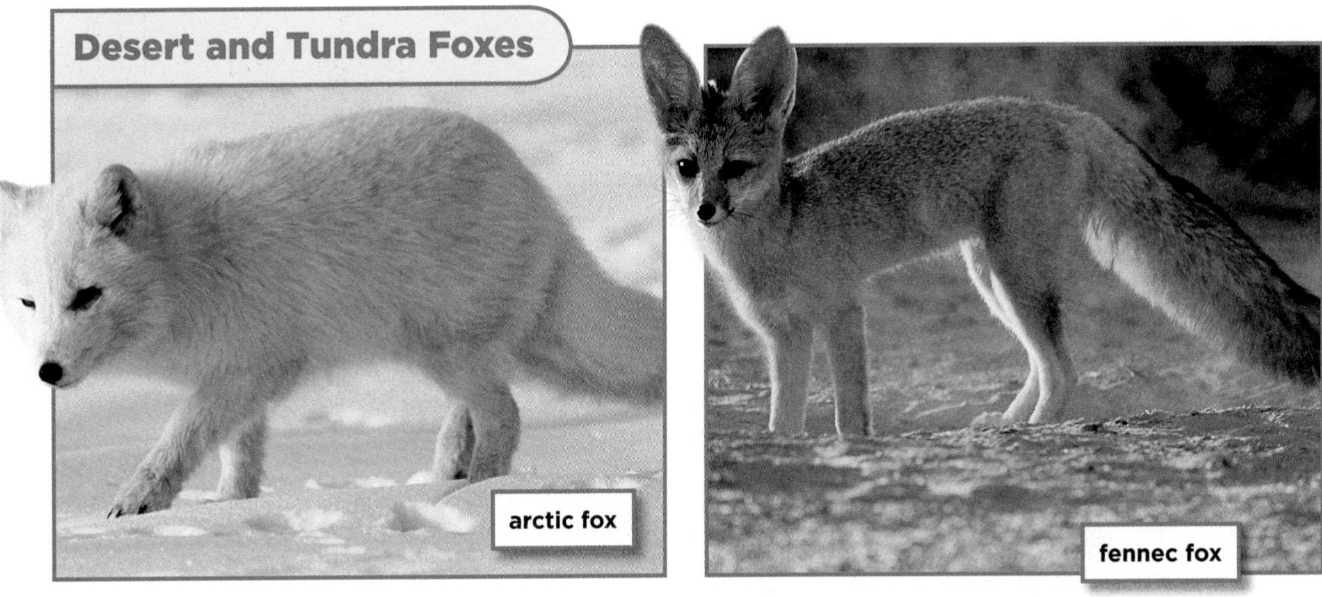

Answer these questions about the photographs.

1. How is the arctic fox adapted to its environment?

____

____

2. How is the fennec fox adapted to the desert?

____

____

3. What might happen if the arctic fox were relocated to the desert?

____

____

____

How do environments change?

These photographs show the same volcano and the surrounding environment at two different points in time. Look for differences between the photographs.

Natural Change in Environments

Mount Saint Helens in 1980

Mount Saint Helens in 1995

Answer these questions about the photographs.

1. Why is the land barren in the first photograph?

____

2. How has the environment changed in the second photograph?

____

3. If you saw a photograph of the same area taken in 1979, what might it look like? Explain.

____

____

____

Read a Diagram

What are forces?

This diagram shows different points on a roller coaster. Study the diagram to understand the different forces at work being illustrated at each point.

Forces at Work

Answer these questions about the diagram.

1. What is the source of energy that pulls the roller coaster to the top of the first hill?

____

2. What is the force that moves the roller coaster from the top of the first hill to the end of the ride? What force stops the roller coaster?

____

3. Would there be any friction if the cars did not have brakes?

____

____

What is acceleration?

To read this diagram, study the number of the pumpkins and the number of people pulling them. The green arrow represents acceleration, and the red arrow represents the amount of force.

Force and Acceleration

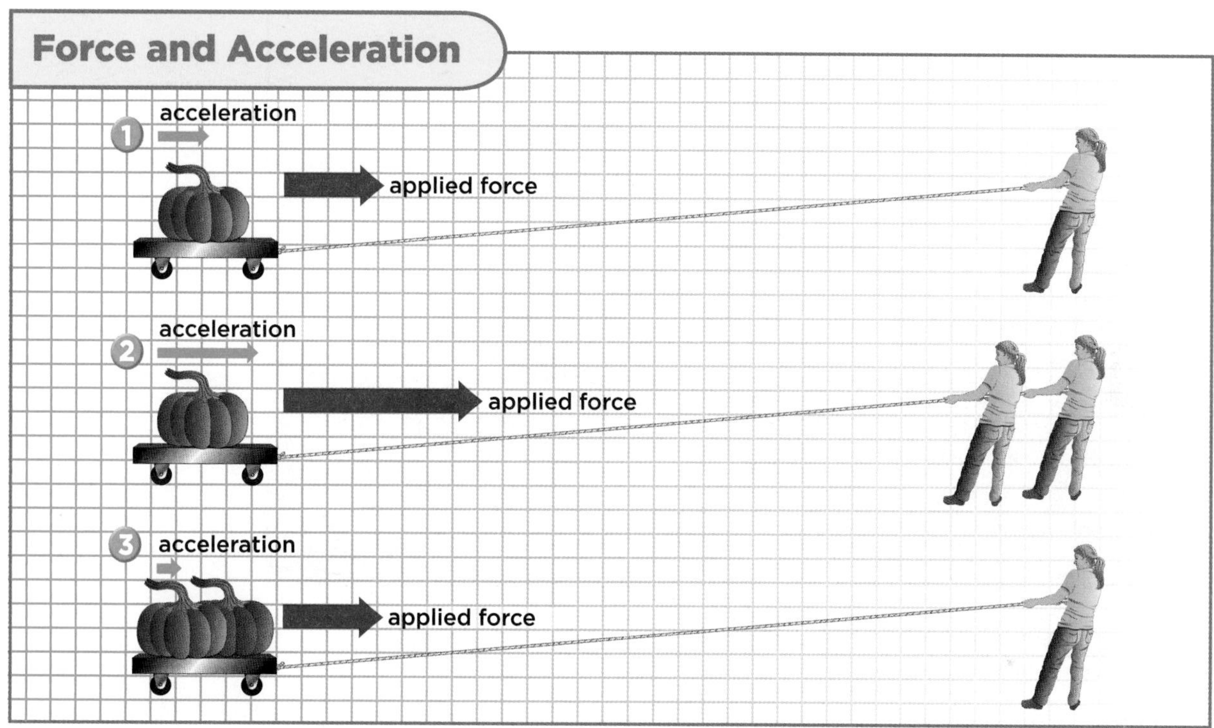

Answer these questions about the diagram.

1. How are the mass, pulling force, and acceleration different in the first and last illustrations?

____

____

2. How are mass, force, and acceleration illustrated in the second drawing?

____

____

____

Read a Photo

How do boats float?

This photo illustrates a steel ship floating in water. Buoyancy acts on the ship to keep it from sinking.

The Force of Buoyancy

Answer these questions about the photograph.

1. What force is buoyancy working against?

____

2. The propeller at the back of the ship pushes the ship forward. What force does the propeller provide?

____

3. There is a force acting on the ship that works against motion. What is this force?

____

4. Draw and label arrows to show how drag, gravity, and thrust are acting on the ship.

What is the design process?

This photograph illustrates a *Gossamer* aircraft. Look at how the aircraft is flying

The Design Process

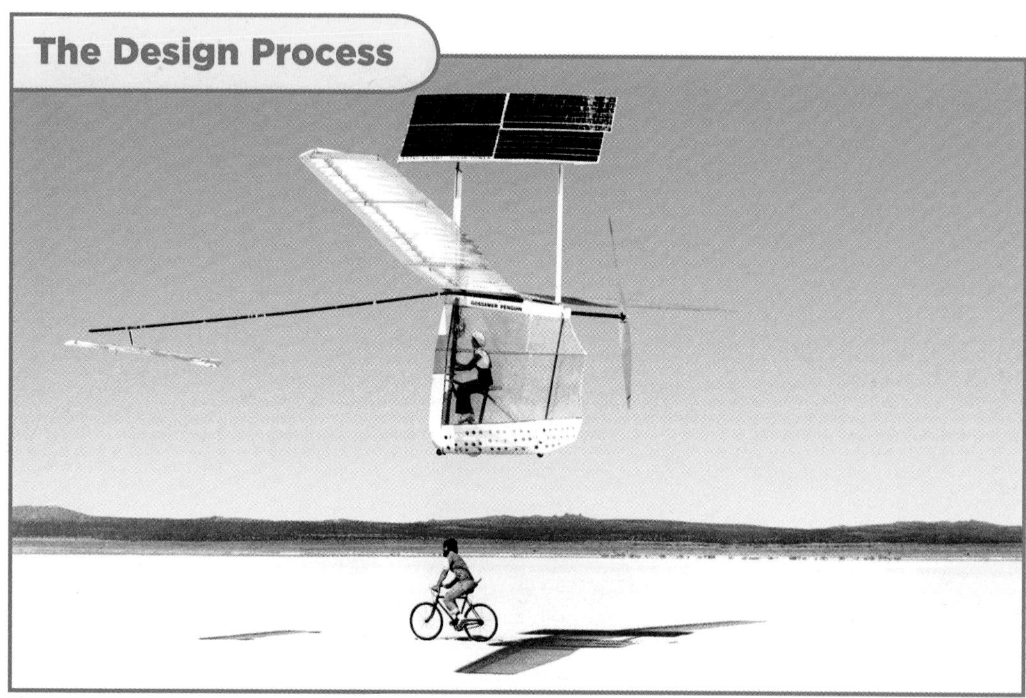

Answer these questions about the photograph.

1. This aircraft was built to solve a problem. What are working models, like this aircraft, called?

___

2. What problem do you think this aircraft is trying to solve?

___

___

3. The propeller is in the rear of the airplane. Is it pushing or pulling? What force is it causing?

___

A Model Volcano

1. **Make a Model** Cover a desk with newspaper. Place a small tube of toothpaste on the desk to model Earth's surface.

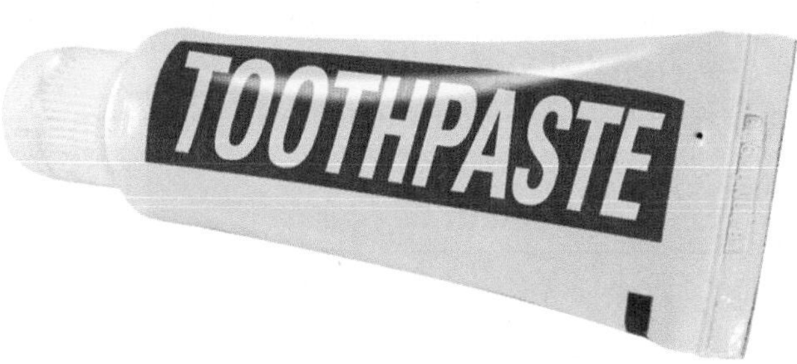

2. Carefully make a hole in the tube on the side opposite the cap. This represents an opening in Earth's surface.

3. **Observe** Press on the tube near the cap. What happens by the hole? What do you think the toothpaste is a model of?

____

____

____

4. **Communicate** Did the same thing happen to everyone's tube? What was different? Why were there differences?

____

____

____

____

Classify Natural Resources

1. **Communicate** Use the table below or make your own table. Record any natural resources that you rely on in your everyday life.

Name of Natural Resource	Renewable or Non-renewable	Ways to Conserve

2. In the second column identify the resource as renewable or non-renewable.

3. **Infer** How could you conserve the resource? Record your answers in the table.

4. **Communicate** Compare your results with those of other classmates. Create a word web that shows how we get what we need from Earth's resource.

Conservation Plan

1. **Observe** How does your school use resources? Find out. Consider water use, energy use, and garbage disposal.

____

____

2. Think of ways your school could conserve resources or produce less waste. Write down your ideas.

____

____

____

3. **Communicate** Share your ideas with your classmates. As a class, write a plan to present to your principal.

Quick Lab

Animal Cards

1. Make two sets of inherited characteristics cards. Use yellow cards for the female parent and orange cards for the male parent.

2. Write an example of a characteristic, such as long fur, on each yellow card. On each orange card, write a different example of the characteristic, such as short fur.

3. **Use Numbers** Choose one card, yellow or orange, for each pair of characteristics. How many combinations of different characteristics can you make?

4. **Infer** How do the cards model reproduction with two parents?

Friction and Motion

1. Tie a piece of string through a book. Place the book on a smooth surface. Attach the string to a spring scale. Stack a second book on top of the first.

2. **Measure** Gently pull on the scale to measure the force of your pull just before the books move. Record your result.

3. Using the scale, drag the books quickly along the surface. Measure and record the force.

4. **Infer** Does an object at rest have more friction than a sliding object? Base your answer on your results from step 3.

___

___

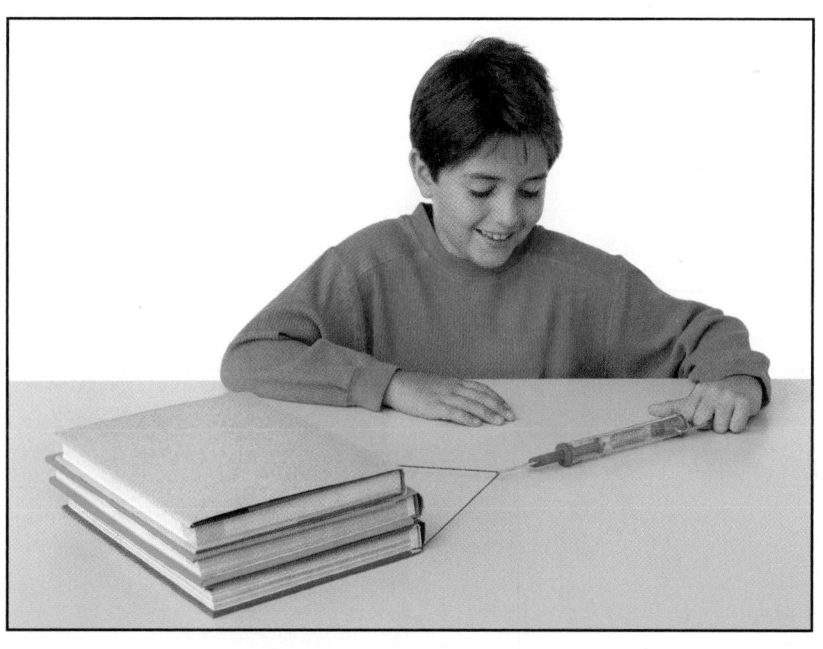

Quick Lab

Observe Gravity

1. **Predict** Does gravity equally affect all objects? Would two plastic bottles with the same volume but different masses be equally affected by gravity?

___

___

___

2. Hold an empty plastic bottle in one hand. Hold an identical bottle full of water in the other hand. Hold each bottle away from your body.

3. **Observe** Describe what you feel. Is each bottle pulled toward Earth with the same force?

___

___

___

4. **Infer** Is the amount of force due to gravity on the two bottles the same? How could you tell?

___

___

___

Design a Paper Airplane

1. Get a piece of paper. If you know how to make a paper airplane and have a design in mind, go ahead and make it. As you do, write down the procedure step by step so someone else can build the same design.

2. If you don't know how to make a paper airplane, simply fold a piece of paper in different ways to experiment with different designs. Ask your teacher or classmates if you need ideas.

3. **Observe** Fly your plane. How well does it perform?

____

4. **Experiment** Refine your design and try it again. Does the plane fly better?

____

5. Put a paperclip on the plane's nose. Does it fly better?

____

6. **Interpret Data** Use a measuring tape to see how far your plane will travel. Record your results. Compare your plane's flight distance to your classmates' planes.

____

Foldables®

by Dinah Zike

Notebook Foldables®

The following pages offer instructions to make Notebook Foldables®. Use a separate sheet of paper to make your Notebook Foldables®. You can use notebook paper, graph paper, or plain paper as appropriate.

1 Half-Book

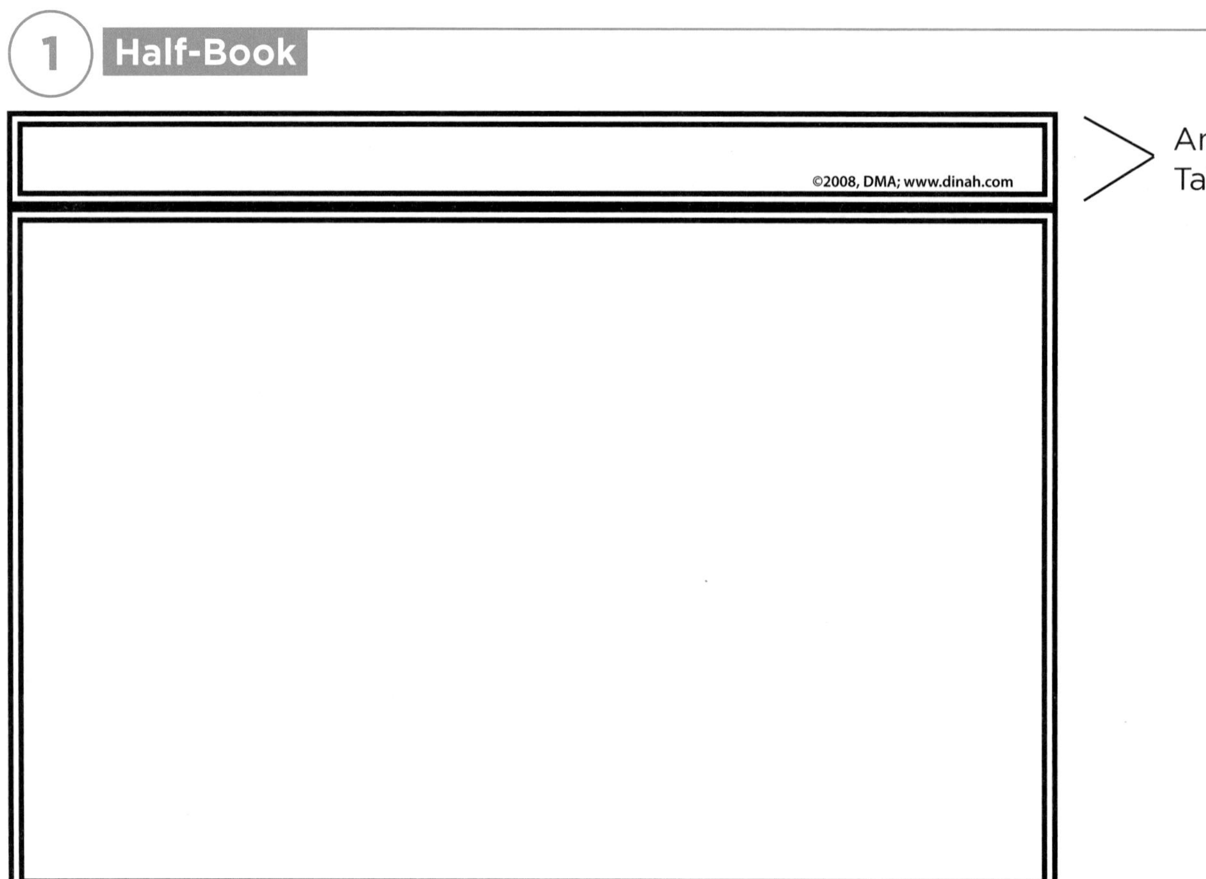

Folding Instructions

1. Fold the anchor tab.
2. Glue the anchor tab along the dotted line on the page in your book.

One-Tab

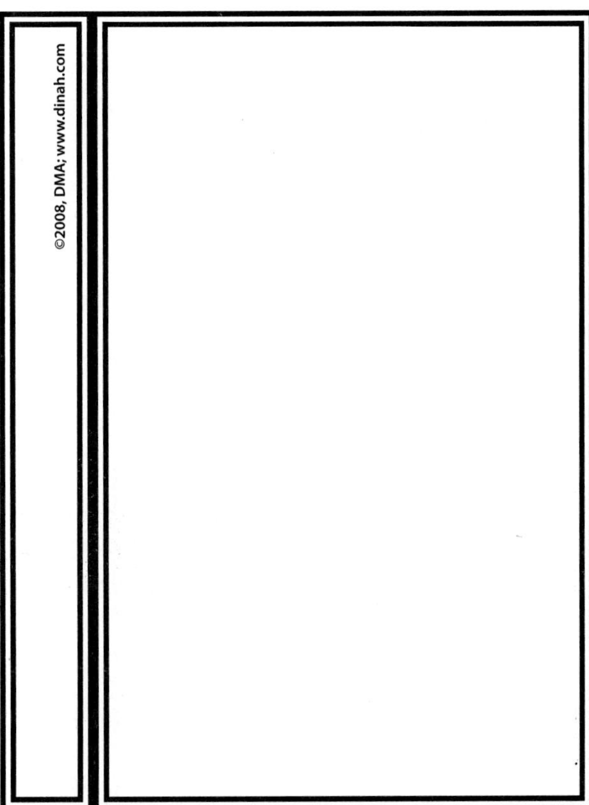

Folding Instructions

1. Fold the anchor tab.
2. Glue the anchor tab along the dotted line on the page in your book.

3 Two-Tab

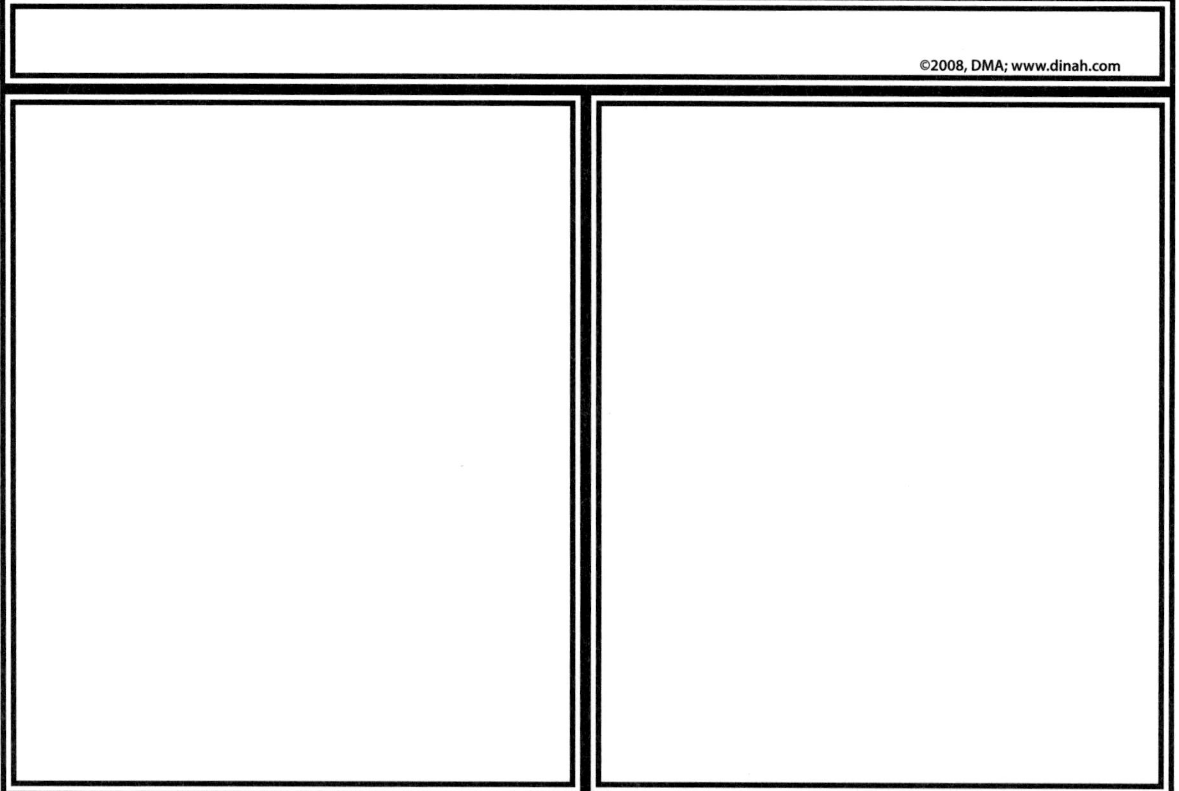

©2008, DMA; www.dinah.com

Folding Instructions

1. Fold the anchor tab.
2. Glue the anchor tab along the dotted line on the page in your book.
3. Cut the Foldable along the middle line to form two tabs.

4 Three-Tab Vertical

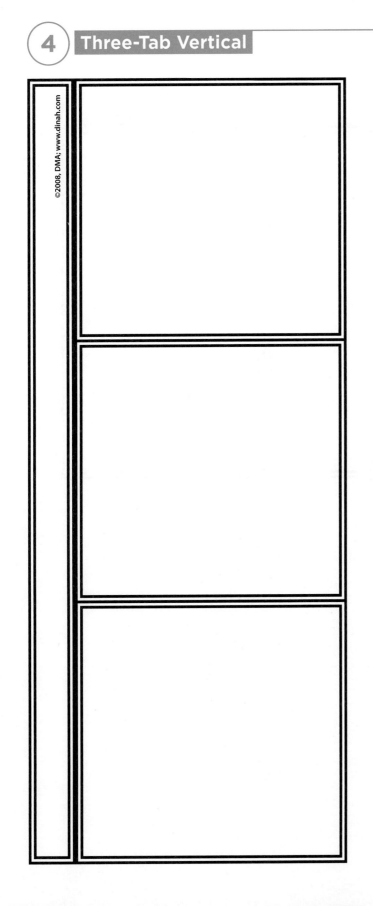

Folding Instructions

1. Fold the anchor tab.
2. Glue the anchor tab along the dotted line on the page in your book.
3. Cut the Foldable along the middle lines to form three tabs.

5 Three-Tab Horizontal

Folding Instructions

1. Fold the anchor tab.
2. Glue the anchor tab along the dotted line on the page in your book.
3. Cut the Foldable along the middle lines to form three tabs.

Mimicry Model

1. **Observe** Look at the photos of the snakes below. The snake on the left is a nonvenomous milk snake. The one on the right is a venomous coral snake. Use these photos to compare the two snakes.

____

____

____

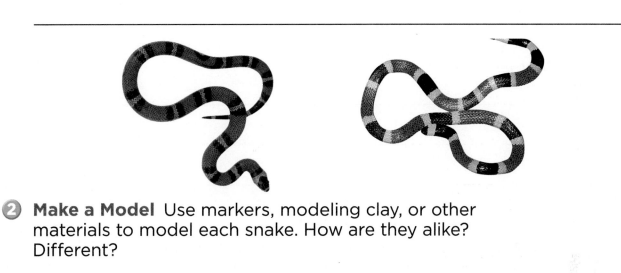

2. **Make a Model** Use markers, modeling clay, or other materials to model each snake. How are they alike? Different?

____

____

____

3. How could this saying save someone's life? "Red touches yellow, kill a fellow. Red touches black, friend of Jack."

____

____

____

____

Quick Lab

Model Pollution

1. **Observe** Look at the shell of a hard-boiled egg. Is it hard or soft? Why do you think the egg has this type of shell?

   ____

2. **Make a Model** Fill a large cup with vinegar. This models polluted land or water. Place your egg inside of the cup.

3. **Observe** Look at the egg and study its shell throughout the day. Do you notice any differences in the egg or its shell?

   ____

   ____

   ____

   ____

4. **Infer** After being placed in vinegar, can the shell still protect the egg?

   ____

5. **Predict** What may happen to eggs near polluted land or water?

   ____

   ____

6. **Infer** What adaptation might protect the egg from pollution?

   ____

   ____

6 Four-Door

Folding Instructions

1. Fold the two anchor tabs.
2. Glue the first anchor tab along the dotted line on the page in your book.
3. Glue the second anchor tab across from the first anchor tab.
4. Cut the each Foldable along the middle line to form two tabs.

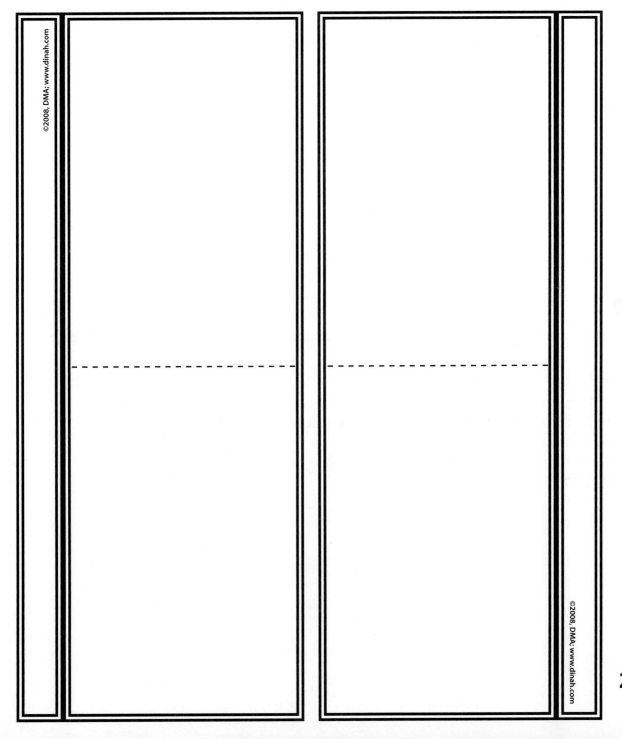

by Dinah Zike

Three-Tab Venn Diagram

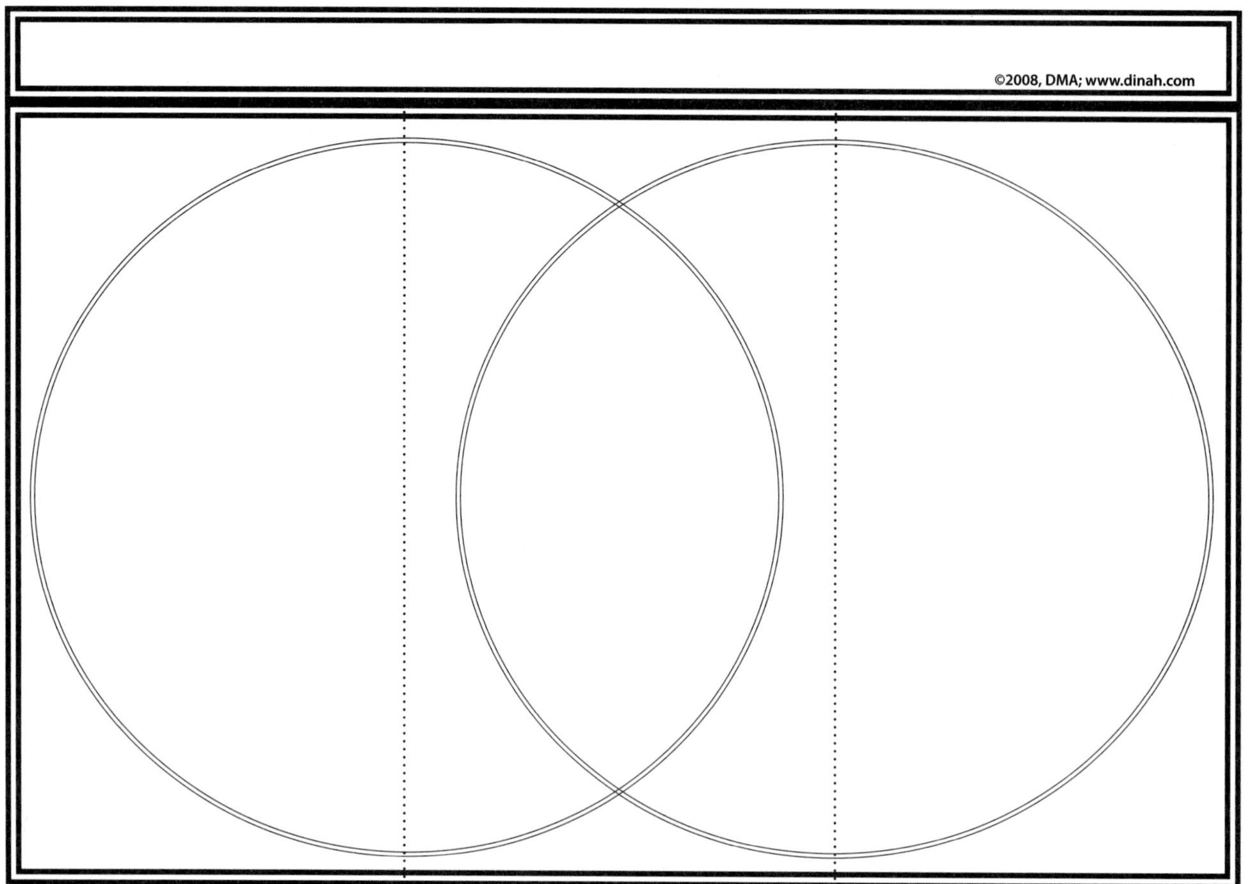

Folding Instructions

1. Fold the anchor tab.
2. Glue the anchor tab along the dotted line on the page in your book.
3. Cut along the dotted lines on the Foldable to form three tabs.

Four-Tab Vertical

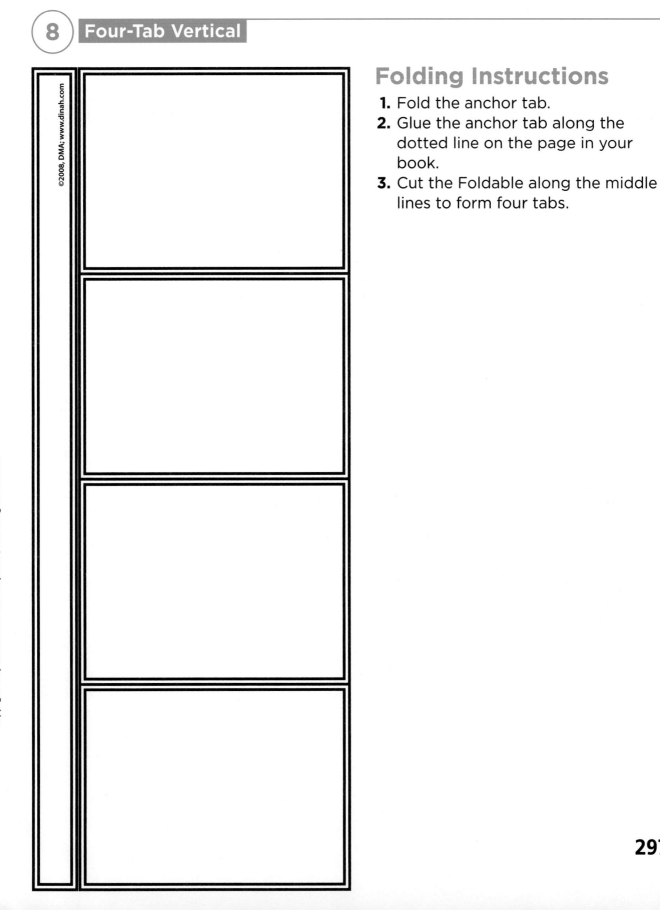

Folding Instructions

1. Fold the anchor tab.
2. Glue the anchor tab along the dotted line on the page in your book.
3. Cut the Foldable along the middle lines to form four tabs.

9 Four-Tab Horizontal

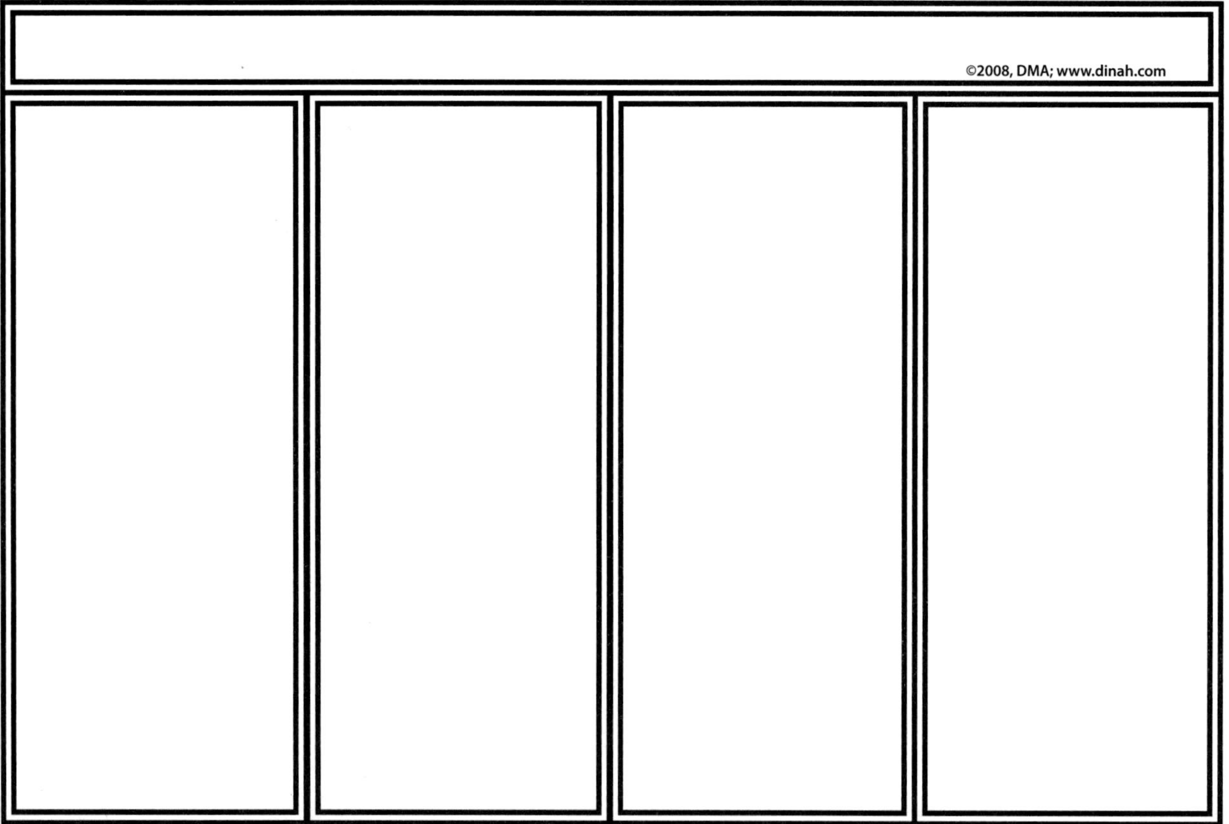

Folding Instructions

1. Fold the anchor tab.
2. Glue the anchor tab along the dotted line on the page in your book.
3. Cut the Foldable along the middle lines to form four tabs.

10 Shutter Fold

Folding Instructions

1. Fold the anchor tab.
2. Glue the anchor tab along the dotted line on the page in your book.
3. Cut the Foldable along the middle lines to form four tabs.

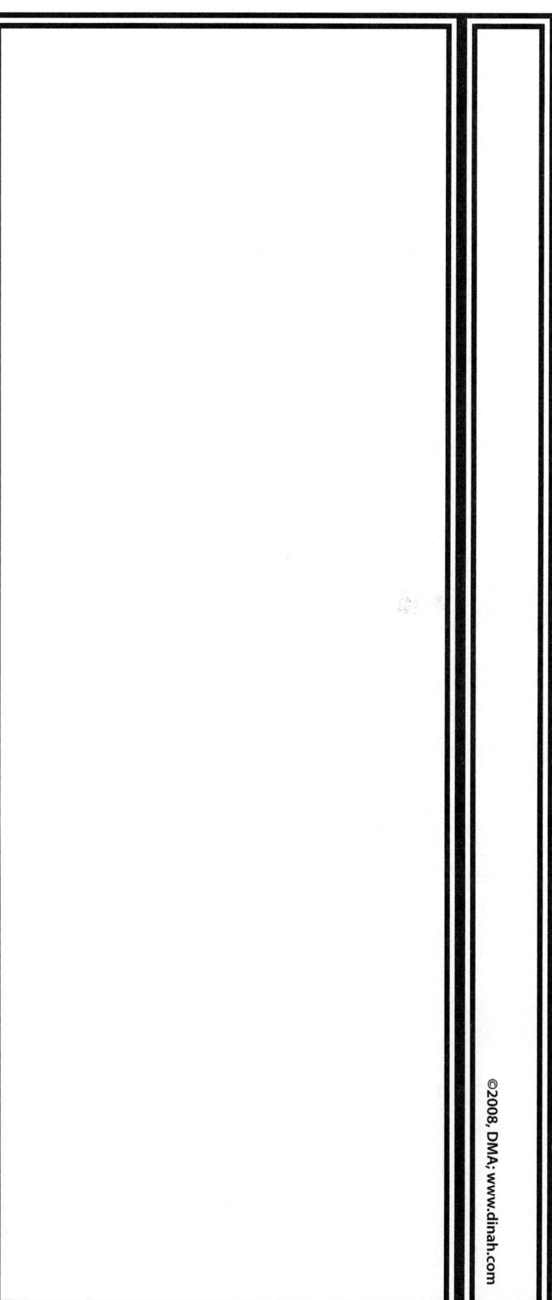

by Dinah Zike

Study Guide Folding Instructions

The following pages offer step-by-step instructions to make the Foldables study guides.

Half-Book

1. Fold a sheet of paper ($8\frac{1}{2}$" x 11") in half.
2. This book can be folded vertically like a hot dog or ...
3. ... it can be folded horizontally like a hamburger

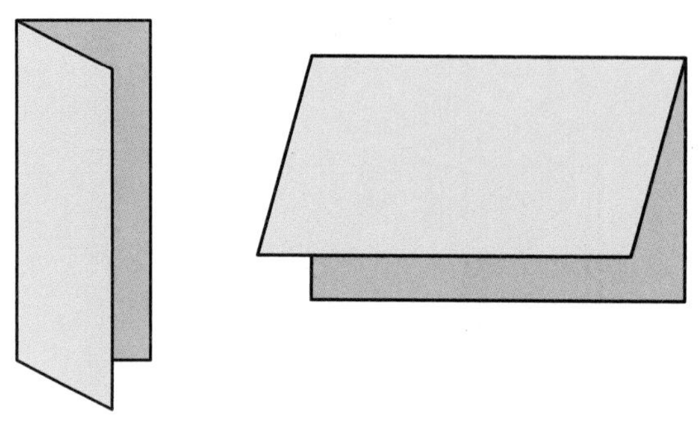

Folded Book

1. Make a Half-Book.
2. Fold in half again like a hamburger. This makes a ready-made cover and two small pages inside for recording information.

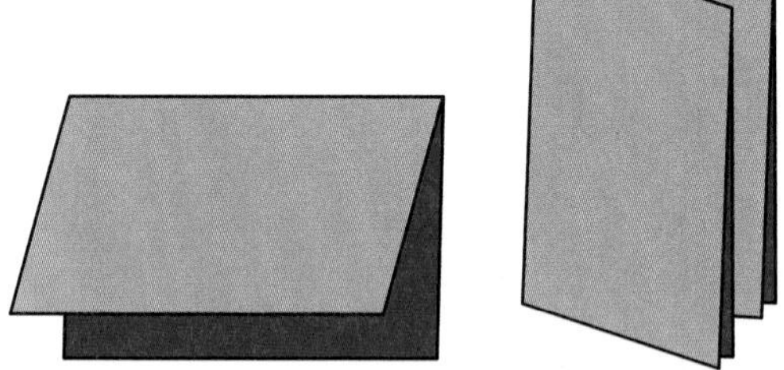

Pocket Book

1. Fold a sheet of paper ($8\frac{1}{2}$" x 11") in half like a hamburger.
2. Open the folded paper and fold one of the long sides up two inches to form a pocket. Refold along the hamburger fold so that the newly formed pockets are on the inside.
3. Glue the outer edges of the two-inch fold with a small amount of glue.

Shutter Fold

1. Begin as if you were going to make a hamburger, but instead of creasing the paper, pinch it to show the midpoint.
2. Fold the outer edges of the paper to meet at the pinch, or midpoint, forming a Shutter Fold.

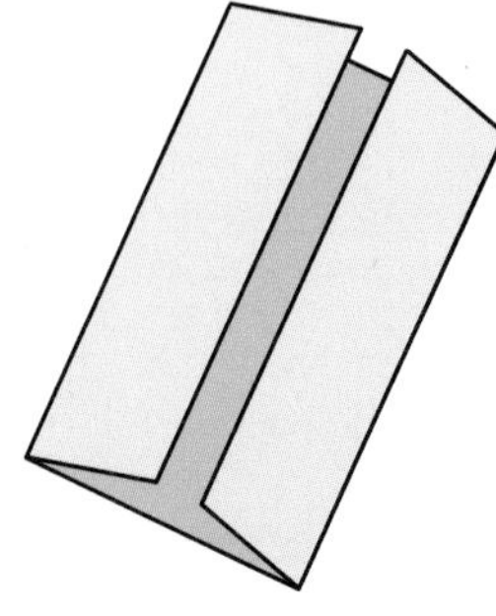

Trifold Book

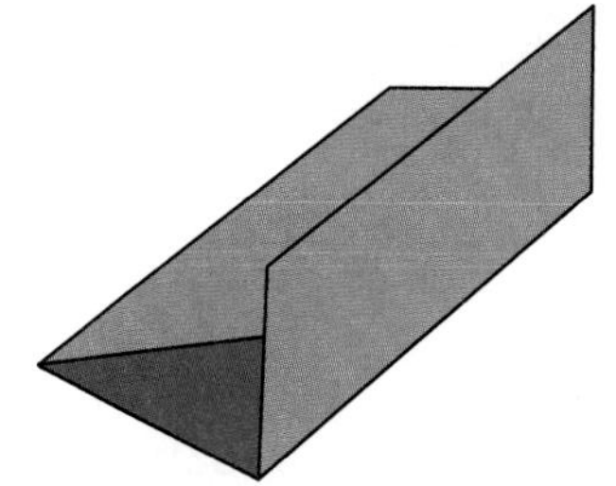

1. Fold a sheet of paper ($8\frac{1}{2}$" x 11") into thirds.
2. Use this book as is, or cut into shapes.

Three-Tab Book

1. Fold a sheet of paper like a hot dog.
2. With the paper horizontal and the fold of the hot dog up, fold the right side toward the center, trying to cover one half of the paper.
3. Fold the left side over the right side to make a book with three folds.
4. Open the folded book. Place one hand between the two thicknesses of paper and cut up the two valleys on one side only. This will create three tabs.

Layered-Look Book

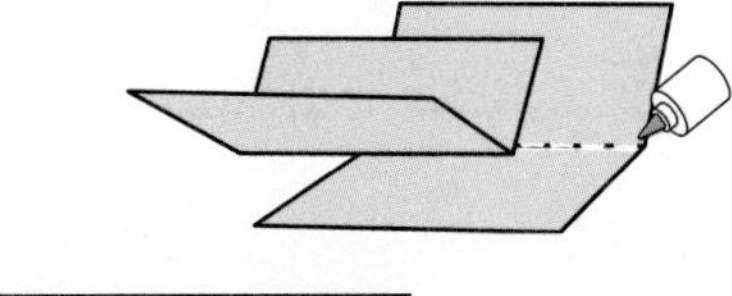

1. Stack two sheets of paper ($8\frac{1}{2}$" x 11") so that the back sheet is one inch higher than the front sheet.
2. Bring the bottoms of both sheets upward and align the edges so that all of the layers or tabs are the same distance apart.
3. When all the tabs are an equal distance apart, fold the papers and crease well.
4. Open the papers and glue them together along the valley, or inner center fold, or staple them along the mountain.

Folded Table or Chart

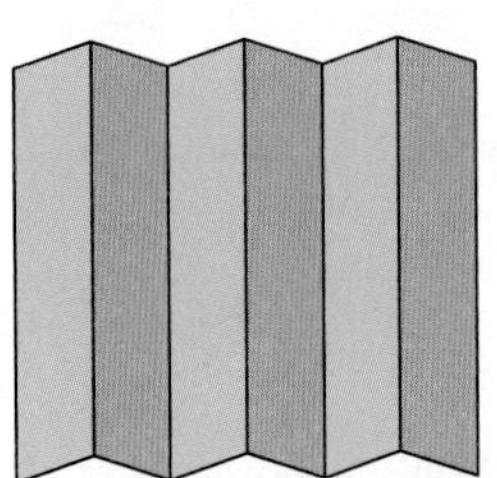

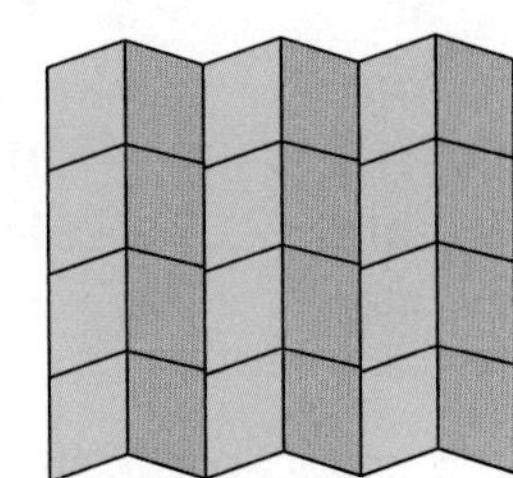

1. Fold the number of vertical columns needed to make the table or chart.
2. Fold the horizontal rows needed to make the table or chart.
3. Label the rows and columns.

Glossary

Use this glossary to learn how to pronounce and understand the meanings of the science words used in this book. The page number at the end of each definition tells you where to find that word in the book.

acceleration (ak·se′lə·rā′shən) any change in the speed or direction of a moving object (p. 202)

adaptation (a′dap·tā′shən) a characteristic that helps a living thing survive in its environment (p. 158)

buoyancy (boi′ən·sē) the upward force of a liquid or a gas on an object (p. 220)

camouflage (ka′mə·fläj′) an adaptation by which an animal can hide by blending in with its surroundings (p. 162)

circuit (sûr′kət) a path through which electric current can flow (p. 41)

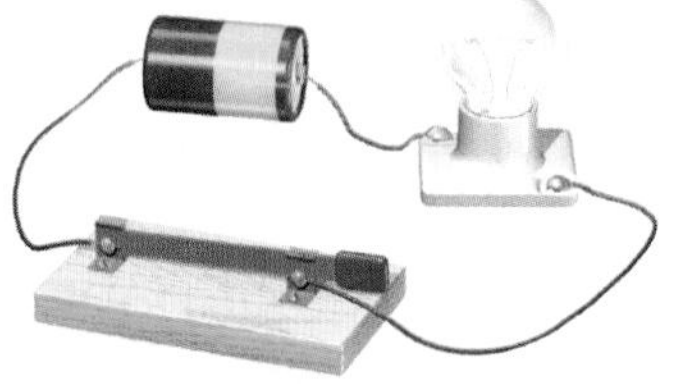

conductor (kən·duk′tər) a material through which heat or electricity flows easily (p. 24, 42)

conservation (kon′sər·vā′shən) the act of saving, protecting, or using resources wisely (p. 122)

convection (kən·vek′shən) the movement of heat through liquids or gasses (p. 27)

Pronunciation Key

The following symbols are used throughout this glossary.

a	**a**t	e	**e**nd	o	s**o**ft	u	**u**p	hw	**wh**ite	ə	**a**bout
ā	**a**pe	ē	m**e**	ō	g**o**	ū	**u**se	ng	so**ng**		tak**e**n
ä	f**a**rther	i	t**i**p	ôr	f**or**k	ü	r**u**le	th	**th**in		penc**i**l
âr	c**a**re	ī	**i**ce	oi	**oi**l	ù	p**u**ll	th (underlined)	**th**is		lem**o**n
ô	l**a**w	îr	f**ear**	ou	**ou**t	ûr	t**ur**n	yü	r**u**le		circ**u**s
								zh	mea**s**ure		

′ = primary accent; shows which syllable takes the main stress, such as **at** in **atmosphere** (at′mə·sfîr′)

′ = secondary accent; shows which syllables take lighter stresses, such as **sphere** in **atmosphere**

deposition (de'pə·zi'shən) dropping off of eroded soil and bits of rock (p. 68)

design process (di·zīn' pro' səs) the process through which an idea becomes an invention (p. 238)

distance (dis'təns) how far apart two points are (p. 198)

drag (drag) a foce acting against the motion of an object travelling through a liquid or gas (p. 214)

earthquake (ûrth'kwāk') a sudden shaking of the rock that makes up Earth's crust (p. 82)

electrical current (i·lek'trō·kal kur'unt) a flow of charged particles through a material (p. 40)

engineer (en·jə'nir) a scientist that designs new technology and modifies old technology (p. 235)

environment (in·vī'rən·mənt) all the living and nonliving things in an area (p. 120)

erosion (i·rō'zhən) the weathering and removal of rock or soil (p. 66)

force (fôrs) a push or pull (p. 200)

fossil fuel (fä'səl fū'əl) a source of energy that formed from the remains of plants and animals that lived million of years ago (p. 108)

friction (frik'shən) a force between surfaces that works against motion by slowing or stopping objects (p. 200)

fuse (fyooz) a device that stops the flow of electrical current when heated (p. 43)

glacier (glā'shər) a large sheet of ice that moves slowly across the land (p. 66)

gravity (gra´və tē) a force that acts over a distance and pulls objects together (p. 201)

H

heat (hēt) the movement of energy from a warmer object to a cooler object (p. 22)

hibernate (hī'bər·nāt) to rest or sleep through a cold winter (p. 159)

inherited characteristic (in·her'ət·əd kâr·ek·tur·rĭs'tĭk) a characteristic that a living thing is born with (p. 144)

instinct (in'stingkt) an inherited behavior that is automatic (p. 148)

insulator (in'sə·lā'tər) a material that does not easily move through (p. 24, 42)

landslide (land'slīd) a sudden movement of rock and soil down a slope (p. 86)

lift (lift) a force that works against gravity and allows planes to fly (p. 216)

moraine (môr'ān) mound of sediment deposited by a glacier (p. 69)

natural resources (na'cha ·rəl rē'sôrs') necessary or useful things we get from nature (p. 106)

nonrenewable resource (non'ri·nü'ə·bəl rē'sôrs') a natural material that is useful to people and cannot be replaced easily (p. 108)

offspring (ôf'sprĭng') an organism's young (p. 144)

physical characteristic (fi'zi·kəl kâr·ek·tur·rĭs'tĭk) a feature that can be observed and measured (p. 145)

pollution (pə·lü'shən) harmful or unwanted material that has been added to the environment (p. 120)

population (po'pyə·lā'shən) all the members of a single type of organism in an area (p. 146)

prototype (prō'tō·tīp) working model of a design that can be tested (p. 236)

radiation (rā'dē·ā'shən) movement of heat by wave energy (p. 26)

recycle (rē·sī'kəl) to make new objects or materials from old objects or materials (p. 123)

-Glossary at www.macmillanmh.com

reduce (ri·düs′) to use less of something (p. 123)

renewable resource (ri·nü′ə·bəl rē′sôrs′) a useful material that is replaced quickly in nature (p. 111)

reuse (rē·ūz′) to use something again (p. 123)

speed (spēd) the distance an object moves in an amount of time (p. 199)

static electricity (sta′tik i·lek′tri′sə·tē) the buildup of electrical charge on an object or material (p. 39)

stimulus (stim′yə·ləs) *sing.*

stimuli (stim′yə·lī) *pl. n.*, things in the environment that causes a living thing to respond (p. 160)

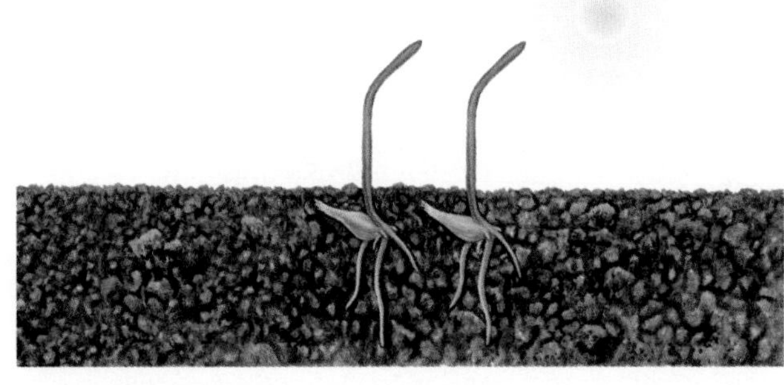

switch (swich) a device that controls the flow of current through a circuit (p. 41)

technology (tek·nôlə·j ē) everything we design, make, or use to solve problems (p. 234)

thrust (thruhst) a force that moves an object forward (p. 214)

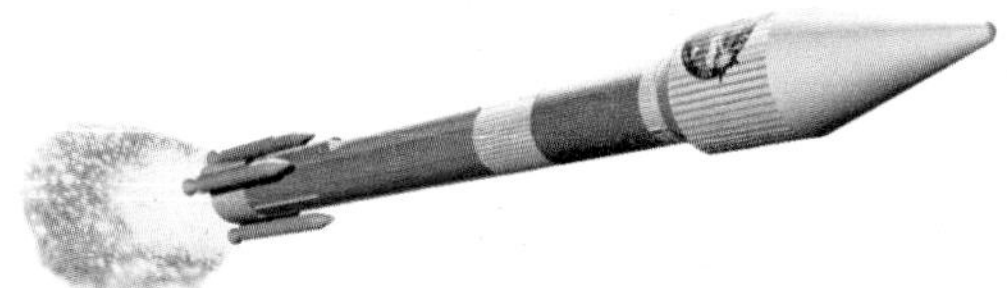

till (til) a mixture of small rocks, sand, and soil deposited by glaciers (p. 69)

velocity (və·lo′sə·tē) the speed and direction of a moving object (p. 199)

volcano (vol·kā′nō) a mountain that builds up around an opening in Earth's crust (p. 84)

weathering (we′thə·ring) the breaking down of rocks into smaller pieces (p. 64)

Index

A

Note: Page references followed by an asterisk indicate activities.

Credits

Photo Credits:

Front COV Bob Elsdale/Getty Images; **COV Back** Stephen Dalton/NHPA; **i** Stephen Dalton/NHPA; **iv** Joe Polillio/Macmillan/McGraw-Hill; **x** Digital Vision/Alamy; **xi** (t)Ingram Publishing/SuperStock, (b)Paul A. Souders/CORBIS; **xiv** (t)Dynamic Graphics Group/IT Stock Free/Alamy, (b)CORBIS; **1** David Trood/Getty Images; **2-3** Diehm/Getty Images; **3** (t)Courtesy of American Museum of Natural History, (b)Denis Finnin/American Museum of Natural History; **4-5** Danilo Donadoni/age fotostock; **5** Courtesy of American Museum of Natural History; **6-7** American Museum of Natural History; **7** Mark A. Schneider/Visuals Unlimited; **8** Courtesy of American Museum of Natural History; **9** Jerry Driendl/Getty Images; **10-11** Game McGimsey/epa/CORBIS; **11** American Museum of Natural History; **12** (t)Michio Hoshino/Minden Pictures, (b)Dave Starett/Macmillan/McGraw-Hill; **13** Ken Karp/Macmillan/McGraw-Hill; **14** Macmillan/McGraw-Hill; **15** Alexey Stiop/Alamy; **16** (tr)Boden/Ledingham/Masterfile, (cl)David Young-Wolff/PhotoEdit, (bl)Brand X Pictures/PunchStock, (br)Steve Cole/Getty Images; **18-19** CORBIS; **20** (t)Macmillan/McGraw-Hill, (c)Frank Bean/Getty Images, (b)Macmillan/McGraw-Hill; **21** Macmillan/McGraw-Hill; **23** (t)Gary Morrison/Getty Images; **24** (l)Brand X Pictures/PunchStock, (r)foodfolio/Alamy; **25** The McGraw-Hill Companies; **26** Frank Cezus/Getty Images; **27** David Young-Wolff/PhotoEdit; **28** (2)The McGraw-Hill Companies, (3)David Young-Wolff/PhotoEdit, (4)Jacques Cornell/Macmillan/McGraw-Hill; **30** Macmillan/McGraw-Hill; **33** TongRo/Beateworks/CORBIS; **34-35** Boden/Ledingham/Masterfile; **36** Macmillan/McGraw-Hill; **38 39** Macmillan/McGraw-Hill; **40** (t)Ken Cavanaugh/Macmillan/McGraw-Hill, (bl)Image Source/Alamy, (br)BananaStock/PunchStock; **42** (t)imagebroker/Alamy, (b)Skip Nall/Getty Images; **43** (t)Steve Cole/Getty Images, (b)Ken Cavanaugh/Macmillan/McGraw-Hill; **44 46 47** Macmillan/McGraw-Hill; **48** (t)Brand X Pictures/PunchStock, (bl)Ken Cavanagh/The McGraw-Hill Companies,(br)Ingram Publishing/SuperStock; **49** (l)Brand X Pictures/PunchStock, (r)Ken Karp/The McGraw-Hill Companies; **50** (t)CORBIS, (b)Boden/Ledingham/Masterfile; **56** A. Ramey/PhotoEdit; **57** Tom Uhlman/Alamy; **58** (tl)Bill Bachman/Alamy,(tr)USGS photo by Walter D. Mooney,(cl)CORBIS,(cr)Toshi Sasaki/Getty Images, (bl)Michael Szönyi/age fotostock, (br)ChinaFotoPress/Getty Images; **60-61** Rod B. Schack/Bruce Coleman USA; **62** Michael Scott/Macmillan/McGraw-Hill; **64** Bill Bachman/Alamy; **65** (t)Marengo Caverns,(b)CORBIS; **66** Ted Mead/Getty Images; **67** CORBIS; **68** Airphoto-Jim Wark; **69** (t)Glow Images/Superstock, (b)Michael Szönyi/age fotostock; **70** (t tl tr b)Indiana DNR/Outdoor Indiana Magazine,(c)Daniel Dempster Photography/Alamy; **72** (t to b)Marengo Caverns,(2)Michael Szönyi/age footstock,(3)The McGraw-Hill Companies; **74** Roland Gerth/zefa/CORBIS; **76** (l)Robert Glusic/Getty Images, (cl)age fotostock/SuperStock,(cr)Gary Braasch/Peter Arnold Inc.,(r)Dennis Frates/Alamy; **77** (l)DEA/PUBBLI AER FOTO/Getty Images, (r)CORBIS; **78-79** USGS photo by Walter D. Mooney; **80** Macmillan/McGraw-Hill; **82** USGS photo by Walter D. Mooney; **85** Toshi Sasaki/Getty Images; **86** Paul A. Souders/CORBIS; **87** ChinaFotoPress/Getty Images; **88** (t to b)Toshi Sasaki/Getty Images, (2)ChinaFotoPress/Getty Images, (3)The McGraw-Hill Companies; **90** American Museum of Natural History; **90-91** (b)Adastra/Getty Images; **91** (t)Sonya Senkowsky/AP Images; **92** S.D. Ellen, U.S. Geological Survey; **94** (t)Rob B. Schack/Bruce Coleman USA, (c)USGS photo by Walter D. Mooney,(b)The McGraw-Hill Companies; **100** (tl)CORBIS,(tr)Digital Vision/PunchStock, (cl)U.S. Coast Guard photo by Petty Officer 3rd Class Patrick Kelley,(c)Todd Bannor/age footstock,(bl)Brand X Pictures/PunchStock, (br)Getty Images; **102-103** Daniel Dempster Photography/Alamy; **104** (t to b 5 6)Jacques Cornell/The McGraw-Hill Companies, (2)Stockbyte/PictureQuest,(3)James H. Robinson/Photo Researchers, Inc., (4)Brand X Pictures/PunchStock, (7)The McGraw-Hill Companies Inc./Ken Cavanagh, (8)Andy Crawford/Getty Images, (9 10)Macmillan/McGraw-Hill; **106** (t)CORBIS, (b)Arthur Tilley/Creatas/Jupiterimages; **107** Digital Vision/Alamy; **109** U.S. Coast Guard photo by Petty Officer 3rd Class Patrick Kelley; **111** Brand X Pictures/PunchStock; **112** (t)Arthur Tilley/Creatas/Jupiterimages,(b)Brand X Pictures/PunchStock; **114** Brian Hagiwara/Brand X Pictures/Getty Images; **115** (tl)Douglas Whyte/CORBIS, (tr)Colin Keates/Courtesy of the Natural History Museum, London/DK Images,(b)Charles D. Winters/Photo Researchers, Inc., (bkgd)Dr. Parvinder Sethi/The McGraw-Hill Companies; **116-117** Juan Carlos Calvin/age fotostock; **118** Macmillan/McGraw-Hill; **120** Oxford Scientific/Photolibrary/Getty Images; **121** Digital Vision/PunchStock; **122** Airphoto-Jim Wark; **123** (l)The McGraw-Hill Companies, (r)Radius Images/Alamy; **124** Noah Addis/Star Ledger/CORBIS; **125** Todd Bannor/age fotostock; **126** (t)Digital Vision/PunchStock, (c)Airphoto-Jim Wark, (b)Noah Addis/Star Ledger/CORBIS; **128** Lester Lefkowitz/CORBIS; **129** James Hardy/Photo Alto/Punchstock; **130** (t)Daniel Dempster Photography/Alamy, (b)Juan Carlos Calvin/age fotostock; **135** CORBIS; **136** Carsten Peter/National Geographic Image Collection; **137** Susan Wiltse/Getty Images; **138** (tl)Masterfile, (tr)Silman Snozyk/age footstock, (cl bl)Brand X Pictures/PunchStock,(br)David Fox/Getty Images; **140-141** David Stoecklein/CORBIS; **142** (t)NaturePL/SuperStock,(c)Brand X Pictures/PunchStock,(b)Brand X Pictures/PunchStock; **144** Masterfile; **145** Sharon Bailey/Stock Connection Distribution/Alamy; **146** Brand X Pictures/PunchStock; **147** (t)USFWS, (b)Courtesy of the Center for Disease Control; **148-149** Ingram Publishing/SuperStock; **149** (t)Russell Illig/Getty Images, (b)Stan Osolinski/Getty Images; **150** (t)Masterfile, (c)Brand X Pictures/PunchStock, (b)Ingram Publishing/SuperStock, (b)Jacques Cornell/Macmillan/McGraw-Hill; **152** Craig Chesek/American Museum of Natural History; **153** (c)Bruce Coleman Inc./Alamy, (b) Nick Garbutt/naturepl.com; **154-155** Danita Delimont/Getty Images; **156** The McGraw-Hill Companies; **158** Silman Snozyk/age fotostock; **159** James Randklev/Getty Images; **161** Rob & Ann Simpson/Visuals Unlimited; **162** (t)Creatas Images/PictureQuest, (b)Bill Beatty/Visuals Unlimited; **163** (t)Martin Siepmann/age footstock, (c)Dynamic Graphics Group/IT Stock Free/Alamy, (bl)Getty Images, (br)Peter Lavery/Masterfile; **164** (t)Jim Brandenburg/Minden Pictures, (b)Image Source/PunchStock; **165** Robert Glusic/Getty Images; **166** (t)Rob & Ann Simpson/Visuals Unlimited, (c)Bill Beatty/Visuals Unlimited, (b)CORBIS; **168** Lynda Richardson/CORBIS; **169** Digital Vision/PunchStock; **170** Creatas Images/PictureQuest; **171** CDC/Edward J. Wozniak D.V.M., Ph.D.; **172-173** George H. H. Huey/CORBIS; **174** (t)Macmillan/McGraw-Hill, (b)Joe Polillio/Macmillan/McGraw-Hill; **176** (l)Larry Fisher/Masterfile, (r)Jack Dykinga/Getty Images; **177** (t)Juan Medina/Reuters/CORBIS, (b)Gary Meszaros/Photo Researchers, Inc.; **178-179** CORBIS; **179** David Fox/Getty Images; **180** (t)Juan Medina/Reuters/CORBIS, (c)CORBIS, (b)David Fox/Getty Images; **182** Daniel L. Geiger/SNAP/Alamy; **182-183** J. A. Kraulis/Masterfile; **183** Gerlach - John/Animals Animals; **184** (t)David Stoecklein/CORBIS, (c)Danita Delimont/Getty Images, (b)George H. H. Huey/CORBIS, (others) The McGraw-Hill Companies; **187** F. Lukasseck/Masterfile; **190** Galen Rowell/CORBIS; **191** (l)CORBIS/Veer, (r)Getty Images; **192** (tl)Charles O'Rear/CORBIS,(tr)Brand X Pictures/PunchStock,(tr)StockTrek/Getty Images, (cr)Paul A. Souders/CORBIS, (bl)Greg Stott/Masterfile, (br)Warren Gretz/DOE/NREL; **194-195** Robert Laberge/Stringer/Getty Images; **196** J. Beckman/Macmillan/McGraw-Hill; **199** (l)Jules Frazier/Getty Images,(cl)Digital Vision, (cr)CORBIS, (r)Digital Vision/PunchStock, (b)Charles O'Rear/CORBIS; **200** Greg Stott/Masterfile; **203** Reuters/Darren Staples; **204** (t)Charles O'Rear/CORBIS, (c)Greg Stott/Masterfile, (b)Reuters/Darren Staples; **206** J. Beckman/Macmillan/McGraw-Hill; **209** Getty Images; **210-211** Timothy Hearsum/Getty Images; **212** Macmillan/McGraw-Hill; **214-215** (inset) Brand X Pictures/PunchStock, (bkgd)StockTrek/Getty Images; **216-217** Paul A. Souders/CORBIS; **218-219** (bkgd)CORBIS, (inset)Richard Wong/Alamy; **219** CORBIS; **220-221** Massimo Borchi/CORBIS; **224** (t)Brand X Pictures/PunchStock, (c)Paul A. Souders/CORBIS, (inset) StockTrek/Getty Images, (inset)StockTrek/Getty Images; **226** Pixtal/SuperStock; **230-231** Phil Meyers/AP Images; **232** (others)Macmillan/McGraw-Hill, (2)F. Schussler/PhotoLink/Getty Images; **234** (t)Fotosearch/PhotoLibrary, (b)Warren Gretz/DOE/NREL; **235** Nick Galante/PMRF/NASA; **236** (bl)Dennis Taylor/NASA, (br)Tom Tschida/NASA; **236-237** (t)Jim Ross/NASA,(bkgd) DAJ/Getty Images; **237** Tom Tschida/NASA; **238-239** Bob Rhine/NASA; **240** (t)Warren Gretz/DOE/NREL,(c)Tom Tschida/NASA, (b)Bob Rhine/NASA; **242** Ken Karp for MMH; **243** Macmillan/McGraw-Hill; **244** Daniel Dempster Photography/Alamy; **246** (t)Robert Laberge/Stringer/Getty Images, (c)Timothy Hearsum/Getty Images, (b)Phil Meyers/AP Images; **252** NASA Marshall Space Flight Center; **253** Stephen Dalton/NHPA; **256** David Young-Wolff/PhotoEdit; **258** CORBIS; **264** Airphoto-Jim Wark; **265** (l)The McGraw-Hill Companies, (r)Radius Images/Alamy; **266** Sharon Bailey/Stock Connection Distribution/Alamy; **268** (l)Jim Brandenburg/Minden Pictures, (r)Image Source/PunchStock; **269** (l)Larry Fisher/Masterfile, (r)Jack Dykinga/Getty Images; **272** Massimo Borchi/CORBIS; **273** Bob Rhine/NASA; **274** Stephen Dalton/NHPA; **276** Ken Karp/Macmillan/McGraw-Hill; **279 280** Michael Scott/Macmillan/McGraw-Hill; **282** C Squared Studios/Getty Images; **284** (l)Image Quest Marine/Alamy, (r)Mitsuhiko Imamori/Minden Pictures; **286** Janette Beckman/Macmillan/McGraw-Hill; **288** Pixtal/SuperStock; **302** Ingram Publishing/SuperStock; **303** (t)CORBIS, (bl)Joe Polillio/Macmillan/McGraw-Hill, (br)Steve Cole/Getty Images; **304** (t)Gary Morrison/Getty Images, (tl)Brand X Pictures/PunchStock, (tr)NaturePL/SuperStock, (bl)Martin Siepmann/age footstock, (br)Juan Carlos Calvin/age fotostock; **305** (tl)Frank Cezus/Getty Images, (tr)Brand X Pictures/PunchStock, (bl)Adrian Sherratt/Alamy, (br)Toshi Sasaki/Getty Images.